Wind forces on buildings and structures:
an introduction

Wind forces on buildings and structures:

an introduction

E. L. Houghton

Associate Dean, School of Engineering, and Director of Studies of
Mechanical and Aeronautical Engineering, The Hatfield Polytechnic

N. B. Carruthers

Senior Lecturer in Aeronautical Engineering, The Hatfield Polytechnic

A Halsted Press Book

**John Wiley & Sons
New York**

First published 1976
by Edward Arnold (Publishers) Ltd

Published in the U.S.A.
by Halsted Press, A Division
of John Wiley & Sons, Inc.
New York

Library of Congress Cataloging in Publication Data

Houghton, Edward Lewis.
   Wind forces on buildings and structures.

   "A Halsted Press book."
   Bibliography: p.
   Includes index.
   1. Buildings—Aerodynamics. 2. Wind-pressure.
I. Carruthers, N. B., joint author. II. Title.
TA654.5.H68.   624'.175   76-16146
ISBN 0-470-15147-1

Printed in Great Britain

Contents

Preface

In the last decade or so, the building and construction industry has seen the advent of new forms of structural and other materials which have allowed greater scope for aesthetic expression and innovation in architectural practice; increasing costs have required engineers to scrutinise the value of each component part; and more and more sophisticated techniques of structural analysis have become available, with concomitant refinement of design technique. All of these trends have resulted in buildings and structures which are more responsive to significant loading influence from the wind — affecting their stability, integrity, and safe life — which makes it imperative that students and practising engineers become familiar with the physical processes involved. At the same time, the industry demands more relevant theoretical experimental information and data from which to derive safe and successful designs.

These data are particularly requested in forms suitable for inclusion in modern design practice and are required to refer not only to static loadings induced by steady wind pressures but to the dynamics of flexible structures and their response to intermittent wind-induced forces.

It is to support the basic studies of students of civil engineering and architecture and to provide a background text for those practising engineers who find themselves concerned with wind loading that the present volume was devised. For several years the authors have been concerned in those aspects of industrial aerodynamics relevant to wind loadings on buildings and structures, through their work in the Hatfield Polytechnic within two broad categories: firstly, in teaching the elements of wind effects to undergraduates of civil and constructional engineering and to postgraduate researchers through the supervision of their projects, and secondly in the provision of wind-tunnel testing and other experimental support to a wide range of industrial projects.

With a few exceptions there is a dearth of support literature for individuals working in either of these categories, apart from the various Codes of Practice and the research and technical papers which emanate from the worldwide scientific and technological support to those aspects of science and technology involved in wind effects. The aim of the present book is to make available in a single volume sufficient basic information on meteorology, fluid mechanics, aerodynamics, structural vibration dynamics, and experimental techniques to guide the student and engineer to a proper identification of the problem and hopefully towards the particular solution associated with wind loadings. With certain necessary but easily identifiable exceptions the work calls for no advanced ability in mathematics, physics, or aerodynamics — all topics originate in fundamental principles. The text is not meant to be a substitute for or indeed an extension of any Code of Practice but aims to help provide knowledge and understanding of some of the topics of science and technology which contribute to a proper interpretation of a Code of Practice and to permit a wider understanding of the phenomena involved.

E. L. H.
N. B. C.

Symbols used in text

A	area
$A_1, \ldots, A_n$	coefficients of a Fourier series
A_e	effective area
a	pipe radius or boundary-layer thickness; an index; acceleration
a_c	centripetal acceleration
B	a dimension; excitation turbulence factor
B_f, B_m	full-scale and model dimensions
b	an index
C	Celsius
C	a constant
C_D	drag coefficient
C_F	force coefficient
C_{F_t}	transverse force coefficient
C_f	surface-friction coefficient
C_L	lift coefficient
C_M	moment coefficient
C_p	pressure coefficient
C_{p_e}	external pressure coefficient
C_{p_i}	internal pressure coefficient
C_x	coefficient of force in x-direction
c	frequency factor; an index
c'	frequency factor
c_p, c_V	specific heats at constant pressure and constant volume
d	diameter; an index
E	east
E	modulus of elasticity
E_f, E_m	modulus of elasticity for full scale and for model
e	eccentricity; an index
F	resultant force or component; resonant turbulence factor

F_n	natural frequency of transverse oscillation
F_x, F_z	forces in x-direction and in z-direction
f	frequency; force; an index
f_c	frequency of oscillation of a cylinder
f_d, f_p	force components
f_v	force component; frequency of vortex formation
f_{vs}	vortex shedding frequency
g	a function; acceleration due to gravity; peak factor
H	total pressure; height above ground
h	spacing between plates
I_θ, I_z	torsional and bending moments of inertia
J	joule
$J_h{}^2, J_z{}^2$	horizontal and vertical aerodynamic acceptances
K	kelvin
K	circulation; a constant
k	roughness coefficient; pressure-drop coefficient
k_a, k_s	aerodynamic and structural damping coefficients
kg	kilogram
km	kilometre
kt	knot
k_1	a constant
L	dimension of length
L	length; lapse rate; characteristic gust length
L_x	gust length in x-direction
l	mixing length; spacing between rods
M	dimension of mass
M	aerodynamic moment; mass per unit length
M_e	equivalent mass per unit length
m	mass per unit length
N	newton; north
N	yawing moment; normal force
n	frequency; an index
n_θ, n_z	torsional and vertical frequencies
$\bar{n}$	reduced frequency $= nL/\bar{V}_{10}$
Pa	pascal
p	static pressure
p_0	free-stream static pressure
p_1, p_2, p_3	pressures on faces 1, 2, 3
q	dynamic pressure $= \frac{1}{2}\rho V^2$
R	radius; resultant force; characteristic gas constant
(Re)	Reynolds number

R_p	wind-speed ratio
S	south
S^f, S^v, S^y	power spectral densities in force, speed and displacement
(Str)	Strouhal number
s	length
T	dimension of time
T	temperature; torsional moment; transverse force; sample time
T_A	applied torsional moment
T_R	resisting torque
t	time
U	average velocity in pipe
U_1	maximum velocity in pipe; velocity at edge of boundary layer
U_∞	velocity in free stream
u	velocity component; velocity in boundary layer
$\bar{u}$	velocity ratio u/U_1; mean velocity
u'	fluctuating component of velocity
V	velocity
V_f, V_m	velocities in full-scale and model tests
V_g, V_z	velocities at heights g and z
V_R	relative wind velocity
$\bar{V}_{10}$	mean wind speed 10 metres above ground
v	wind velocity; incremental velocity; velocity component
v_g	gust velocity
$\bar{v}$	steady velocity component
v'	fluctuating velocity component
W	west
W	weight
w	velocity component
$\bar{w}$	steady velocity component
w'	fluctuating velocity component
$X_a{}^2, X_m{}^2$	aerodynamic and mechanical admittances
x	distance along surface; characteristic length
Y	side force
Y_0	deflection under forced vibration
$\bar{Y}$	mean deflection
y_s	deflection under steady force
y_n	amplitude of nth oscillation
$\bar{y}$	incremental deflection
z	vertical displacement
α (alpha)	power-law exponent

β (beta)	damping factor
γ (gamma)	ratio of specific heats, c_p/c_V
δ (delta)	logarithmic decrement
δ_c	critical damping decrement
δ_θ, δ_z	angular and linear deflections
ϵ (epsilon)	eddy viscosity
κ (kappa)	bulk modulus
ζ_0 (zeta)	deflection ratio
θ (theta)	dimension of temperature; an angle
λ (lambda)	wavelength
μ (mu)	absolute coefficient of viscosity
μ_w	coefficient of viscosity at wall
ν (nu)	kinematic coefficient of viscosity; effective frequency
ξ (xi)	displacement per unit length
ξ_0	frequency factor
ρ (rho)	density
Σ (sigma)	summation sign
σ (sigma)	structural density
σ^2	variance
τ (tau)	shear stress, time difference
τ_w	shear stress at wall
$\bar{\tau}$	turbulent shear stress
ϕ (phi)	an angle
ψ (psi)	correlation coefficient
Ω (omega)	frequency of forced angular motion
ω (omega)	angular velocity; frequency of angular motion

1

Units, dimensions, and relevant dimensional analysis

1.1 Units and dimensions

A study in any science must include measurement and calculation, which presuppose an agreed system of units in terms of which quantities can be measured and expressed. There is one system which has come to be accepted for most branches of science and engineering, and for meteorology and aerodynamics in particular, in most parts of the world. That system is the Système International d'Unités, commonly abbreviated to SI units, and it is used throughout this book, except in a very few places as specially noted. The conversion of imperial units to SI units is discussed in section 1.1.5.

It is essential to distinguish between the terms 'dimension' and 'unit'. For example, the dimension 'length' expresses the *qualitative* concept of linear displacement, or distance between two points, as an abstract idea, without reference to actual quantitative measurement; the term 'unit' indicates a specified amount of the quantity. Thus a metre is a unit of length, being an actual 'amount' of linear displacement, and so also is a mile. The metre and mile are different *units*, since each contains a different *amount* of length, but both describe length and therefore are identical *dimensions*.

Expressing this in symbolic form,

x metres = $[L]$ (a quantity of x metres has the dimension of length);
x miles = $[L]$ (a quantity of x miles has the dimension of length);
x metres $\neq x$ miles (x miles and x metres are unequal quantities of length);
$[x$ metres$]$ = $[x$ miles$]$ (the dimension of x metres is the same as the dimension of x miles).

Quite often the word 'dimension' appears in the form 'a dimension of 8 metres', and thus means a specified length. This meaning of the word is therefore closely related to the engineer's 'unit' and implies linear extension

1

only. Another common example of its use is in 'three-dimensional geometry', implying three linear extensions in different directions. References to three-dimensional bodies and two-dimensional flow in later chapters illustrate this. The original meaning must not be confused with either of these uses.

1.1.1 The fundamental dimensions and units.   There are four fundamental *dimensions* in terms of which the dimensions of all other physical quantities may be expressed. They are mass $[M]$, length $[L]$, time $[T]$, and temperature $[\theta]$ *. A consistent set of *units* is formed by specifying a unit of particular value for each of these dimensions. In engineering, the accepted units are respectively the kilogram, the metre, the second, and the kelvin or degree Celsius (see below). These are identical with the units of the same names in common use, and are defined by international agreement.

It is convenient and conventional to represent the names of these units by abbreviations, namely:

kg for kilogram,
m for metre,
s   for second,
$^\circ$C for degree Celsius, and
K for kelvin.

For most practical purposes, the degree Celsius is one one-hundredth part of the temperature rise involved when pure water at freezing temperature is heated to boiling temperature at standard pressure. In the Celsius scale, pure water at standard pressure freezes at 0°C and boils at 100°C.

The kelvin (K) is identical in size with the degree Celsius ($^\circ$C), but the Kelvin scale of temperature is measured from the absolute zero of temperature, which is approximately -273°C. Thus a temperature in K is equal to the temperature in $^\circ$C plus 273 (approximately).

1.1.2 Multiples and sub-multiples.   Sometimes, the fundamental units defined above are inconveniently large or inconveniently small for a particular case. In such cases, the quantity can be expressed in terms of some multiple or sub-multiple of the fundamental unit. Such multiples and sub-multiples are denoted by appending a prefix to the fundamental unit. Three prefixes most often used, are, with their abbreviations,

mega (M), denoting one million;
kilo (k), denoting one thousand;
milli (m), denoting one one thousandth part.

---

* Some authorities express temperature in terms of length and time.

Thus

   1 MW = 1 000 000 W,
   1 mm = 0·001 m.

A prefix attached to a unit makes a new unit; for example,

   $1 \text{ mm}^2 = 1 \text{ (mm)}^2 = 10^{-6} \text{ m}^2$, not 10^{-3} m^2.

For some purposes, the hour or the minute can be used as the unit of time.

Note: there could be confusion between the use of m for milli and its use for metre. This is avoided by use of spacing; thus ms denotes millisecond while m s denotes the product of metre and second.

1.1.3 The units of other physical quantities. Having defined the four fundamental dimensions and their units, it is possible to establish units of all other physical quantities (see Table 1.1).

   Speed, for example, is defined as the distance travelled in unit time; it therefore has the dimension LT^{-1} and is measured in metres per second (m/s). It is sometimes desirable and permissible to use 'kilometres per hour' or 'knots' (nautical miles per hour, see section 1.1.5) as units of speed, and care must then be exercised to avoid errors of inconsistency.

   To find the dimensions and units of more complex quantities, appeal is made to the principle of *'dimensional homogeneity'*. This means simply that, in any valid physical equation, the dimensions of both sides must be the same. Thus if, for example, (mass)^n appears on the left-hand side of the equation, (mass)^n must also appear on the right-hand side, and similarly this applies to length, time and temperature. This is considered in more detail later in this chapter, where the wider applications of dimensional analysis are also discussed.

   Thus, to find the dimensions of *force*, use is made of the equation

   force = mass x acceleration

while acceleration is speed ÷ time.
   Expressed dimensionally, this is

$$\text{force} = [M] \times \left[\frac{L}{T} \div T \right] = [MLT^{-2}]$$

Writing in the appropriate units, it is seen that a force is measured in units of kg m/s^2. Since, however, the unit of force is given the name 'newton' (abbreviated usually to N), it follows that

   $1 \text{ N} = 1 \text{ kg m/s}^2$

TABLE 1.1 *Units and dimensions*

Quantity	Dimension	Unit (name and abbreviation)
Length	L	metre (m)
Mass	M	kilogram (kg)
Time	T	second (s)
Temperature	θ	degree Celsius ($^\circ$C); kelvin (K)
Area	L^2	square metre (m^2)
Volume	L^3	cubic metre (m^3)
Speed	LT^{-1}	metre per second (m/s)
Acceleration	LT^{-2}	metre per second per second (m/s^2)
Angle	1	radian or degree ($^\circ$) [The radian is expressed as a ratio and is therefore dimensionless]
Angular velocity . . .	T^{-1}	radians per second (s^{-1})
Angular acceleration . .	T^{-2}	radians per second per second (s^{-2})
Frequency	T^{-1}	hertz; cycles per second (Hz; s^{-1})
Density	ML^{-3}	kilograms per cubic metre (kg/m^3)
Force	MLT^{-2}	newton (N)
Stress	$ML^{-1}T^{-2}$	pascal (Pa; 1 Pa = 1 N/m^2)
Strain	1	(none, expressed as %)
Pressure	$ML^{-1}T^{-2}$	pascal (Pa; 1 Pa = 1 N/m^2)
Energy; work	ML^2T^{-2}	joule (J)
Power	ML^2T^{-3}	watt (W)
Moment	ML^2T^{-2}	newton metre (Nm)
Absolute viscosity . .	$ML^{-1}T^{-1}$	kilogram per metre second (kg/m s)
Kinematic viscosity . .	L^2T^{-1}	metre squared per second (m^2/s)
Bulk elasticity	$ML^{-1}T^{-2}$	newtons per square metre (N/m^2)

1.1.4 Imperial units.   Until about 1968, engineers in some parts of the world, the United Kingdom and the USA in particular, used a set of units based on the Imperial set of units. In this system, the fundamental units were:

>   mass − the pound
>   length − the foot
>   time − the second
>   temperature − the degree Centigrade or kelvin.

Since many valuable texts and papers exist using those units, factors for converting from the Imperial system to the SI system are given in Table 1.2.

1.1.5 Conversion of Imperial units to SI units. The conversion between
Imperial units and SI units is based on the fact that the fundamental units
(pound mass, foot, second, and degree Centigrade) of the Imperial system
have now been *defined* in terms of the corresponding units of the SI.

These definitions are as follows:

1 foot = 0·3048 metres,
1 pound - 0·453 592 37 kilograms,

while the second and the degree Celsius (degree Centigrade or kelvin) are
identical in the two systems.

TABLE 1.2 *Conversion factors between Imperial units and SI units*

One of these	is equal to this number	of these
ft	0·3048	m
in	0·0254	m
in	25·4	mm
st. mile	1609·3	m
n. mile	1853·2	m
ft^2	0·0929	m^2
in^2	$6·4516 \times 10^{-4}$	m^2
in^2	645·16	mm^2
ft^3	0·028 32	m^3
in^3	$1·6387 \times 10^{-5}$	m^3
in^3	16 387	mm^3
lb	0·4536	kg
lb/ft^3	16·0185	kg/m^3
lbf	4·4482	N
lbf/ft^2	47·880	N/m^2
lbf/in^2	6894·8	N/m^2
ft lbf	1·3558	J
hp	745·70	W
lbf ft	1·3558	N m
ft/s	0·3048	m/s
mile/h	0·447 04	m/s
knot	0·514 77	m/s

1.2 Dimensional analysis

The theory of dimensional homogeneity has additional uses to that described above. By predicting how one variable may depend on a number of others, it may be used to direct the course of an experiment or the analysis of experimental results. For example, when fluid flows past a circular cylinder whose axis is perpendicular to the stream, eddies are formed behind the cylinder at a frequency which depends on a number of factors, such as the size of the cylinder, the speed of the stream, etc.

1.2.1 Dimensional theory applied to eddy shedding. In an experiment to investigate the variation of eddy frequency, the obvious procedure is to take several sizes of cylinder, place them in streams of various fluids at a number of different speeds, and count the frequency of the eddies in each case. No matter how detailed, the results apply directly only to the cases tested, and it is necessary to find some pattern underlying the results. A theoretical guide is helpful in achieving this end, and it is in this direction that 'dimensional analysis' is of use.

In the above problem, the frequency of the eddies, n per second, will depend primarily on:

i)   the size of the cylinder, represented by its diameter, d m;
ii) the speed of the stream, V m/s;
iii) the density of the fluid, ρ kg/m^3 ; and
iv) the viscosity of the fluid, v m^2/s.

Note that either μ or v may be used to represent the viscosity of the fluid (see section 3.1.4).

The factors should also include the geometric shape of the body. Since the problem here is concerned only with long circular cylinders with their axes perpendicular to the stream, this factor will be common to all readings and may be ignored in this analysis. It is also assumed that the speed is low compared to the speed of sound in the fluid, so that compressibility may be ignored; also, gravitational effects are excluded.

Then $n = \mathrm{f}(d,\ V,\ \rho,\ v)$

and, assuming that this function f(. . .) may be put in the form

$$n = \Sigma C d^a V^b \rho^e v^f \qquad \cdot \quad \cdot \quad \cdot \quad \cdot \quad \cdot \quad \cdot \quad \cdot \quad \cdot \quad \cdot \quad \cdot \quad (1.1)$$

where C is a constant and a, b, e, and f are some unknown indices, not necessarily rational or real, putting eqn 1.1 in dimensional form leads to

$$[T^{-1}] = [L^a (LT^{-1})^b (ML^{-3})^e (L^2 T^{-1})^f] \qquad \cdot \quad \cdot \quad \cdot \quad \cdot \quad \cdot \quad \cdot \quad (1.2)$$

where each factor has been replaced by its dimensions. Now the dimensions of both sides must be the same, and therefore the indices of M, L, and T on the two sides of the equation may be equated as follows:

mass (M) $0 = e$.   .   .   .   (1.3.1)

length (L) $0 = a + b - 3e + 2f$.   .   .   .   .   (1.3.2)

time (T) $-1 = -b - f$.   .   .   .   .   .   (1.3.3)

Here are three equations in four unknowns. One unknown must therefore be left undetermined; f, the index of v, is selected for this role, and the equations are solved for a, b and e in terms of f.

The solution is, in fact,

$$b = 1 - f \quad\quad\quad\quad\quad\quad\quad\quad (1.3.4)$$

$$e = 0 \quad\quad\quad\quad\quad\quad\quad\quad\quad (1.3.5)$$

$$a = -1 - f \quad\quad\quad\quad\quad\quad\quad\quad (1.3.6)$$

Substituting these values in eqn 1.1,

$$n = \Sigma C d^{-1-f} V^{1-f} \rho^0 v^f \quad\quad\quad\quad\quad (1.4)$$

Rearranging eqn 1.4, it becomes

$$n = \Sigma C \frac{V}{d} \cdot \left(\frac{Vd}{v}\right)^{-f} \quad\quad\quad\quad\quad (1.5)$$

or, alternatively,

$$\frac{nd}{V} = \mathrm{g}\left(\frac{Vd}{v}\right) \quad\quad\quad\quad\quad\quad (1.6)$$

where 'g' represents some function which, as it includes the undetermined constant C and index f, is unknown from the present analysis.

Although it may not appear so at first sight, eqn 1.6 is extremely valuable, as it shows that the values of nd/V should depend only on the corresponding value of Vd/v, regardless of the actual values of the original variables. This means that if, for each observation, the values of nd/V and Vd/v are calculated and plotted as a graph, all the results should lie on a single curve, this curve representing the unknown function 'g'. This curve can now be published, and a person wishing to estimate the eddy frequency for some given cylinder, fluid, and speed need only calculate the value of Vd/v, read from the curve the corresponding value of nd/V, and convert this to eddy frequency n. Thus the results of the series of observations are now in a usable form.

This was done, for example, by Relf and Simmons[1], whose results are shown in fig. 1.1, where the compound variable nd/V (the Strouhal number (*Str*), sometimes referred to as the *reduced frequency*) is plotted against the logarithm of the compound variable Vd/ν (the Reynolds number (*Re*)). Some authors use the reciprocal of the Strouhal number, i.e. V/nd, which is referred to as the *reduced velocity*.

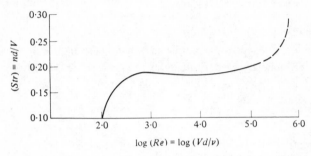

Fig. 1.1 The frequency of vortex shedding from a circular cylinder, after Relf and Simmons

The Strouhal number is of major importance as a parameter in the problems associated with the wind-excited oscillations of stacks, masts, towers, etc., and is dealt with more fully in Chapter 5.

Consider for a moment the two compound variables derived above.

a) nd/V, the Strouhal number.   The dimensions of this are given by

$$nd/V = [T^{-1} \times L \times (LT^{-1})^{-1}] = 1$$

b) Vd/ν, the Reynolds number.   The dimensions of this are given by

$$Vd/\nu = [(LT^{-1}) \times L \times (L^2 T^{-1})^{-1}] = 1$$

Thus the above analysis has collapsed the five original variables n, d, V, ρ and ν into two compound variables, both of which are non-dimensional. This has a great advantage, namely that the values obtained for these two quantities are independent of the consistent system of units used.

There are certain problems (e.g. the frequency of vibration of a stretched string) in which all the indices may be determined, leaving only the constant C undetermined. It is, however, usual to have more indices than equations, requiring one index or more to be left undetermined as above.

It must be noted that, while dimensional analysis may show which factors are not relevant to a given problem, the method cannot indicate which relevant factors, if any, have been left out. It is, therefore, advisable to include all factors likely to have any bearing on a given problem, leaving

out only those factors which, on *a priori* considerations, can be shown to
have little or no relevance.

1.2.2 Dimensional theory applied to forces on bodies in moving streams.
Another problem which is amenable to an approach by dimensional
theory and which is of considerable importance in the following chapters
concerns the wind force likely to be experienced by a building or object
immersed in a stream of air.

Assume, then, that the wind force, or one of its components, is denoted
by F and depends on the following quantities: air density ρ, air kinematic
viscosity ν, and wind speed V. The force and moment will also depend on
the shape and size of the body and its orientation to the stream. If,
however, attention is confined to geometrically similar bodies (e.g. spheres,
or models of a given building to different scales) the effects of shape as
such will be eliminated, and the size of the body can be represented by a
single typical dimension (e.g. the sphere diameter, or the roof span of the
model building, say) denoted by D. Then, following the method above,

$$F = f(V, D, \rho, \nu)$$

$$= C \cdot V^a D^b \rho^c \nu^d \quad \cdot \qquad \cdot \qquad \cdot \qquad \cdot \qquad \cdot \qquad \cdot \qquad \cdot \qquad (1.7)$$

In dimensional form this becomes

$$\left[\frac{ML}{T^2}\right] = \left[\left(\frac{L}{T}\right)^a (L)^b \left(\frac{M}{L^3}\right)^c \left(\frac{L^2}{T}\right)^d\right]$$

Equating indices of mass, length, and time separately leads to the three
equations:

(mass) $\quad 1 = c \quad \cdot \qquad \cdot \qquad \cdot \qquad \cdot \qquad \cdot \qquad \cdot \qquad (1.8.1)$

(length) $\quad 1 = a + b - 3c + 2d \quad \cdot \qquad \cdot \qquad \cdot \qquad \cdot \qquad (1.8.2)$

(time) $\quad -2 = -a - d \quad \cdot \qquad \cdot \qquad \cdot \qquad \cdot \qquad \cdot \qquad (1.8.3)$

With four unknowns and three equations it is impossible to determine
completely all the unknowns, and one must be left undetermined. This will
be d.
Equations 1.8 may then be solved for a, b and c in terms of d, giving

$$a = 2 - d$$
$$b = 2 - d$$
and $\quad c = 1$

Substituting these in eqn 1.7 gives

$$F = V^{2-d} D^{2-d} \rho^1 \nu^d$$

$$= \rho V^2 D^2 \left(\frac{\nu}{VD} \right)^d \qquad\qquad (1.9)$$

Therefore eqn 1.9 may be written as

$$F = \rho V^2 D^2 . \mathrm{g} (VD/\nu) \qquad . \qquad . \qquad . \qquad . \qquad . \qquad (1.10)$$

where $\mathrm{g}(VD/\nu)$ is some undetermined function of the stated compound variable.

Thus it can be concluded that the aerodynamic forces acting on a family of geometrically similar bodies (the similarity including the orientation to the stream) obey the law

$$F/\rho V^2 D^2 = \text{function } (VD/\nu) \qquad . \qquad . \qquad . \qquad . \qquad . \qquad (1.11)$$

This relationship is usually known as Rayleigh's equation.

The term VD/ν may also be written, from the definition of ν, as $\rho VD/\mu$, and was met previously in the problem relating to the eddy frequency in the flow behind a circular cylinder. It is a very important parameter in fluid flows, and, it will be recalled, is the *Reynolds number*.

Now consider any parameter representing the geometry of the flow round the bodies at any point relative to the bodies. If this parameter is expressed in a suitable non-dimensional form, it can easily be shown by dimensional analysis that this non-dimensional parameter is a function of the Reynolds number only. If, therefore, the values of (Re) (a common symbol for Reynolds number) of a number of flows round geometrically similar bodies are each the same for all the flows, it follows that all the flows are geometrically similar in all respects, differing only in geometric scale and/or speed. This is true even though some of the fluids may be gaseous and the others liquid. Flows which obey these conditions are said to be 'dynamically similar', and the concept of 'dynamic similarity' is essential in wind-tunnel experiments.

It has been found, for most bodies of present interest, in steady motion that the Reynolds number is an important criterion of dynamic similarity.

Graphs showing the variation in drag-force (windward-force) coefficient for a circular cylinder and for a sphere are given in fig. 3.12, and are accompanied by a fuller description of the flow around these bodies.

2

Relevant meteorology

2.1 The atmosphere

The earth's atmosphere extends about 1000 km above the earth's surface, to where the gas (particle) density is barely perceptibly greater than that of interplanetary space. (Other effects of the proximity of the earth, such as gravity or the concentration of radiation, are experienced even further away than that.)

The atmosphere is conventionally divided into five layers. The outermost layer, the *exosphere,* extends down to about 200 km above the earth. In this region the gas density is so low that it is measured in terms of the number of particles per unit volume, and the gas behaviour is that of its individual particles in separate elliptical orbits, seldom colliding with one another and occasionally escaping from the earth's gravitational field altogether.

Next underneath is the *thermosphere,* down to 100 km above the surface, and below this is the *mesosphere* down to about 25 km altitude. These regions absorb most of the incident solar ultraviolet radiation and within them are the ionised regions known as 'D', 'E', 'F' layers etc. which are important for example in radio communications, as they affect the degree to which radio waves may be reflected back to earth. In these regions also appear the *aurorae polaris* and meteor tracks (or shooting stars). Sounding balloons and airborne aircraft can penetrate the lower few kilometres of this region from the *stratosphere,* which is the next-to-inner-most region of the atmosphere and extends down to 11 km, below which, down to the surface, is the *troposphere.*

The outer edge of the troposphere is known as the *tropopause* and is defined as the height where the air temperature ceases to decrease with height.

The natural phenomenon of most direct interest in this book is the surface wind, that is the movement of the lower kilometre or so of the air adjacent to the ground or sea. The behaviour of the surface wind is, however, only a part of the circulation of the lower atmosphere as a whole, which takes place mostly within the troposphere. It is instructive to think of the surface winds as those air movements which can be perceived by the inhabitants dwelling at the bottom of an ocean of air which in reality is in continuous motion, washing about the surface of the globe in great tidal waves many kilometres thick.

2.1.1 The composition of the lower atmosphere. The main constituent gaseous elements that form clean dry air in the troposphere are, by volume, nitrogen 78%, oxygen 21%, argon 0·93%, with traces of neon, helium, krypton, hydrogen, and xenon, together with ozone, and the compound carbon dioxide. But, in the lower levels particularly, 'foreign' constituents such as fog, cloud, dust, pollen, and smoke may exist in varying proportions. Of these, water vapour forms the largest 'foreign' component and indeed constitutes from time to time a considerable percentage of the lower atmosphere *in toto*. Owing to its dependence on temperature, the percentage of water vapour may vary from about 3% by volume near the equator to 1% at mid latitudes, and it is reckoned that sufficient water exists in the atmosphere to cover the entire globe with a layer of water about 2·5 cm deep were it all to condense at the same time.

2.1.2 Temperature change with height. It is a matter of common experience that, over a few hundred metres of height, the air temperature changes perceptibly so that in general it gets cooler as one goes upwards. This negative gradient of temperature with height, or lapse rate of temperature as it is known in meteorology and aeronautics, is on average fairly constant for the first 10 km or so, changing only slightly with seasonal variations.

The vertical temperature change in the lower atmosphere at large is due primarily to two reasons. Firstly, because of its transparency to most of the solar radiation, the atmosphere is heated at the bottom, i.e. by the surface of the warm earth which absorbs radiation; and, secondly, at normal temperatures the atmosphere emits more radiation than it absorbs. These together cause density changes which bring about vertical convectio As the air rises into a region of lower pressure it expands and cools; conversely, as it falls it warms up. The net effect in the gross lower atmosphere is to produce a cooling at the 'standard' rate of 6·5 K per kilometre of height, or 1 K per 150 metres.

The lapse rate given here is that of the International Standard Atmosphere, an agreed standard for international comparison purposes in aeronautics, approximating to the atmospheric conditions prevailing for most of the year in temperate latitudes such as Europe and North

America. There are two other Standard Atmospheres: the *Tropical maximum*, with the same lapse rate but higher temperatures, and the *Arctic minimum*, with much lower temperatures, whose lapse rate is − 10 K/km (i.e. a temperature inversion, see section 2.1.4) over the first 1·5 km and 4·7 K/km from 3 km up to the start of the stratosphere. These represent the two global extremes of atmospheric-temperature variation with height, reduced to a standard for comparative purposes mainly in aeronautics, see fig. 2.1.[1]

In meteorology, the temperature lapse rate is a topic of primary importance; it is a vital factor in the evaluation of the movement of air masses, in the understanding and predictions of weather, in its relation to

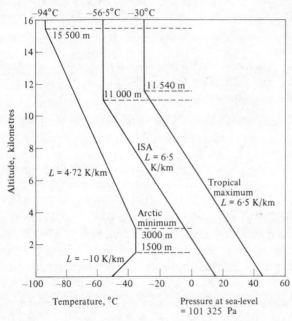

ig. 2.1 Variation of temperature with height in the International Standard, Tropical Maximum, and Arctic Minimum atmospheres

the climate of the region, and it is by no means taken to have a constant value. Indeed, to postulate a 'standard' value for a certain purpose implies that the normal occurrence of the quantity is variable, and that is the case for the vertical variation in temperature from place to place on the earth's surface.

It will be seen below (page 18) that the lapse rate has a profound effect on the stability or otherwise of the local atmosphere, and hence of the weather, since some of the most spectacular storms and associated high winds are due to the rapid and violent vertical convection of air masses in an unstable atmosphere.*

2.1.3 Horizontal temperature changes in the atmosphere are also a matter of common knowledge as are, in addition, the significant temporal change night to day and summer to winter. Perhaps the most easily recognised spatial temperature change around the globe is from the high-temperature region in the equatorial belt to the temperate zones in the mid latitudes on to the cold polar zones.

While on average the overall tendency is for the temperature to decrease towards the poles, regional and local conditions — the presence of land masses for example — and the movement of the atmosphere can modify and sometimes reverse the rate at which the temperature changes along any meridian. This is usually graphically illustrated by joining points of identical temperature by smooth lines on the map. These lines are known as *isotherms*. Of course, the local temperature data need to be suitably corrected to allow for variation due to, for example, the height of the recording station.

2.1.4 Temperature inversions. It often happens that for one or more reasons the air temperature at a certain layer stays constant or even increases with height. This is known as a *temperature inversion*. One such inversion of temperature is mentioned above — the International Arctic Minimum Standard Atmosphere — and it is general in most polar air masses, particularly as they travel towards mid latitudes and are heated from underneath by the warmer oceans and land. Another typical temperature inversion exists, for example, on still clear nights when the earth and adjacent air cool more rapidly then the free atmosphere, or when, throughout a layer, high turbulence causes rapid vertical convection so that the top of the turbulent layer may be cooler than the next layer above it at the interface. The running of a cool air flow under a warm wind is another cause of temperature inversion. As a rule, the presence of an inversion implies a highly stable atmosphere: one in which vertical air movements are rapidly damped out. In such a situation, fog and airborne pollutants collect — being unable to move freely or be dissipated by convection.

2.1.5 Atmospheric pressure. The pressure at a point in the atmosphere arises directly from the weight of the air above it and thus is greater lower down than higher up. What complicates the workings of the *hydrostatic laws* beyond those familiar from hydraulics is that the fluid

*See, for example, Barry, R. G., and Chorley, R. J., *Atmosphere, weather and climate*, London, Methuen, 1971.

volved, air, is compressible and changes its density in proportion to the
essure and inversely with the temperature. These laws, their derivation
d development both for compressible fluids − such as the atmosphere −
d for incompressible fluids − water, oils, and the like − are discussed
the next chapter.

In the meantime, accept that a relatively large vertical-pressure increase
ists positively downwards in the atmosphere (i.e. lower altitude, higher
essure). In still air, the buoyancy force which therefore exists on an
ment of air is balanced by the gravitational force exerted on the mass of
e air. At the same time, the atmospheric pressure varies from point to
int on the same level, and a horizontal pressure difference is felt on
e air. This horizontal pressure difference, or horizontal *pressure
adient* as it is known, is of major significance in generating and sustaining
otion of the air − in short, it is of first importance in raising wind.

It is shown below (page 26) that the equilibrium wind speed is
early proportional to the horizontal pressure gradient, so that high
inds are experienced where the pressure gradient is high, which will
where *isobars* are closest together.

1.6 Isobars are lines drawn on a map which join points of equal atmos-
eric pressure and from which the horizontal pressure gradient may be
tained (see below); this is of major interest in meteorological
timation of winds and climate. Since, as shown in section 2.2.2, the
essure changes significantly with height, it is necessary to specify (or
ow for) a standard height above sea level when the results from the
rious countrywide or international meteorological stations are collected
provide the isobars.

The isobars and atmospheric pressure are usually quoted in units of
illibars, one bar being equivalent to 10^5 N/m^2 which is very close to an
erage atmospheric pressure (1·0132 bar at sea level) − hence its appeal.

An alternative method of graphically indicating the change in atmos-
eric pressure on a map is to make direct appeal to the atmospheric
essure−height relationship and plot the height contours for a given
nstant atmospheric pressure; hence the appearance in meteorology
geographical or topographical terms such as trough, ridge, or col,
e first and second of which imply abrupt lowering or raising of atmos-
eric pressure over the land.

2 Circulation in the atmosphere

2.1 Vertical convection. Vertical convection of the atmosphere may be
vided into two groups: (a) mechanically forced convection and (b)
avity-induced convection.

Mechanically forced convection arises from the stirring of the flowing atmosphere from beneath by the obstructions arising from the surface of the earth, whether occurring naturally as in the case of mountains, hills, and forests, or man-made, for example buildings, towers, terraces, etc. The scale and rapidity with which the convection is forced decides the quality of the turbulence which may be induced in the atmosphere and the consequent gustiness felt locally in the wind; but, for the present, the movement of air up and down the windward and leeward (respectively) sides of a mountain may simply be considered as examples of mechanical forced convection in the lower atmosphere.

Gravity-induced convection is by far the more important phenomenon of the two and is ultimately responsible for the generation of all atmospheric movements. Stated at its simplest, it acts as follows: if for some reason, usually but not always heating or cooling, a volume of air becomes lighter (or heavier) than its surroundings, it will rise (or fall); this then sets in train any of the many phenomena associated with wind and weather. For example, if the oversimplified model of a column of rising air adjacent to a column of sinking air is taken, a surface wind will be generated at the bottom of the column (the surface of the earth) as the down-flowing air is drawn into the up-going column. A similar flow will proceed at the top from the 'lighter' column to the 'heavier'. Thus a circulation of air has taken place within the lower atmosphere.

Now, *thermal convection* as briefly described above is the most important but not the only mechanism for inducing vertical convections. The *composition* of the atmosphere and its *velocity* (speed and direction) also contribute to the vertical forces that may act on a given volume of air.

The effect of *change of composition* becomes apparent if the presence of water vapour in a given volume is considered. The molecular weight of water is 18, that of dry air about 29, so that the sample volume of atmosphere becomes less heavy as the proportion of water vapour in it increases. Extreme changes of humidity from dry to fully saturated do not occur, but 50% changes in the absolute humidity are not unknown in certain climatic situations, in which case a 1% change in mass per unit volume is produced, which is equivalent to the buoyancy induced by a 3 K temperature change.

Much smaller are the vertical forces associated with air moving with horizontal velocity over the surface of the globe. These involve motion of air in curved paths and arise from 'centrifugal' effects.

Consider a mass of air 'at rest' on the surface of the globe at P (fig. 2.2). As it is at rest relative to the surface, it will be spinning in space with the same speed as P; that is, moving with a tangential velocity of

$= \omega \, . \, R \cos \theta$ m/s about the N–S axis of spin, where ω is the angular elocity of the earth and $R \cos \theta$ is the radius of P from the axis of spin, being the radius of the globe which is about 6300 km.

This rotational velocity requires the centripetal acceleration $a_c =$ $^2/R \cos \theta$, which has a normal-to-surface (or vertical) component of $_c \cos \theta = V^2/R$.

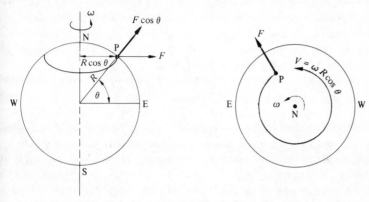

Fig. 2.2

Under still conditions, a volume of air of mass m near the earth's urface has a vertical downwards force or 'weight' equal to $m(g - v^2/R)$, where g is the acceleration towards the earth's centre due to gravity.

If now the air is in motion in an west–east direction, that is a westerly vind is blowing with velocity v, say, then the 'weight' of the air is *reduced* o $m\{g - (V + v)^2/R\}$, that is the westerly wind is lighter. Equally the asterly (east-to-west-flowing) wind is heavier, having its 'weight' increased o $m\{g - (V - v)^2/R\}$. The increase or decrease is quite small, being of the rder of 0·2% for a westerly of gale force 8 blowing in the wind latitudes; evertheless, it is sufficient to cause a westerly wind to overrun an adjacent asterly wind.

But, as indicated above, the most significant type of gravity-induced onvection is thermal convection, and all large winds and indeed all large-cale atmospheric circulations (even in the case of hurricanes, for example) we their continuance to heating (in general from below) and cooling (from bove) whether the heating or cooling is induced locally or is very wide-pread.

It is convenient to classify winds by the nature and magnitude of the hermal convections involved, dealing on the one hand with the global tmospheric circulation and the large-scale air movements peculiar to hem and on the other with the local winds which in the main are forced y the temperature differences due to peculiarities of the local terrain or geography but which may in their locality be more significant than the widespread circulation.

Before attempting a classification of winds and how they arise, it is worthwhile to consider some of the natural laws of mechanics which, applied to the atmosphere in motion, may help to explain the relevant phenomena associated with air movements and winds.

It is easy to fall into the habit of thinking of a wind, say, as blowing straight across a flat surface when in reality it is moving in a highly curved path over the surface of a spinning globe. Nowadays, photograph taken of observations from above the atmosphere assist not only the scientist in his work but all of us the more readily to accept the 'three-dimensional' concept of the atmosphere.

2.2.2 The stability of the atmosphere.   It is not hard to visualise conditi under which large vertical currents might exist in the lower atmosphere and, indeed, such currents are detected by aircraft as bumps and rough a On the ground in some parts of the world, the effects of violent up and down currents may be seen in the spectacular weather conditions generated, waterspouts and dust devils being among some of the smaller effects that are observed. Whether an atmosphere permits such motions to persist or whether the local conditions inhibit and damp them out are respectively, the physical manifestation of what meteorologists and flyer understand by the terms 'unstable' or 'stable' atmosphere.

The idea of stability, as far as an element of air in vertical motion is concerned, is similar to that of more common notions of mechanical static stability. For example, a solid cone resting on its base is said to be in *stable equilibrium* for, if its displacement is disturbed, i.e. if it is tilted slightly, it tends to return to its original position. If, on the other hand, it is balanced on its point and slightly displaced, it will tend to topple further and not to return to its original (on-the-point) condition and is seen to be in *unstable equilibrium.* The intermediate state of *neutrally stable equilibrium* obtains in this case with the cone lying on its side when, after a rolling displacement, no tendency to move either way is experienced. The same notions are involved in the case of an element of air being displaced up and down.

Figure 2.3 shows an element of air initially at level z_1 displaced upwards vertically to level z_2 in the atmosphere. Three possibilities exist:

i) the displaced section may tend to return to its original position (as it will if it becomes denser than the surrounding air);

ii) it will tend to continue upwards (if it is then less dense than the surroundings);

ii) it will remain in its new position (if its density becomes that of the air around it).

These three cases correspond, respectively, to *positive stability*, *instability*, and *neutral stability* of the atmosphere.

There are certain physical conditions of the atmosphere which encourage one state of stability or another, and, due to the importance

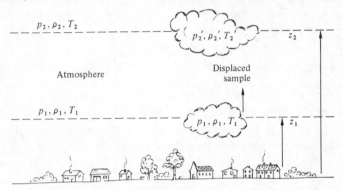

Fig. 2.3

of atmospheric instability in the generation of weather and storms, it is worthwhile to look more closely at them.

If the atmosphere is at rest, then the gravitational force on a specimen sample is exactly balanced by the buoyancy forces on it. If the gravity force changes, an out-of-balance force arises. Now, over a small height the acceleration due to gravity remains appreciably constant but the mass of a unit volume (i.e. its density) may not, since it is so closely related to temperature, which, as shown above, has significant vertical changes.

Refer back to fig. 2.3 and assume that the displaced sample had initially the conditions of pressure, density, and temperature (p_1, ρ_1, T_1) of the atmosphere at large at height z_1. After displacement to a height z_2 where the atmospheric conditions are p_2, ρ_2, T_2, the sample properties are p_2', ρ_2', T_2'.

Now, the pressure and density are related by a law which is conventionally expressed as

$$p = k\rho^n \tag{2.1}$$

This, combined with the equation of state $p = R\rho T$, allows the temperature ratio to be expressed in terms of the pressure ratio, viz., from the equation of state,

$$T_2/T_1 = (p_2/p_1)\rho_2/\rho_1 \tag{2.2}$$

From eqn 2.1,

$$\rho_2/\rho_1 = (p_2/p_1)^{1/m} \tag{2.3}$$

whence by substitution

$$T_2/T_1 = (p_2/p_1)^{(n-1)/n} \tag{2.4}$$

If the displaced element moves so quickly that no heat is gained or lost, it will expand adiabatically — that is, with the index of expansion, n, equal in value to the ratio of specific heats* (γ) — and the temperature of the element at the new height is given by

$$T_2'/T_1 = (p_2'/p_1)^{(\gamma-1)/\gamma} \tag{2.5}$$

As there is no constraint on the size of the element as it moves, a further valid assumption is that the pressure (p_2') in the element at z_2 will be p_2 — that of the atmosphere at z_2 — in which case

$$T_2'/T_1 = (p_2/p_1)^{(\gamma-1)/\gamma} \tag{2.6}$$

To find the ratio of the temperature in the element (T_2') and the temperature outside (T_2), combine eqns 2.4 and 2.6 thus:

$$\frac{T_2'}{T_2} = \frac{T_2'}{T_1}\frac{T_1}{T_2} = \frac{T_2'/T_1}{T_2/T_1}$$

or

$$\frac{T_2'}{T_2} = \frac{(p_2/p_1)^{(\gamma-1)/\gamma}}{(p_2/p_1)^{(n-1)/n}} = \left(\frac{p_2}{p_1}\right)^{(\gamma-n)/\gamma n} \tag{2.7}$$

The inverse of this ratio gives the density ratio between the air in the displaced sample and that outside, and hence the buoyancy of the sample at its new height,

i.e. $\quad \dfrac{\rho_2'}{\rho_2} = \dfrac{p_2'T_2}{T_2'p_2} = \dfrac{1}{T_2'/T} \qquad$ since $p_2' = p_2$

Then

$$\rho_2'/\rho_2 = (p_1/p_2)^{(\gamma-n)/\gamma n} \tag{2.8}$$

There are three possibilities which in turn determine the stability:

i)   If $n < \gamma$, $(\gamma-n)/\gamma n$ is a positive number, $=+a$ say.

Then, since $p_2 < p_1$,

$$\rho_2'/\rho_2 = (p_1/p_2)^a > 1$$

---

* See for example, Houghton, E. L., and Brock, A. E., *Aerodynamics for engineering students*, London, Edward Arnold, 2nd edn 1970.

Thus, after displacement, the air is denser than the atmosphere surrounding it and it will tend to sink back to its original level. The atmosphere is therefore *stable*.

ii) If, $n > \gamma$, $(\gamma - n)/\gamma n$ is negative, $= -b$ say.

Then $\quad \rho_2'/\rho_2 = (p_1/p_2)^{-b} < 1$

Thus, after displacement, the density of the small element is less than that of its surroundings and the element will tend to rise further. The atmosphere is therefore *unstable*.

iii) If $n = \gamma$, $(\gamma - n)/\gamma n = 0$

and therefore $\quad \rho_2'/\rho_2 = (p_1/p_2)^0 = 1$

The displaced air is therefore at all times equal in density to the surrounding atmosphere at the same level and will tend neither to sink nor to rise but will remain in its displaced position. The atmosphere is therefore *neutrally stable*.

Thus the three cases $n < \gamma$, $n > \gamma$ and $n = \gamma$ correspond respectively to stable, unstable, and neutrally stable atmospheres.

It is easily shown[1] that the index of expansion n is related to the lapse rate L by the relationship $n = g/(g - LR)$, where g is the acceleration due to gravity and R is the gas constant.

When $n = \gamma = 1\cdot4$ for dry air, $R = 287\cdot26$ J/kg K, and $g = 9\cdot807$ m/s^2,

$$L = \frac{0\cdot4 \times 9\cdot807}{1\cdot4 \times 287\cdot26} = 0\cdot009\ 75\ \text{K/m}$$

or $\quad L = 9\cdot75$ K/km $\hfill$ (2.9)

This is termed the *adiabatic lapse rate*. If the lapse rate exceeds this, i.e. the atmosphere becomes even more cool with height, the atmosphere is *unstable*.

It will be noted that in the International Standard Atmosphere the lapse rate in the troposphere is $6\cdot5$ K/km (the corresponding expansion index $n = 1\cdot235$) and the atmosphere is stable, as is also the 'standard' stratosphere where $n = 1$ and the lapse rate is zero.

As far as dry air is concerned, instability is reached only over hot surfaces where the heating from underneath is very severe. The rapid small-scale surface convection causes a shimmering effect particularly noticeable over asphalt on a hot summer's day.

It would seem from the above that an atmosphere will be stable if its lapse rate is less than the dry adiabatic lapse rate (seen to be about $9\cdot75$ K/km), and the standard average lapse rate is only about $6\cdot5$ K/km. This would imply a fairly stable normal atmosphere, but the degree of stability the atmosphere experiences — the frequency of the type of weather normally associated with unstable atmospheres – would belie this assumption. This is because only dry air has been considered in the demonstration above, and as a rule the atmosphere is more or less humid with water vapour.

The presence of water vapour saturating a sample of gas expanding without heat exchange across its boundaries causes the temperature of the sample to drop more slowly as latent heat of vaporisation is given up to the gas when the vapour condenses, as it must do when the temperature drops. The wet or *saturated adiabatic lapse rate* is about 5 K/km to 6 K/km at normal temperatures, which is less than the standard lapse rate of 6·5 K/km. As a rule the atmosphere is not fully saturated, so that an element of atmosphere in vertical motion may behave in a 'stable' way (the actual lapse rate of the surroundings being less than the dry adiabatic lapse rate of 9·75 K/km) until its temperature has dropped sufficiently for it to be fully saturated with water vapour. Subsequent upward movement condenses out some water and the element behaves in an unstable way (the actual lapse rate of the surroundings now being greater than the saturated adiabatic lapse rate of about 5·5 K/km). Meteorologists call this *conditional instability* in the atmosphere, since it is conditional on the presence of water vapour in the region of atmosphere concerned. It will come as no surprise to weather observers in the mid-latitudes that this is a 'normal' state of the atmosphere and does much to explain how large convective currents causing cumulus clouds, showers, and thunderstorms might grow from initially quite small vertical displacements.

The initiating displacement can be due to any one of several different causes which are properly the province of the meteorologist. They include uplift at the 'fronts' of weather systems, where cool heavy air runs under and lifts warm lighter air; heating from below; large-scale turbulence; and uplift caused by large barriers to the wind, such as ranges of hills and mountains.

2.2.3 The rotation of the local atmosphere.   Wind is air in motion due to the horizontal pressure difference caused by heating and cooling of the atmosphere; but it should be borne in mind that air has mass, is in motion on the surface of a spinning sphere, and consequently behaves in accordance with the laws of mechanics. Even in the absence of obstructions, further thermal disturbances, and, for simplicity in the theory, viscosity, the full prediction of the flow path is complicated, though not so much so as to prevent an understanding of some of the effects that may be induced in an air flow over the globe.

Consider the skin of atmosphere to be spinning with the earth so that it is at rest relative to the earth, fig. 2.4. The tangential velocity of the

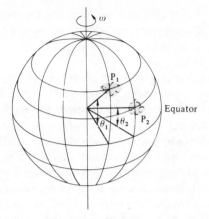

Fig. 2.4

earth's surface at the equator is $V = R\omega$, where R is the radius and ω the angular velocity about the axis of spin. At any other latitude the tangential velocity is $V \cos \theta$.

Now an element of the atmosphere at P_1 on latitude θ_1 having mass m will have an angular momentum about the axis of spin given by $mV \cos \theta_1 \, R \cos \theta_1$. If this mass of air moves to another point P_2 at latitude θ_2, where the radius of spin is $R \cos \theta_2$, for its angular momentum to be conserved it must have its tangential velocity changed to $V \cos^2 \theta_1 / \cos \theta_2$.

But in the latter case the 'still' tangential velocity at the point P_2 is $V \cos \theta_2$, so that on shifting latitude the mass of air acquires a velocity relative to the point on the surface to which is has moved of

$$V \frac{\cos^2 \theta_1}{\cos \theta_2} - V \cos \theta_2 = V \left(\frac{\cos^2 \theta_1 - \cos^2 \theta_2}{\cos \theta_2} \right)$$

A simple example will suffice to give a sense of the directions involved. Air moving with the surface of the earth at the equator where $\theta_1 = 0$, $\cos \theta_1 = 1$ has a tangential velocity of about

$$\frac{2 \pi \times 6370\,000}{24 \times 3600^*} = 465 \text{ m/s}$$

If moved to a latitude of $30°$ it would acquire a tangential velocity of $465/\cos 30° = 537$ m/s, according to the law of conservation of momentum. But the air locally at rest on the surface at latitude $30°$ has a tangential velocity of $465 \cos 30° = 410$ m/s, so that the required increase is a

* Note that a sidereal day has 86 164 seconds, *not* 24 x 3600 = 86 400 seconds as assumed above, which is for a calendar day.

velocity $537 - 410 = 127$ m/s in the direction of spin, which is from west to east. Similarly, working the other way, air moved from a latitude of $30°$ to the equator would acquire a velocity of 127 m/s against the direction of spin, that is from east to west.

Now these values of wind speed are very large and, if for example other latitudinal shifts were considered, it could be shown that even larger values could be produced. But, as indicated above, this simple theory ignores all of the real effects which go to producing those wind speeds actually occasioned by poleward and equatorward drifts and which prevent any credence being given to the values determined by the simple theory. Although for a particular case the absence of consideration of the most significant effects invalidates the theory, it is a noted fact that planetary winds flow from the west in middle latitudes and from the east on the equator and that poleward-moving air generally acquires an easterly drift whereas air flowing from the poles tends to acquire a westerly direction.

2.2.4 Wind deflection force due to the earth's rotation.   Some indication of the force acting on a mass of air due to the rotation of the globe underneath it may be obtained by the following simple extension of mechanics.

Figure 2.5 (a) shows a point P_1 at latitude θ_1 in the northern hemisphere. From a point in space just above the north pole N, the globe rotates at ω rad/s. From above any other point P_1 at latitude θ_1, the globe appears to rotate at $\omega \sin \theta_1$ around an axis through $P_1 O$.

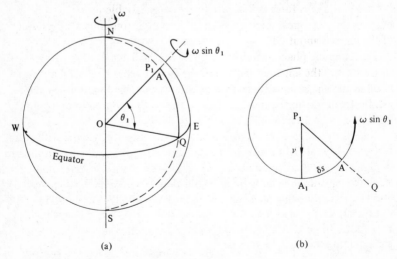

(a)   (b)

Fig. 2.5

Consider now a mass of air in space just above P_1, ignore any viscous or other effects which may constrain its motion, and let it begin to move with velocity v southwards along the meridian $P_1 Q$, fig. 2.5 (b). If there are no constraints, it will move during an interval of time δt along the straight line $P_1 A$ of length $v \delta t$. In the meantime, the earth has rotated under the mass of air so that in the same time interval the meridian has moved through an angle $\omega \delta t \sin \theta$ or, from the figure, the length $\delta s = A_1 A$. In other words, as the mass of air moves through $v \delta t$ to A_1, A moves through $A_1 A$, a distance of

$$\delta s = V \omega (\delta t)^2 \sin \theta_1 \qquad (2.10)$$

Looked at by an observer moving round the meridian, the air seems to be accelerating away westwards at right angles to the meridian. If this acceleration is a, the length δs in time δt is

$$\delta s = a(\delta t)^2 / 2 \qquad (2.11)$$

Equating eqns 2.10 and 2.11 gives the value of the normal-to-meridian acceleration to be

$$a = 2V\omega \sin \theta_1 \qquad (2.12)$$

Thus, to keep the air over the same meridian on its way south would demand a sideways force of

$$f = \text{mass} \times \text{acceleration} = m \times 2 v \omega \sin \theta_1 \qquad (2.13)$$

Note that the meridian through P_1 was taken in this demonstration but the same sideways force would be equally demonstrable if the air mass moved along any great circle through P_1, since the component of rotation of the earth is about OP_1.

Restating the phenomenon from the more usual assumption of a still earth reverses the apparent motion of the force so that in general a mass m of air moving along a great circle at latitude θ with velocity v sustains a deflective force to the right due to the *earth's rotation* given by eqn 2.13.

One or two consequences may briefly be described. Since the deflecting force is always at right angles to the direction of motion, the magnitude of the velocity v is unaffected but the direction will change so that, other things being equal, the air will move over the globe in a series of curves. Now, a particle moving on a curve of radius r has a radial acceleration of

$$a = V^2 / r \qquad (2.14)$$

and equating this to 2.13 yields

$$r = v / 2 \omega \sin \theta_1 \qquad (2.15)$$

Thus the radius of curvature is large when the wind speed is high and in low latitudes (on and near the equator) and small, that is the curvature is more pronounced, at higher latitudes. The actual *directional change of the wind* may be found straight away from the expression for the rotation due to the earth at any point P_1 quoted above as $\omega \sin \theta_1$.

2.2.5 'Centrifugal' effects have already been noted above as contributing to the change of weight of air due to its motion round a great circle on the earth. If, in addition, the airflow is curved in the horizontal sense, the plane of the resulting curve is inclined to the plane of the earth's diameter and the centripetal inertia force acting along a radius in the plane of the orbit will have a surfacewise or sideways component. This force is that required to press the air mass into the curved path; without it the mass would tend to continue in straight (or tangential) motion.

2.2.6 Resultant horizontal deflecting force. In general, the *resultant horizontal deflecting force* on the moving air mass will be the algebraic sum of the rotational and 'centrifugal' forces. The deflecting forces are additive when the wind flow is clockwise in the southern hemisphere or anticlockwise in the northern, and vice versa.

Of course, and it may not be repeated too often, all the above generalisations embody the grossest of simplifying assumptions but nevertheless yield important indications of the natural tendency to motion of an airstream otherwise generated in the earth's atmosphere.

An airstream in steady motion along a curved path will ostensibly be in equilibrium under the action of the resultant horizontal deflecting force and the force due to the pressure gradient arising from gravity-induced convection. In point of fact, viscous effects compounded by stirring by surface obstructions contribute significantly to the wind flow in the lower levels. At higher levels, however, at about $\frac{1}{2}$ km altitude, the lower atmosphere circulation is clear of the surface-induced turbulence and the wind is free to take up the equilibrium speed and direction. The height at which this takes place and the wind velocity at that height are known as the *gradient height* and the *gradient velocity* respectively. The latter is very nearly the wind speed that would be taken up on a smooth sphere in the absence of viscosity.

It is instructive to work out that wind direction likely to be obtained from a horizontal pressure distribution, that is to reach a state of equilibrium which satisfies a horizontal pressure distribution. For the moment, assume that *vertical* stability exists — that the vertical pressure difference or buoyancy is balanced by gravity.

Consider a mass of air for convenience in a rectangular volume between the isobars (lines of constant pressure) p_1 and p_2 which are separated by a distance s, fig. 2.6 (a). The horizontal pressure gradient acting is $(p_1 - p_2)/s$, where p_1 is greater than p_2. (In the limit this is defined as $\delta p/\delta s$, where δp is the pressure rise over the elemental distance δs).

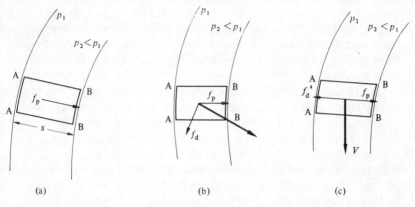

(a)   (b)   (c)

Fig. 2.6

The pressure force tending to move the air *from* the direction of the higher pressure p_1 *towards* the lower pressure p_2 is

pressure p_1 × area of surface AA − pressure p_2 × area BB

which for a rectangular box whose ends are of equal area A is $(p_1 - p_2)A$ away from the direction of the rise in pressure, or $-(p_1 - p_2)A$ *towards* the pressure rise. This pressure force accelerates the air from high to low pressure such that the applied (pressure) force (f_p) equals the product of the mass of air and its acceleration

i.e. $-(p_1 - p_2)A = (\rho A s)a$ (2.16)

where ρ is the air density and As is the volume of the 'box', a being the resulting acceleration.

Thus the acceleration induced by the pressure gradient is

$$a = -(p_1 - p_2)/\rho s \qquad\qquad (2.17)$$

which is more generally written as

$$a = -(1/\rho)\mathrm{d}p/\mathrm{d}s \qquad\qquad (2.18)$$

This, then, is the initial motion, with the air acquiring acceleration and then velocity in the direction of the lower pressure. Left to itself, this motion would so continue but, as noted above, as soon as the air acquires

a velocity of motion over the surface of the globe it also acquires a
deflecting force f_d which acts at right angles to its direction of motion,
and the force f_d (which is, remember, the algebraic sum of the rotational
and 'centrifugal' forces mentioned above) combines with the pressure
force to act on the air as shown in fig. 2.6 (b). The imbalance must
continue with the air being accelerated along the resultant of the two
forces f_p and f_d; but, all the time, as the wind direction swings round so
does the deflecting force until a state of equilibrium exists with the air
moving *along* the isobars, with the deflecting force balancing the pressure
force fig. 2.6 (c).

Left to itself under the action of pressure force and deflecting force,
the air will move at a velocity whose direction is *along* the isobars (higher
pressure on the right) and whose magnitude is sufficient for the deflecting
force to balance the pressure (gradient) force. This is the situation which
most nearly obtains at the *gradient height* to produce the *gradient
velocity* as mentioned above, at the height sufficiently far removed from
the surface to be free from surface-friction effects.

In what has gone before, the isobars p_1 and p_2 are shown curved with,
as it happens, the centre of curvature towards the *low* pressure. The
gradient wind will consequently be somewhat lower than might be
expected were the isobars curved the other way, that is if the centre of
curvature were towards the *high* pressure. This may be explained as follows
by taking first the case of fully developed friction-free flow along straight
isobars, fig. 2.7 (a), in equilibrium under the pressure force f_p and
deflecting force f_d. Since the centripetal acceleration is zero, the deflecting
force f_d is (from eqn 2.13, $f_d = m\,2V\,\omega \sin\theta$) required only to balance
the pressure force, given from eqn 2.18 as $f_p = -m(1/\rho)dp/ds$. Thus

$$2V\,\omega \sin\theta = -(1/\rho)dp/ds$$

The wind speed at sufficient height to be free from turbulence effects
is given directly for flow along parallel isobars as

$$V = -\left(\frac{1}{2\rho\,\omega \sin\theta}\right)\frac{dp}{ds} \tag{2.19}$$

and is directly proportional to the magnitude of the horizontal pressure
gradient, since, for a given locality, the density (ρ), the earth's rotational
speed (ω), and the latitude (θ) are constant. This velocity is referred to as
the *geostrophic velocity*.

But in general the isobars are curved around either a lower pressure
area (fig. 2.7 (b)) or a higher pressure area (fig. 2.7 (c)), in which cases the
resultant deflecting force f_d needs, respectively, to be less than or
greater than the rotational deflection force above for equilibrium, and the
wind velocity for equilibrium is consequently less than or greater than the

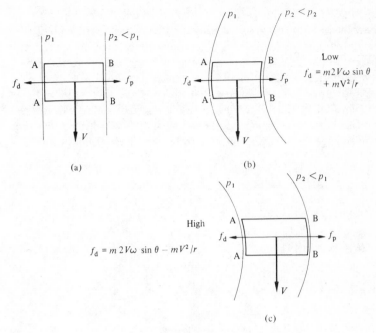

Fig. 2.7

geostrophic wind. That is, the force balance is now

$$2V\omega \sin\theta \pm V^2/r = -(1/\rho)dp/ds \quad (+\text{low}, -\text{high})\tag{2.20}$$

and the resulting wind velocity (free from viscous effects) depends also on the radius of curvature (r) of the streamlines, which in equilibrium flow is that of the isobars.

The gradient wind flowing round a low-pressure region (cyclonic) is less than the geostrophic wind, and that around a high-pressure region (anticyclonic) will be greater since in this case it is required to accelerate towards the higher pressure whereas around the low-pressure region the pressure gradient assists.

2.2.7 Frictional forces. So far in this book the effects of viscosity, which is an inherent property of any real fluid, have in the main been ignored. At the interface between a moving fluid and a solid surface, viscosity manifests itself in the creation of shear forces aligned in opposition to the direction of motion of the fluid. In the case of the surface of the earth and the atmosphere above it, the same effect occurs, although, in the context of this book, the shear forces imparted to the surface are of less

consequence than is the reaction of the fluid. If one thinks, for
convenience, of the earth's surface as at rest with a wind stream passing
over it, the action of viscosity is to reduce to almost zero the air velocity
adjacent to the surface. In fact, at the actual surface of separation between
solid and fluid, consideration of the intermolecular forces leads to the
assumption that at the boundary there is a condition of 'no slip' and the
relative velocity of the fluid tangential to the surface is everywhere zero.
However, close to the smooth surface in a wind, the wind velocity is very
low, and large shearing gradients and stresses are developed in the air.

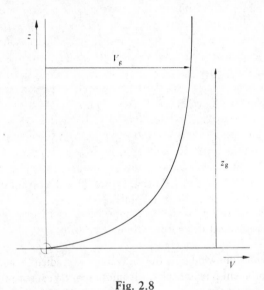

Fig. 2.8

These have the effect of retarding the layers near the ground, and these
layers, in turn moving more slowly than those beyond them, will
influence the outer ones and tend to slow them down in their turn, and
so on outwards until the effect is negligibly small.

It is evident that the velocity increase which takes place along a
vertical line must be continuous from zero on the surface to a maximum
some distance away, and a graph of this velocity plotted against height is as
shown in fig. 2.8. The height at which the velocity ceases to increase and
the velocity at that point are, as stated earlier, the gradient height and the
gradient velocity respectively. This state of affairs will be seen to be
similar to that discussed in the boundary-layer theory in aeronautics,
say, but care must be taken not to take the analogy too far: the
mechanics of the flow are the same, but the scale and growth

of the earth's boundary layer are very different from those of boundary layers encountered in aeronautics.

The effect of viscosity on the air close to the surface is to slow it down, i.e. to apply a retarding or frictional force to it. In mechanics, this could be stated as causing a rate of change of streamwise momentum of the air. Now, although viscosity starts the momentum loss in the layers close to the surface, and continues throughout the layers above to contribute a certain amount to the frictional force, away from the surface another mechanism — turbulence — is of greater significance for causing a momentum transfer. In turbulent flow, considerable random motion exists not only along the mean streaming direction but also perpendicular to it — up, down, and sideways. As a result, appreciable transportation of mass takes place between adjacent layers. If there is a mean velocity gradient in the flow there will be corresponding interchanges of stream-wise momentum between adjacent layers, and resisting shears will be built up*. These are known as Reynolds stresses, as distinct from viscous stresses already shown to exist close to the surface.

The shape and size of the curve shown in fig. 2.8 will depend less on viscosity than on the type and predominance of the turbulent and random eddying motions in the wind, which will in turn be affected by the type of terrain over which the wind is blowing. Figure 2.9, taken from the classic work of Davenport[2], illustrates the point.

For the present, recognise that near the ground a frictional force is present which opposes the wind motion and increases towards the surface.

2.2.8 The equilibrium wind direction.
Below the gradient height, the viscous and turbulent phenomena of the air in motion causes a frictional force, which impairs the balance of the two forces discussed in section 2.2.6.

The frictional force is generated as soon as motion starts, so that equilibrium is eventually reached with the wind direction tilted towards the lower pressure isobars, fig. 2.10. As shown above, the frictional force steadily decreases with height, from a maximum at the surface to zero at the gradient height, so that not only does the wind speed increase with height but also its *direction* shifts with height to become more nearly parallel to the isobars with increasing altitude, fig. 2.11.

The curve of the wind vectors on the horizontal plane is known as the Ekman spiral, after Ekman's analogous work in *Influence of the earth's rotation on ocean currents*[3]. The layer of the atmosphere in which the wind shifts in this way is known as the *Ekman layer*, the actual shift

* See, for example, Houghton, E. L., and Boswell, R. P., *Further aerodynamics for engineering students,* London, Edward Arnold, 1969.

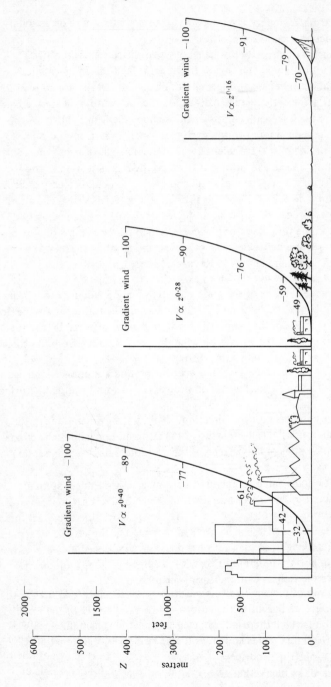

Fig. 2.9 Profiles of mean wind velocity over level terrains of differing roughness

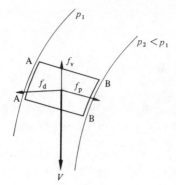

Fig. 2.10

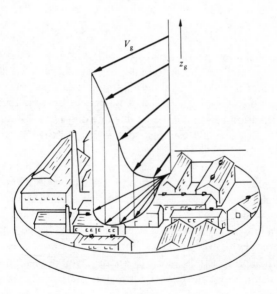

Fig. 2.11

being about 30° over land to about 15° over the sea, where frictional forces are lower.

More recently, workers in this field have defined a *surface layer* of 10–30 metres adjacent to the ground (opinions differ as to the mean height) over which the wind properties – wind direction, for example – remain constant.[4] One can recall numerous particular situations where, even in a gale, the wind speed is zero for several metres of height due to the presence of blanketing obstructions such as tall timber stands or high-density buildings. These surely affect wind loadings and are dealt with separately below.

2.3 Classification and types of wind

For much of its wind terminology, modern meteorology relies on maritime history in describing the global circulation and on folklore in describing specific recurring local winds associated with particular geographical or topographical situations.

Long-distance sailors were quick to recognise the occurrence of steady winds blowing for a long period in the same direction, and the names given by these early mariners have remained − e.g. trade winds, westerlies, roaring forties − as indeed have the names of the regions where for long periods the winds are fitful and weak, i.e. the doldrums and horse latitudes.

2.3.1 The general atmospheric circulation. It was convenient, following these early 'observations', to incorporate the prevailing wind systems into a theoretical model of the general lower atmospheric circulation such as shown in fig. 2.12. As this purports to be in essence the simplification of years of observation of wind, it has a value in giving a broad indication of the flow in the lower levels resulting from the general circulation of the atmosphere.

While not pursuing modern thermodynamic theories of the origin of the earth's circulation, it is still of value to recall less sophisticated geographical explanations. Near the equator, the lower atmosphere is warmed and rises, depositing much precipitation and creating a uniform low-pressure area into which flow the (trade) winds drawn from northern and southern hemispheres. The air going aloft flows counter to the trades to descend in the horse latitudes, creating a wide region of high pressure (the horse latitudes over the oceans, the major desert areas on the continents). Flowing northwards and southwards from these horse latitudes in the northern and southern hemispheres respectively are the prevailing westerlies, which meet the cold dense air flowing away from the poles in a low-pressure region characterised by stormy variable winds. It is this interface between cold dense and warm moist air which is of main interest to the climatology of Northern Europe and North America.

This oversimplified picture may be used as little more than a means of classifying broad climatic regions over the globe, and even this use must be treated with care − particularly in the Northern hemisphere where, for example, the incidence of large land masses causes considerable deviations from the simple model above.

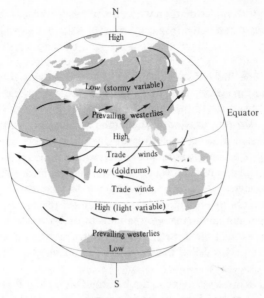

Fig. 2.12

Many other observations also belie the 'steady-state' impression given by the above simple general circulation—the successive cyclones and anti-cyclones which are generated and swept along in the westerlies, the large and regular air movement associated with the monsoons, and the tropical cyclonic disturbances which reach enormous proportions have all been discounted here. Owing to the influence of the first on the wind structure in mid-latitudes, they are described briefly below. The remainder should be referred to in the literature.

2.3.2 Air masses. Notwithstanding the strictures implied above, the effect of the general circulation is to produce in motion over the surface of the earth large masses of air in which the physical properties are more or less uniform. The air masses originate in, and are named after, their geographical source region where the large-scale uniformity of the mass first appears. For example, air which is relatively quiet for several weeks over many thousands of square kilometres of the cold snow- and ice-covered Arctic wastes will become very cold and dry (and consequently heavy). On the other hand, if the surface over which air rests for any length of time is warm and moist the air will become warm and humid, and so on. As the masses move about the globe, their properties gradually change according to the conditions of the surface over which they travel. If one recalls the simplified general-circulation model above, the UK, for example, would seem to be in a situation where at any one time the local atmosphere may have originated in the tropical regions of the horse latitudes or alternatively in the cold polar regions. In point of fact, climatologists in the UK recognise some sixteen* or so categories of air mass arriving over western Europe, most of them being subdivisions of the four broad groups: Tropical Maritime (mT), Tropical Continental (cT), Polar Maritime (mP), and Polar Continental (cP).

Tropical Maritime air is warm and humid and forms the majority of the tropical air flowing polewards, originating as it does over the large oceans. As it travels polewards over cooler waters, it undergoes cooling from below and an inversion occurs at lower levels, which makes for a stable atmosphere.

A *Tropical Continental* air mass is a much less frequent visitor to the UK, although common in many other parts of the world. It is formed chiefly over low-latitude deserts. The air, particularly that near the ground, has a high temperature, and the whole mass, although quite dry, is very unstable.

Of the cold masses arriving in the UK, the *Continental Polar* mass originates over the large northern land masses of Europe and Asia, which in winter are intensely cold. Air close to the surface has a very low temperature, and a strong temperature inversion exists above, so that a very stable air mass is produced. The *Maritime Polar* type is the commoner mass to visit the UK and often has markedly unstable characteristics since, having originated in the intensely cold high latitudes, its passage over relatively warmer seas both warms and humidifies the lower layer. The warming generates a steep lapse rate, while the humidity provides the precipitation.

As the air masses proceed along their tracks, they become modified by thermal or mechanical processes so that the length, shape, and features under their paths, the season of the year, and the condition and temperature of the land or sea on arrival all have an influence on the state of the local atmosphere at the time.

2.3.3 Features of secondary atmospheric circulation (fronts).   It has become customary to group the atmospheric circulation into primary and secondary states. The primary circulation involves the transport of energy and momentum in the atmosphere on a global scale and refers to large relatively permanent features in the overall pressure distribution,

---

* Belasco, J. E., 'Characteristics of air masses over the British Isles' *Air. Min. Met. Office Geophys. Mem.* 87 MO 5306, 1952, differentiates 19 types of air mass.

whereas the secondary circulation concerns those elements of air movement which are relatively short lived and which frequently originate from the interference of widely different types of air mass at their frontiers or interfaces. Very broadly, the *primary* circulation may be said to determine the *climate* of an area, whereas the *secondary* circulation is responsible for the *weather.*

A fairly recent (early twentieth century) discovery was that the changes in weather in mid-latitudes could be associated with the way in which the interface regions between different air masses were moving and behaving. These interfaces were named *fronts,* and the study of the formation, life, and eventual dissolution of fronts has become a cornerstone of modern climatology, some of the terminology of which has become common usage in discussion of weather.

The interface between two dissimilar air masses is called the *frontal surface,* and it is the intersection of this surface with the earth's surface which is the *front* proper. It has become general in the mass media to represent fronts as curved lines on maps, being identified as warm fronts, cold fronts, or occluded fronts as the case may be by making the advancing line with half rounds, spikes, or alternately the one and the other, fig 2.13.

While it has become customary to look at the development of, for example, a depression from above as a movement of the fronts, it must not be forgotten that the real disturbance is taking place in three

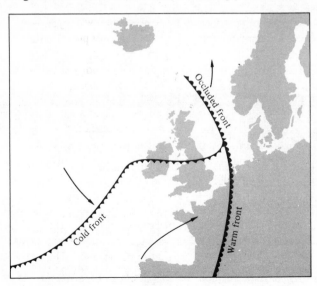

Fig. 2.13

dimensions and has a vertical shape; as will be seen, the vertical changes may have a considerable effect on the surface wind generated.

A cold air mass, being much more 'heavy' than a warmer mass, will, even if they are both in motion parallel to the interface, tend to move under the latter so that the frontal surface is quite curved and upward and downward components of velocity are induced, fig. 2.14.

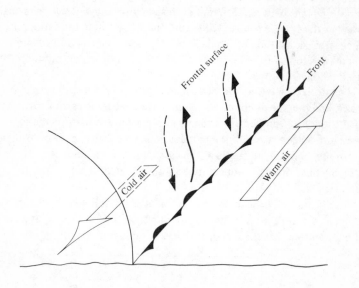

Fig. 2.14

Now, in reality the frontal surface is a surface of separation between fluids of different density moving with inertia in a gravitational field. If there is much relative motion at the interface, shearing stresses will build up a wave motion (directly analogous to waves created by the shearing forces of wind on a water surface, which is physically the surface of separation between fluids of (vastly) different densities).

Under certain conditions, the waveform generated develops as shown by the frontal distortions in fig. 2.15. In fig. 2.15 (b), the cold front advances behind the warm air trapped in the crest of the wave, lifting it upwards *en masse* as the cold front catches up with the warm front. At this stage the fronts merge and are said to be *occluded*. The warm entrapped air is lifted off the surface and the swirl of cold air sweeps underneath to form on the surface a low-pressure centre whose isobars and isoclines are closed and near-circular loops. The whole process may take three to four days and, since large-scale vertical convection of, very often, humid air is induced, much precipitation may well be encouraged.

Of more interest in the context of this book is that the growth of the depression, historically called a cyclone – a name nowadays usually reserved for the deep depressions generated in tropical zones – and the movement of the associated fronts often give rise to strong surface gusts and lulls, i.e. 'squalls'. The intensity of these is directly attributable to the vertical movements induced before and behind the advancing front, the pressure gradient, and the stability of the advancing air mass.

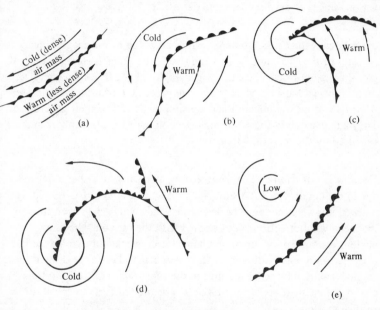

Fig. 2.15

If air is being raised at a front, the surface air moving to replace it has to overcome the effects of surface friction and will move more slowly than the downward-flowing air which might in any case be moving with near gradient velocity. At the same time, if the advancing air flow has a higher pressure gradient, an increase in wind speed is to be expected as the front passes; conversely, a lull will be experienced if the following pressure gradient is weak. Finally, an overtaking air mass which is unstable is prone to induce gusts of stronger intensity than if it were stable.

It is evident, then, that those frontal systems which have these three factors all present at the same time will produce severe gusting conditions and as a general rule they will be cold fronts preceding an unstable air mass whose pressure gradients are much larger than those of the stable warm mass being overtaken.

Such depressions rarely occur in isolation, The depressions in the mid-latitudes of the northern hemisphere at the interface of the polar and tropical air masses are generated in what have been dubbed 'cyclone families'. A fresh disturbance is created on the frontal surface behind the trailing cold front as the initial depression grows into maturity, and that in turn develops from a wave into a depression and again in its turn causes yet another disturbance in the frontal surface to follow along behind. A 'world-wide' chart would show a string of depressions in various stages of development and decay, fig. 2.16.

2.3.4 Local winds.   A number of winds arise due to the geographical features of the surrounding area and their occurrence is so regular as to give them a definitive place in the geography of the region and very often a special local name. It is not the present intention to enumerate these but rather to indicate the conditions which force their generation. They all arise due to local warming or cooling of the atmosphere and are canalised by the relevant topography.

Canalisation of wind.   The wind roaring up a canyon, either a natural one in the country or the man-made canyon of a street of tall buildings, is a well-known experience of pedestrians on a windy day, even though the mean wind direction is not aligned with the canyon. This is an obvious example of an air stream being locally canalised by obstructions. It is less commonly realised that the lower atmosphere as a whole is more readily canalised by relief features in the topography of the land than would at first sight appear, with the 'sky as the limit', so to speak, to vertical motion.

In fact, a sheet of air moving over the earth's surface is reluctant to rise in the face of an obstacle such as a hill or mountain and, if the topography is suitable, will tend to flow around rather than over the obstruction. There are good physical reasons for this tendency. As a rule, the energy changes required to accelerate the flow round the obstacle at the same level are less than those involved in increasing the potential energy of the air in lifting it, with, additionally, the concomitant rarefaction and compression of the air going up and down. Generally, if there is a gap in the line of obstruction to an air stream, the air will try to flow through the gap, causing a characteristic high wind. Of course, air is forced to rise over wide ranges of obstructions and the local climate is determined as a consequence; nevertheless, as a general rule, air will stream into a valley and over passes where an opportunity presents itself, and care should be taken on site to recognise the possibility of a predominant wind.

In a similar way, wind coming in off the sea will be canalised between headlands and will tend to follow the estuary, sea loch, or fiord as the case may be, giving local wind directions at water level somewhat at variance with the mean wind direction. An example of this on the South Coast of the UK is in those breezes found in the Solent, and much favoured by yachtsmen, due to the wind being canalised between the Isle of Wight and the mainland coast of Hampshire.

Land and sea breezes.   As stated above, winds may arise due to local warming or cooling of the atmosphere. Perhaps the most well-known examples of this phenomenon are *land* and *sea* breezes, which occur due to the discontinuity in air temperature at the coast at certain times of the night or day respectively.

Shortly after mid-morning on a clear summer day, the land temperature is raised by the sun and in turn raises the temperature of the air above it, lowering its density. Meanwhile, over the sea the temperature has remained very much the same. The warm air mass over the land rises to be replaced by the denser cooler air flowing in off the sea. At night, if it is at all clear, the land cools off rapidly; the adjacent air also cools to a temperature lower than that above the sea and a reverse, though less marked, air movement takes place from the land out to sea. The same types of wind are generated at lakesides and, indeed, at any boundary where a differential temperature may be caused, for example at the edge of a forest which may warm up less than the adjacent plain.

Mountain breezes and glacier winds.   Another form of wind is generated by a widespread cooling of areas where there is considerable geographical relief. These *mountain breezes* may at certain places under exceptional conditions become quite large. On a still clear night, say, mountain and valley sides may cool so that the adjacent air, becoming heavier, drains down the slopes into the valley. If the head of the valley terminates in a large plateau-like area of snow and ice, the flow of air at the lower end of the valley can assume high-wind proportions. *Glacier winds* have the same mechanism, the cool air adjacent to the surface, or within crevasses, draining towards the foot of the glacier and on downwards.

When a similar situation exists on a very much larger scale, the resulting winds affect a large territory and have been called fall winds. Among the

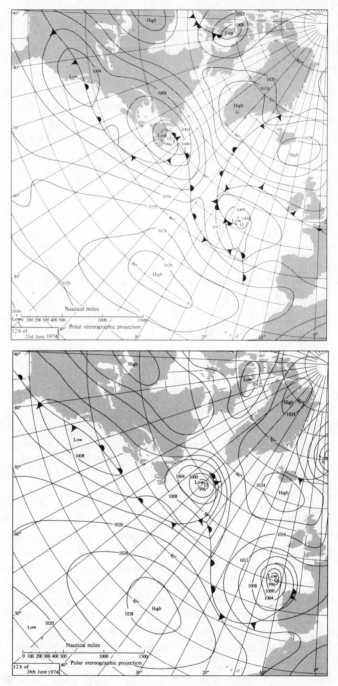

Fig. 2.16 A world-wide chart of family of lows

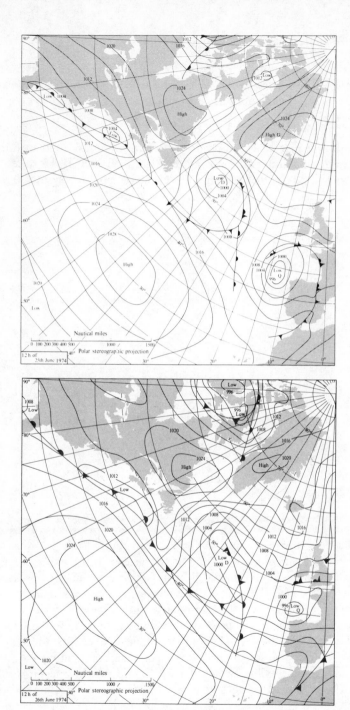

Fig. 2.16 (*continued*)

best known in Europe is the *Mistral,* caused by the dense air cooled over the high winter-snow-covered plateaus of southern-central France flowing as a northerly wind down the Rhône valley to the (warmer) Mediterranean.

Whirlwinds are common, for example, over very hot plains and are caused by the local uprush of the hot and very light surface air. This surface air is much less dense than that immediately above it but is prevented from

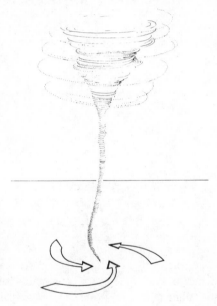

Fig. 2.17

rising piecemeal over the surface by the blanketing effect of the heavier air just above it *until* a gap appears in the blanket. This gap then in effect becomes an orifice allowing the light surface air to jet upward in a well-defined chimney. The surface air rushing towards the bottom of the chimney acquires a velocity slightly offset from the exact centre so that when it is drawn up the 'spout' it possesses a component of spin about the axis of the column and hence produces the characteristic whirl, fig. 2.17. Over land, dust and small surface debris are drawn into the whirlwind to give the well known 'dust-devil'. These vertical vortices have all the classical properties of cyclones and tornadoes on a miniature scale, with the exception of course of the precipitation due to the changes in humidity.

The tornado is a cyclonic storm of a few tens to hundreds of metres diameter whose surface winds are of such ferocity that much structural damage results from its passing. Very common in parts of large land masses such as the USA, the tornado is also not unknown in the UK. Tornados exhibit the same stability once generated as do, on their tinier scale, the dust devils mentioned above, but they are generated in the lower atmosphere away from the surface. The initiating mechanism is much the same. A large, warm lighter air mass is blanketed by a region of much denser air, perhaps by overrunning of an adjacent cold mass. A gap appears above, and massive vertical convection begins, fed and maintained by condensation of water vapour into rain or ice droplets. The horizontal velocities induced in the warm lower layer as the up flow through the 'gap' develops have no surface-friction effects to reduce them, so they arrive at the base of the chimney with very high values. For this reason, coupled with that of the much larger scale involved, the horizontal air flow acquires a curved path which contributes much angular momentum to the 'chimney' as the flow is drawn upwards, and a large vertical-vortex core is created. This swirl started at a point above the surface gradually takes in air at lower and lower levels until it is terminated by the surface, over which the winds blow in tight concentric circles.

Other mechanisms exist for generating the vertical vortices; for example, two different air masses flowing in opposite directions beside each other would cause vortices to spin up between them. Subsequent condensation within would lead to warming and convection which in turn feeds the vortex. Small tornadoes are usually accompanied and are caused by violent thunderstorms. Thunderstorms are characterised by the rapid vertical downwards movement of cold air due to a combination of evaporation of and cooling by the falling rain or ice droplets. This cold air thrusts forward on reaching the surface, running under and forcing upwards the warm humid air in front of the thunderstorm. It is this convection which may generate the swirling tornado which stands ahead of and precedes the thunderstorm.

The passage of a (weak) tornado in the UK in January 1971 and a survey of the considerable damage it wreaked is reported by K. J. Eaton.[5] At the time, the mean wind speed was 12 m/s (force 6), the maximum gust recorded at the Meteorological Office anamometer nearest to the tornado was 17 m/s (force 8), but an estimate of the maximum wind speed was twice as much.

As for the weather at the time, there was no cold front but a deep region of unstable air due to a cold upper trough, and it was thought likely that the tornado descended from one of the thundery storms plotted over the region.

The trail of damage went 250 km from the Isle of Wight north east to Upminster in Essex, and the trail of destruction was 100 to 200 m across.

By no means could a *hurricane* be called a local wind, but its mechanics are similar. At yet another order of magnitude, larger in scale than the tornado, the *tropical cyclone, hurricane,* or *typhoon* — which may be hundreds of kilometres in diameter — feeds itself from the same process of energy conversion. These storms originate in the shallow depressions associated with the disturbed oceanic regions of the doldrums.

The properties and structure
of fluid flows

1 The relevant properties of a fluid

The basic feature of a fluid is that it can flow, and this is the essence of any definition of it, but this property is shared by substances which are not true liquids, e.g. a fine powder piled on a sloping surface will also flow. However, fine powder, such as flour, poured in column onto a flat surface will form a roughly conical pile, with a large angle of repose, whereas water — a true liquid — poured onto a fully wetted surface will spread uniformly over the whole surface. Also, a powder may be heaped in a bowl, whereas, away from the edges, a still liquid will always form a level surface. A definition of a fluid must allow for these facts; thus a fluid may be defined as 'matter capable of flowing and either finding its own level (if a liquid) or filling the whole of its container (if a gas)'.

1.1 Pressure.

At any point in a fluid, whether liquid or gas, there is a pressure. If a body is placed in a fluid, its surface is bombarded by a large number of molecules moving at random. Under normal conditions the collisions on a small area of surface are so frequent that they cannot be distinguished as individual impacts: they appear as a steady force on the area. The intensity of this 'molecular-bombardment' force is the static pressure.

For large bodies moving or at rest in the fluid (air, say) the pressure is not uniform over the surface, and this gives rise to aerodynamic force or aerostatic force respectively.

Since pressure is intensity of force, it has the dimensions

$$[\text{Force}] \div [\text{area}] = [MLT^{-2}] \div [L^2] = [ML^{-1}T^{-2}]$$

and is expressed in units of pascals (Pa) or of millibars (mb).

1.2 Temperature.

In any form of matter, the molecules are in motion relative to each other. In gases the motion is random movement of appreciable amplitude ranging from about 76×10^{-9} metres under normal conditions to some tens of millimetres at very low pressures. The distance of free movement of a molecule of gas is the distance it can travel before colliding with another molecule or the walls of the container The mean value of this distance for all the molecules in a gas is called the 'mean molecular free path'.

By virtue of this motion the molecules possess kinetic energy, and this energy is sensed as temperature of the solid, liquid, or gas. In the case of a gas in motion, it is called the 'static temperature'.

Temperature has the *dimension* $[\theta]$ and the *units* K or $^\circ$C (Chapter 1). In practically all calculations in aerodynamics, temperature is measured in K, i.e. from absolute zero.

3.1.3 Density.   The density of a material is a measure of the amount of the material contained in a given volume. In a fluid, the density may vary from point to point. Consider the fluid contained within a small spherical region of volume δV centred at some point in the fluid, and let the mass of fluid within this spherical region be δm. The density (ρ) of the fluid at the point on which the sphere is centred is then defined by

$$\rho = \lim_{\delta V \to 0} (\delta m/\delta V) \tag{3.1}$$

The dimensions of density are thus $[ML^{-3}]$, and it is measured in units of kilograms per cubic metre (kg/m^3).

At standard temperature and pressure (288 K, 101 325 Pa) the density of dry air is $1 \cdot 2256$ kg/m^3.

Difficulties arise in applying the above definition rigorously to a real fluid composed of discrete molecules, since the sphere, when taken to the limit, either will or will not contain part of a molecule. If it does contain a molecule, the value obtained for the density will be fictitiously high; if it does not contain a molecule the resultant value for the density will be zero.

This difficulty can be avoided in two ways over the range of temperatures and pressures normally encountered:

i) the molecular nature of a gas may for many purposes be ignored and it may be assumed that the fluid is a continuum, i.e. does not consist of discrete particles; or

ii) the decrease in size of the imaginary sphere may be supposed to be carried to a limiting minimum size. This limiting size is such that, although the sphere is small compared with the dimensions of any physical body placed in the fluid, it is large compared with the fluid molecules and therefore contains a reasonable number of whole molecules.

The properties and structure of fluid flows 49

3.1.4 Viscosity. This is often regarded as the 'stickiness' of a fluid and is its tendency to resist sliding between layers or, more rigorously, a rate of change of shear strain.

There is very little resistance to the movement of a knife blade edge-on through air, but to produce the same motion through thick oil needs much more effort; this is because the viscosity of oil is high compared with that of air.

Dynamic viscosity. Consider two parallel flat plates placed a distance h apart, the space between them being filled with fluid. One plate is held fixed and the other is moved in its own plane at a speed V (see fig. 3.1).

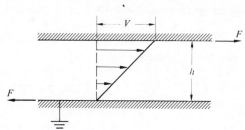

Fig. 3.1

The fluid immediately adjacent to each plate will move with that plate (i.e. there is no slip); thus the fluid in contact with the lower plate will be at rest while that in contact with the upper plate will be moving with speed V. In the absence of other influences, the speed of the fluid between the plates will vary linearly as shown in fig. 3.1. As a direct result of viscosity, a force F has to be applied to each plate to maintain the motion, the fluid tending to retard the moving plate and to drag the fixed plate to the right.

If the area of fluid in contact with each plate is A, the shear stress (τ) is $\tau = F/A$. The sliding strain (rate of slide) of the upper plate over the lower is V/h.

These quantities are connected by Maxwell's equation, which serves to define the dynamic viscosity. This equation is

$$\tau = F/A = \mu(V/h) \tag{3.2}$$

Hence $[ML^{-1}T^{-2}] = [\mu][LT^{-1}L^{-1}] = [\mu][T^{-1}]$

Thus $[\mu] = [ML^{-1}T^{-1}]$

and the units of μ are therefore kg/m s or N s/m^2.

At $0°$C (273 K) the dynamic viscosity of dry air is $1·714 \times 10^{-5}$ kg/m s.

The relationship of eqn 3.2 with μ constant does not apply for all fluids. For an important class of fluids, which includes blood, some oils, some paints, and so-called thixotropic fluids, μ is not constant but is a function of $\mathrm{d}V/\mathrm{d}h$. The derivative $\mathrm{d}V/\mathrm{d}h$ is a measure of the rate at which the fluid is shearing.

Kinematic viscosity.   This is a convenient form in which the viscosity of a fluid may be expressed. It is formed by combining the density ρ and the dynamic viscosity μ according to the equation.

$$v = \mu/\rho$$

and has the dimensions L^2 T and the units m^2/s. It may be regarded as a measure of the relative magnitudes of viscosity and inertia of the fluid and has the practical advantage, in calculations, of replacing two numbers representing μ and ρ by a single number.

3.1.5 Compressibility.   This is a measure of how easily the fluid may be compressed, and is defined as the ratio of a change in pressure to the volumetric strain produced thereby.

If a certain bulk of fluid, under a pressure p, has a volume V and the pressure is then increased to $p + \delta p$, the volume will decrease to $V - \delta V$.

The volumetric strain produced by the pressure increase δp is $-\delta V/V$, and so the modulus of bulk elasticity is given by

$$\kappa = -\delta p/(\delta V/V) \tag{3.}$$

Since $\delta V/V$ is the ratio of two volumes it is non-dimensional, and thus the dimensions of κ are identical with those of pressure, namely $ML^{-1} T^{-2}$, and it is measured in units of Pa.

3.1.6 Heat properties.   Heat has the dimensions of energy, namely $M L^2 T^{-2}$, and is measured in units of joules (J).

Specific heat.   The specific heat of a material is the amount of heat necessary to raise the temperature of unit mass of the material by one degree. Thus it has the dimensions $L^2 T^{-2} \theta^{-1}$ and is measured in units of $J/kg\,°C$ or $J/kg\,K$.

With a gas, there are two distinct ways in which the heating operation may be performed: at constant volume and at constant pressure.

Specific heat at constant volume.   If unit mass of the gas is enclosed in a cylinder sealed by a piston, and the piston is locked in position, the volume of the gas cannot change, and any heat added is used solely to raise the temperature of the gas. (It is assumed that the cylinder and piston do not receive any of the heat.) The specific heat of the gas under these conditions is the specific heat at constant volume, c_V.

For dry air at normal aerodynamic temperatures,

$c_V = 718$ J/kg K*.

Specific heat at constant pressure. Assume that the piston referred to above is now freed and is acted on by a constant force. The pressure of the gas is that necessary to resist the force, and is therefore constant. The application of heat to the gas causes its temperature to rise, which leads to an increase in the volume of the gas in order to maintain the constant pressure. Thus the gas does mechanical work against the force. It is therefore necessary to supply the heat required to increase the temperature of the gas (as in the case at constant volume) and, in addition, the amount of heat equivalent to the mechanical work done against the force. This total amount of heat is called the 'specific heat at constant pressure', c_p, and is defined as 'that amount of heat required to raise the temperature of unit mass of the gas by one degree, the pressure of the gas being kept constant while heating'. In view of the foregoing, it will be realized that c_p is always greater than c_V. For dry air at normal aerodynamic temperatures, $c_p = 1005$ J/kg K.

The ratio of specific heats. This is a quantity important for example in the stability of the atmosphere and is defined by the equation

$$\gamma = c_p/c_V \tag{3.4}$$

The value of γ for air depends on the temperature, but for dry air it may be regarded as constant at about 1·403; this value in turn is often approximated to by $\gamma = 1·4$ ($\gamma = 1·4$ is, in fact, the theoretical value for an ideal diatomic gas).

The gas constant, R. This is the amount of mechanical work which is obtained by heating unit mass through unit temperature rise at constant pressure. It is derived from the definitions of c_p/c_V:

$$c_p - c_V = R \tag{3.5}$$

* See, for example, Mayhew, Y. R., and Rogers, C. F. C., *Thermodynamic and transport properties of fluids (SI units)*, Oxford, Blackwell, 2nd edn 1968.

It follows that R is measured in the units of J/kg K or J/kg °C. For air over the range of temperatures and pressures normally encountered, R has the value 287·26 J/kg K.

From eqns 3.4 and 3.5, the following relationships can be derived:

$$c_p = \frac{\gamma}{\gamma - 1}\ R \qquad (3.6\text{a})$$

and

$$c_V = \frac{1}{\gamma - 1}\ R \qquad (3.6\text{b})$$

3.2 Types of flow

3.2.1 A comparison of steady, unsteady, laminar, and turbulent flows.
Aerodynamicists use the words 'steady' (uniform), 'unsteady' (non-uniform), 'smooth' (laminar), and 'turbulent' (eddying) to describe the different characteristics of fluids in motion. Meteorologists additionally use such terms as 'gust' and 'squall', so it is necessary to review the general meaning of these words as they relate to the present text.

Although the adjectives 'steady', 'uniform', and 'smooth' are all partly synonymous in the context of fluid flows — as are their opposites: 'unsteady', 'non-uniform', and 'turbulent' — a difference is usually implied and may be thought of as distinguishing a distant event from a close or proximate one.

For example, consider the flow around the bluff body in fig. 3.2 (a). This is the usual wind-tunnel situation where the wind is appearing from a long way upstream, moving around the surface of the body, and departing to a long way downstream. Now, independently of the behaviour of the fluid flowing past P, that coming from Q is arriving in a steady or uniform way while that departing to R, even though it is somewhat disturbed, is, as a whole, departing in a steady or uniform way. Even if there were seeds of irregularities in the approaching flow, as if it were locally disturbed somewhere upstream, fig. 3.2 (b), as far as P were concerned it would be appearing and disappearing in a uniform or steady way. In other words, the mean incident flow is steady and has a constant or uniform velocity.

An unsteady flow is one in which the incident mean stream velocity is fluctuating in some way, either with time or in direction. The net result experienced at P may not be to change the 'quality' of the flow felt at P but to alter the overall characteristics of mean speed or direction.

Look now at the particle behaviour in the vicinity of P. The flow may be smooth and regular, behaving very much like laminae (or layers) sliding over each other, fig. 3.2 (c); hence the associated name 'laminar' flow. In contrast, the particle behaviour may be entirely random, with individual particles and groups of particles spinning and rotating and moving first in one direction then in another with no order or method except that the whole aggregate is proceeding in the streaming direction, fig. 3.2 (d). This is described as 'turbulent' flow. It is clearly non-uniform or unsteady in a local sense, but, paradoxically, it can be seen from the previous discussion to be part of a steady or uniform general flow system.

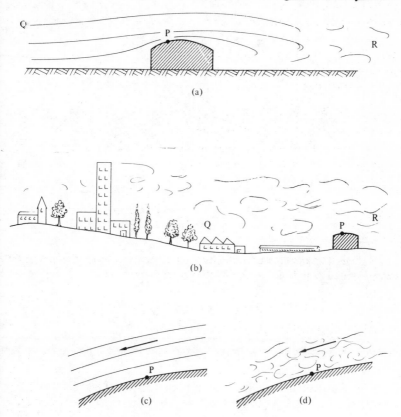

Fig. 3.2

Now the use of the concept of distant events to describe the type of flow felt locally in fact embodies the idea of scale or size, for what may appear to conventional scale as a uniform stream slowly changing in direction may in fact be part of a huge disturbance moving slowly over the surface. Figure 3.3 shows in a very stylised way three situations of different orders of scale.

In the first, fig. 3.3 (a), a large vortex spinning in the anticlockwise sense moves past a building P. The building experiences a wind which

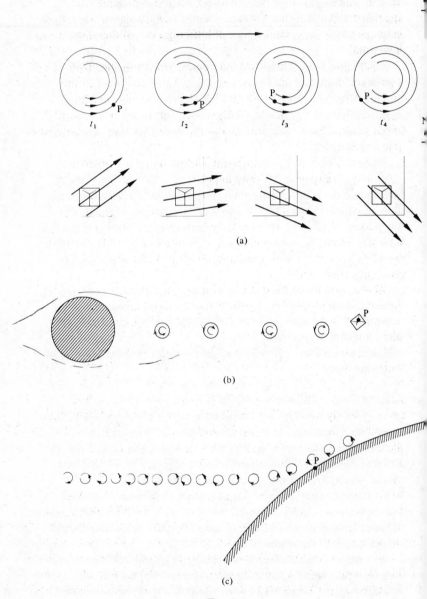

(a)

(b)

(c)

Fig. 3.3

changes slowly in magnitude and shifts in direction from south west through west to north west.

In the second example, fig. 3.3 (b), a large bluff building sheds a series of eddies or vortices into its wake, where the building P is situated. The building has the same order of scale as the vortices which envelope it in an alternating series of buffeting gusts as they flow downwind.

Finally, fig. 3.3 (c) shows a similar series of vortices shed from somewhere upstream but whose size is very small compared to the surface P over which they flow. In this case they would contribute significantly to the turbulence in the stream but would be too small to act as other than a trigger to change the boundary-layer characteristics in the vicinity of P.

Of course, each of the examples illustrated above is unlikely to occur in such a symmetrical way in practice, but one of them might well supply the majority behaviour of a particular three-dimensional flow situation. For example, the first could represent schematically the passage of a depression over the countryside; the second illustrates a possible buffeting sequence typical of an urban area; while the third would be typical of the flow around a body behind a coarse grid or gauze in a wind tunnel.

All may strictly be described as unsteady or disturbed flows, yet the experience at the typical point P may be more adequately represented in the short term by the descriptions 'steady', 'unsteady', and 'turbulent' respectively.

For rigorous analytical purposes, a more formal distinction of flow state is required.

Laminar flow, as its name implies, is flow in which layers of fluid move smoothly over or alongside adjacent layers. It is flow in which the streamlines are smooth curves (a *streamline* is an imaginary line drawn in the fluid such that there is no flow across it at any point). It is possible, as shown above, for smooth flow to be *unsteady,* as is the case if its value V gradually increases or decreases with time.

To postulate that a flow is laminar admits large areas of classical fluid mechanics to the solution of flow problems, the Bernouilli equation discussed later being an example of a useful working equation derived from such classical mathematics.

However, fluid in motion does not stay in the smooth laminar state for long. Many things conspire to break up the ordered motion, and instabilities which may occur locally due to temporary aberrations in the flow soon spread and infect the whole flow so that its particle motion is random and diffuse. This is the 'preferred' ultimate state of motion in nature and its general name is *turbulence*.

Turbulence.   A succinct definition of turbulence is difficult to contrive, except in a negative form such as, 'a turbulent flow is one which does not exhibit laminar flow characteristics'. Perhaps 'random particle motion and distortion superimposed on a general streaming motion' describes in a short phrase the essential unpredictable nature of turbulence.

Lumley and Panofsky[1] list and discuss seven properties evident in turbulent motion. They include three-dimensionality, non-linearity, randomness, diffusion, dissipation, transport, etc.

After several pages in his first chapter, Bradshaw[2] reaches the following definition of turbulence: 'Turbulence is a three-dimensional time-dependent motion in which vortex stretching causes velocity fluctuations to spread to all wavelengths between a minimum determined by viscous forces and a maximum determined by the boundary conditions of the flow. It is the usual state of fluid motion except at low Reynolds numbers.'

It is evident that here is a physical phenomenon of great complexity – and one which is paramount in many of the flow situations arising from the action of the wind. That is not to imply, however, that the complexity is too great for simplifications of one degree or another to be made in order to arrive at some meaningful predictions of the behaviour of certain flow states, and much of the section below attempts this. In so doing, further aspects of the nature of turbulence will be described, and it is hoped that a fuller comprehension of this very common, very important, but so very complicated flow process will be acquired by the reader.

3.2.2 Boundary-layer flow.   Nowhere is the quality of the flow of greater importance than in the region immediately adjacent to a solid surface. It is here that the character of the separated flow downstream is decided, and it is *through* this region that all reaction between the fluid and the body must take place. It is worthwhile taking a closer look at this flow regime which may model not only the flow around discrete bodies but also that of the lower atmosphere (the earth's boundary layer).

Consideration of the intermolecular forces between solids and fluids leads to the assumption that at the boundary between a solid and a fluid (other than a rarified gas) there is a condition of 'no slip': in other words, the relative velocity of the fluid tangential to the surface is everywhere zero. Since the mainstream velocity at a small distance from the surface may be considerable, it is evident that appreciable shearing velocity gradients may exist within this boundary region.

In fig. 3.4, AB represents a portion of body some distance from its upstream edge. The particles of the gas have a general streaming motion from left to right, but, superimposed on this, each particle has an individual velocity which is random in speed and direction. As a result, each particle is moving at a speed and in a direction which differ from those for all the other particles; the general streaming motion is, in fact, merely the statistical mean of all the different velocities of the various particles. The exception to this is when particles at any instant are in contact with the surface and at rest.

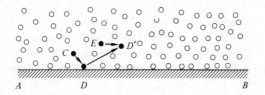

Fig. 3.4

Consider the particle C: its individual velocity is such that it moves towards the plate, striking particle D and knocking D off the surface and back into the stream, while C adheres to the plate in its stead. Thus C has lost all its momentum. Some of this has been imparted to D, and the remainder is lost when C adheres to the plate. This loss of momentum by C is felt by the plate as a small impulse from left to right.

Particle D has been returned to the stream, as shown at D', but has a very low speed and is overtaken and struck by particle E. As a result of this collision, D is speeded up and E slowed down. E in turn may move outwards from the plate at its now low speed, being struck by a faster moving particle in the next 'layer'.

This elementary argument has considered only a few particles. When this type of behaviour applies to the millions of particles present in the gas, producing millions of collisions per second, it is easy to see that the overall effect produces

a) a speed of flow which increases from zero at the surface to the full streaming speed away from the body; and

b) a summation of a very large number of small impulses on the surface per unit time, or, in other words, an apparently steady force acting on the body in the direction of flow. This force is called 'surface-friction drag'.

The region of reduced speed is called the 'boundary layer', and it is seen that it is a direct result of viscosity. If the fluid had no viscosity, i.e. were 'inviscid', there would be no boundary layer.

Boundary-layer thickness.   In order to make the idea of a boundary layer realistic, an arbitrary decision must be made as to its extent, and the usual convention is that the boundary layer extends to a distance δ from the surface such that the velocity u at that distance is 99% of the local main-stream velocity U_1 which would exist there in the absence of the boundary layer. Thus δ is the physical thickness of the boundary layer so far as it needs to be considered, and when defined specifically as above it is usually designated the '99%', or 'general', thickness – fig. 3.5 (a).

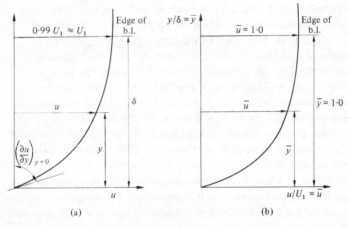

(a)   (b)

Fig. 3.5

Velocity profile.   Further thought about the thickening process will make it evident that the velocity increase that takes place along a normal to the surface must be continuous. Let y be the perpendicular distance from the surface at any point and let u be the corresponding velocity parallel to the surface. If u were to increase discontinuously with y at any point, then at that point $\partial u/\partial y$ would be infinite. This would imply an infinite shearing stress (since the shear stress $\tau = \mu \partial u/\partial y$), which is untenable.

Non-dimensional profile.   In order to compare boundary-layer profiles of different thickness, it is convenient to express the profile shape non-dimensionally. This may be done by writing $\bar{u} = u/U_1$ and $\bar{y} = y/\delta$ so that the profile shape is given by $\bar{u} = f(\bar{y})$. Over the range $y = 0$ to $y = \delta$, the velocity parameter $\bar{u}$ varies from 0 to 0·99. For convenience when using $\bar{u}$ values as integration limits, negligible error is introduced by using $\bar{u} = 1 \cdot 0$ at the outer boundary, and considerable arithmetical simplification is achieved. The velocity profile is then plotted as in fig. 3.5 (b).

Types of boundary layer. Closer experimental study of boundary-layer flows discloses that there are two different regimes which can exist: (i) laminar flow and (ii) turbulent flow.

In laminar flow the layers of fluid slide smoothly over one another and there is little interchange of fluid mass between adjacent layers. The shearing tractions which develop due to the velocity gradients are thus due entirely to the viscosity of the fluid, i.e. the momentum exchanges between adjacent layers are on a molecular scale only.

In turbulent flow, considerable random motion exists in the form of velocity fluctuations both along the mean direction of flow and perpendicular to it. As a result of the latter, there are appreciable transports of mass between adjacent layers. If there is a mean velocity gradient in the flow, then there will be corresponding interchanges of streamwise momentum between the adjacent layers and this will result in shearing stresses between them. These shearing stresses may well be of much greater magnitude than those which develop as the result of purely viscous action, and the velocity profile in a turbulent boundary layer is very largely controlled by these 'Reynolds stresses' as they are termed; see page 61.

As a consequence of the essential differences between laminar- and turbulent-flow shearing stresses, the velocity profiles which exist in the two types of layer are also different. Figure 3.6 shows a laminar-layer profile and a turbulent-layer profile plotted to the same non-dimensional scale; these profiles are typical of those on a flat plate where there is no streamwise pressure gradient.

In the laminar layer, energy from the main stream is transmitted towards the slower moving fluid near the surface through the medium of viscosity alone, and only a relatively small penetration of energy to the layers close to the surface results; consequently an appreciable proportion of the boundary-layer flow has a considerably reduced velocity. Throughout the layer, the shearing stress τ is given by $\tau = \mu(\partial u/\partial y)$ and the wall shearing stress is thus $\tau_w = \mu_w(\partial u/\partial y)_y = 0 = \mu_w(\partial u/\partial y)_w$, say.

In the turbulent layer, as detailed below, large Reynolds stresses are set up due to mass interchanges in a direction perpendicular to the surface, so that energy from the main stream may easily penetrate to fluid layers quite close to the surface. This results in these layers having a velocity which is not much less than that of the main stream. However, in layers which are very close to the surface (considered smooth at this stage of the discussion) it is obviously impossible for velocities to exist perpendicular to the surface, so in a very limited region immediately adjacent to the surface the flow approximates to laminar flow.

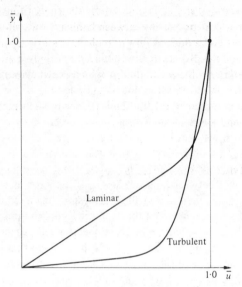

Fig. 3.6

In this *laminar sub-layer*, the shearing action once again becomes purely viscous and the velocity falls very sharply (and almost linearly) within it, to zero at the surface. Since at the surface the wall shearing stress now depends on viscosity, i.e. $\tau_w = \mu_w(\partial u/\partial y)_w$, the surface friction stress under a turbulent layer will be far greater than that under a laminar layer of the same thickness, since $\partial u/\partial y$ is much greater.

The viscous shearing stress at the surface, and thus the surface-friction stress, depends only on the slope of the velocity profile at the surface, whatever the boundary-layer type.

Reynolds stresses; eddy viscosity.   In the understanding of the physical world, streaming flows are most easily visualised in their smooth or laminar state which is a form of sinuous fluid motion referred to above as streamline motion. Turbulent flows bear little resemblance to laminar flows in that frictional effects, mean velocity distributions, and all diffusive mechanisms are totally different from those of laminar flows.

The transfer of all fluid properties throughout the turbulent region is more a consequence of the random nature of the local fluid movements ᵃⁿᵈ owes less to molecular forces. However in order to quantify the motion of a bulk of turbulent fluid, a *mean motion* is imagined in which the turbulent properties are ignored and the fluid is assumed to behave in a fictitious 'laminar' way. Further, the fluid is assumed to possess bulk properties of viscosity and conductivity to account for the difference in transport properties between laminar flow, whose transport properties are due entirely to molecular motions, and turbulence, where the diffusivity is aided by the turbulent motions.

Semi-theoretical profiles of the mean velocity throughout the boundary layer follow from these considerations.

As indicated in section 3.1.4, a viscous fluid is one in which a shear stress exists given by the relationship

$$\tau = \mu(\partial u / \partial y) \tag{3.7}$$

where τ is the (viscous) shear stress, μ the absolute coefficient of viscosity and $\partial u / \partial y$ the velocity gradient *across* the streaming direction.

This relationship exists only for fluids in laminar motion, and the shear stress is the result of the rate of change of streamwise momentum arising from cross-stream particle interchange due to molecular motions.

For fluids in turbulent motion, the random process superimposed on streaming flow provides another mechanism for cross-stream particle interchange which also produces a rate of change of streamwise momentum which in turn appears as a shear stress aligned along the direction of motion.

This *turbulent shear stress* ($\bar{\tau}$) or Reynolds stress may be shown[3] to have a value

$$\bar{\tau} = \rho \overline{u' v'} \tag{3.8}$$

the symbols being defined in section 3.3.3. Mixing-length theories permit this equation to be expressed in the form

$$\bar{\tau} = \rho l^2 (\partial u / \partial y)^2 \tag{3.9}$$

which allows the appearance of a quantity termed *eddy viscosity* (ϵ):

$$\epsilon = \rho l^2 \, \partial u / \partial y \tag{3.10}$$

Eddy viscosity is directly analogous to the dynamic viscosity; thus,

$$\bar{\tau} = \epsilon(\partial u / \partial y) \tag{3.11}$$

and for a fluid in general the total shear stress at large is the sum of the viscous and Reynolds stresses:

$$\bar{\tau}_{\text{total}} = \tau + \bar{\tau} = (\mu + \epsilon)(\partial u / \partial y) \tag{3.12}$$

The logarithmic velocity distribution.   In turbulent boundary layers, the contribution to the total stress due to viscosity diminishes considerably away from the surface, and this is particularly true for the atmospheric boundary layer.

This being so, eqn 3.9 above may be integrated to give the velocity u as a function of y. Several assumptions have to be made, for example in the variation of l (the mixing length), and Prandtl's[4] hypothesis will serve as an illustration.

Prandtl assumed that l is proportional to y

i.e. $l = k_1 y$ 　　　　　　　　　　　　　　　　　　　　　(3.13)

Substituting this in eqn 3.9 and rearranging,

$$\partial u / \partial y = (1/k_1 y) \sqrt{(\bar{\tau}/y)}$$ 　　　　　　　(3.14)

which on integrating yields

$$u = (1/k_1) \sqrt{(\bar{\tau}/\rho)} \ln y + \text{constant}$$ 　　　(3.15)

Von Karman's[5] hypothesis and Squire's[6] dimensional theory yield results which differ from eqn 3.15 only in the value of the constant k_1, which leads to the conclusion that a logarithmic form approximates to the mean velocity distribution in the turbulent layer away from the surface.

As it happens, partly because of the limitations of the assumptions involved and partly because of the inhibiting nature of the close surface, the logarithmic profiles are found to be valid only for a relatively thin region of the full turbulent layer, the relevant region being from just away from the surface (where viscous effects are more likely to predominate over turbulent mechanisms) to about 20% of the thickness of the whole layer. While of limited validity, the approaches above have provoked further work of a semi-empirical nature designed to extend the range of use of the mathematical relationships for the velocity distribution throughout the layer. These analyses have lead to the concept of Prandtl's 'law of the wall' for the near surface region and Von Karman's 'velocity-defect' law for the outer region where the turbulent properties are of paramount importance. Most recently, the form of turbulent boundary-layer profiles between the logarithmic section and the 'main stream' has led Coles[7] to propose a 'law of the wake' which, as it implies, seeks to relate the turbulent characteristics of a free wake to the outer region of the layer.

The major range of interest of the aeronautical boundary-layer work, which has been the dominant spur to the development of this knowledge and from which, for example, the theories quoted above have appeared, has resided in the flow properties near and surface friction on aerodynamic surfaces which are smoothly aligned to the flow and which have only a limited roughness.

The surface over which the atmospheric boundary layer moves may be far from smooth and may have a scale of roughness of the same order as the height of the boundary layer; nevertheless, some authorities have employed the logarithmic velocity distribution to describe the vertical change of mean wind speed, and it is likely that some 'composite' profile as above gives a reasonable approximation.

The power law for velocity distribution.   The British Code of Practice on wind loads (CP3: Chapter V: Part 2: 1972) employs a power law to relate the wind speed to the height above ground; this law has its roots in the older literature of aerodynamics. The great usefulness of the power laws as theoretical expressions for the velocity distributions throughout turbulent boundary layers was that they could be made to approximate to experimentally observed values of mean velocity and, perhaps of greater value to the aeronautical designer, yield values of resistance or drag which were reasonably correct.

They have their origin in the early work of Blasius (1913), who found empirical resistance formulae for the turbulent flow of fluids through smooth circular pipes in terms of the Reynolds number:

$$\overline{C}_{\mathrm{f}} = 0.0791/(\overline{Re})^{1/4} \tag{3.16}$$

where $\overline{C}_{\mathrm{f}}$ is the local surface-friction coefficient on the surface $(\overline{C}_{\mathrm{f}} = \tau_{\mathrm{w}}/\tfrac{1}{2}\rho\overline{U}^{2})$ and $(\overline{Re})$ is the Reynolds number based on the average flow velocity $\overline{U}$.

Prandtl proposed a velocity profile of the form

$$u/U_{1} = (y/\delta)^{n} \tag{3.17}$$

where u is the local streaming velocity, U_{1} is the maximum velocity (i.e. at the centre of the pipe or the edge of the boundary layer) and δ is the pipe radius or boundary-layer thickness.

By relating eqns 3.16 and 3.17, with appropriate assumptions for τ_{w} based on steady-flow considerations, the index n was found to be $1/7$.

A full discussion of Prandtl's 'seventh-root' power law is given in reference 4, but it is a particular example of the more general power law for the velocity profile given by

$$u/U_{1} = (y/a)^{\alpha} \tag{3.18}$$

where, in the aeronautical literature, a is either the pipe radius or the boundary-layer thickness but for present purposes may be regarded as the gradient height.

The 'seventh-root' law is useful for values of $(Re)_{\mathrm{a}} \approx 1.5 \times 10^{5}$. For larger values the exponent α is progressively decreased to 1/8 for $(Re)_a$ = 4 x 10^5, 1/9 up to $(Re)_a$ = 1·2 x 10^6. Such profiles apply to flow over smooth walls; for flow over rough surfaces the index becomes larger, with a value approaching 1/3 for very rough walls.

Now the turbulent shear stress τ increases with the scale and intensity of the turbulence for a given velocity gradient, so the effect of an increased surface roughness and hence of shears in the adjacent flow is to increase the scale and intensity of the turbulence and, as a consequence, change the shape of the lower part of the profile.

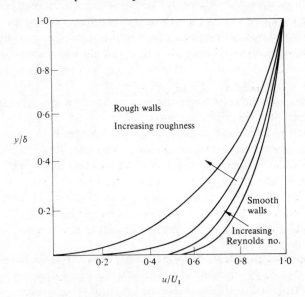

Fig. 3.7 Turbulent-boundary-layer velocity profiles

No single curve exists for velocity distributions *across* flows; these depend on two different parameters, namely Reynolds number and roughness.

Figure 3.7 shows experimental curves for the velocity profiles of turbulent boundary layers on flat walls which are smooth or rough. (A surface is considered to be aerodynamically smooth if the height of surface irregularities is less than the thickness of the laminar sub-layer — in this case the surface was artificially roughened by embedding wire gauzes along the surface.)

It must be appreciated that these profiles refer to boundary layers in flows where the streamwise pressure gradient is small to non-existent and no vertical convections exist. In the atmospheric boundary layer, both of these phenomena can occur to a greater or lesser extent and the flow correspondingly changes, but, as a general rule, especially away from the immediate vicinity of the roughnesses, a power law for variation of wind speed with height is appropriate.

Boundary-layer growth along a flat surface. If the boundary layer which develops on the surface of a flat plate which is held edgeways on to the free stream is studied, it is found that, in general, a laminar layer starts to develop from the leading edge. This laminar layer grows in thickness along the surface, from zero at the leading edge, until at some point a sudden transition to a turbulent layer occurs. This transition is accompanied by a corresponding rapid thickening of the layer. Beyond this transition region, the turbulent layer continues to thicken steadily

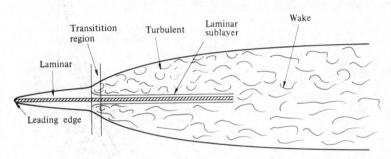

Fig. 3.8 (Note: scale normal to surface is greatly exaggerated.)

as it proceeds towards the trailing edge. Because of the greater shearing stresses within the turbulent layer, its thickness increases much more rapidly than that of the laminar layer – near the surface the turbulent layer is more readily able to influence the main-stream flow at the outer edge of the boundary layer. At the trailing edge the boundary layer joins with that from the other surface of the plate to form a wake of retarded velocity which also tends to thicken slowly as it flows away downstream (see fig. 3.8).

Boundary-layer growth along a curved surface. In most aerodynamic problems, if it is not highly curved or 'bluff', the body exhibits some degree of curvature which causes a departure from the flat-plate boundary-layer growth described above. The major difference affecting the boundary-layer flow in these cases is that the main-stream velocity, and hence the static pressure in a streamwise direction, is no longer constant.

Over the fore or leading part of the body the pressure gradient is negative; that is, the static pressure of the free stream *decreases* along the flow direction. This inhibits the growth of the laminar layer which is as a rule thinner than its counterpart on the flat plate.

Over the rear portion, and indeed in any flow situation where the pressure gradient is positive in the flow direction, that is *increasing* pressure in the flow direction, the boundary layer thickens rapidly and the flow may *separate* from the surface of the body before the rearmost point is reached.

The effect of an adverse pressure gradient – separation.   The behaviour of a boundary layer in a positive pressure gradient may be considered with reference to fig. 3.9. This shows a length of surface which has a

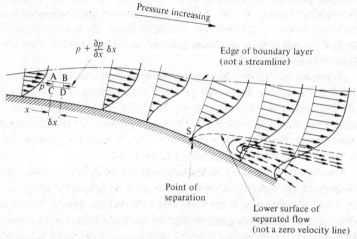

Fig. 3.9

gradual but steady convex curvature, such as the downstream part of a curved roof. In such a flow region, because of the retardation of the main-stream flow, the static pressure in the main stream will rise (conservation of energy). The variation in static pressure along a normal to the surface through the boundary layer is essentially zero, so that the pressure at any point in the main stream, adjacent to the edge of the boundary layer, is transmitted unaltered through the layer to the surface. In the light of this, consider the small element of fluid, marked ABCD, fig. 3.9. On face AC, the pressure is p, while on face BD the pressure has increased to $p + (\partial p/\partial x)\delta x$, where $\partial p/\partial x$ is the streamline pressure gradient. Thus the net pressure force on the element is tending to retard its velocity. This retarding force is in addition to the viscous shears which act along AB and CD and it will continuously slow down the element as it progresses downstream.

This slowing-down effect will be more pronounced near the surface, where the elements are remote from the accelerating effect (via shearing actions) of the main stream, so that successive profile shapes in the streamwise direction will change as shown.

Ultimately, at a point S on the surface, the velocity-profile slope $\partial u/\partial y$ becomes zero. Apart from the change in shape of the profile, it is evident that the layer must thicken rapidly under these conditions in order to satisfy continuity within the layer. Downstream of point S, the flow adjacent to the surface may well be in an upstream direction, so that a circulatory movement, in a plane normal to the surface, may take place near the surface. A line (shown dotted in fig. 3.9) may be drawn from the point S such that the mass flow above this line corresponds to the mass flow ahead of point S. The line represents the continuation of the lower surface of the upstream boundary layer, so that, in effect, the original boundary layer separates from the surface at point S, which is termed the *separation point*.

Reference to the velocity profiles for laminar and turbulent layers (fig. 3.6) shows that, due to the greater extent of fluid of lower energy near the surface in the laminar layer, the effect of a positive pressure gradient on such a laminar layer will cause separation of the flow much more rapidly than if the layer were turbulent. A turbulent layer is said to 'stick' to the surface better than a laminar one.

The result of separation on the rear half of a body is to increase the thickness of the wake flow, with a consequent reduction in the pressure rise which should occur at the rear. This latter means that the forward-acting pressure-force components on the rear part of the body do not develop to offset the rearward-acting pressures near the front stagnation point, and the pressure drag increases. In fact, if there were no boundary layer, there would be a stagnation point towards the rear and the boundary-layer pressure drag (as well as the surface-friction drag) would be zero. If the curvature is sufficiently large, the separation may take place not far downstream of the minimum-pressure point, and a very large wake will develop.

Transition. It has been mentioned above that transition from laminar to turbulent flow usually occurs at some point along the surface. The process of transition and the factors which determine its position are still not fully understood, although it is known that a shearing velocity gradient is essential to the generation of turbulence.

Up to certain values of Reynolds number, typically 9×10^4 (here[8] defined as $(Re)_x = U_1 x/v_1$, where U_1 is the local mainstream velocity, v_1 is the kinematic viscosity in the mainstream, and x is the distance along the surface in a streamwise direction, measured from the leading edge (or stagnation point), small disturbances in the laminar flow may be damped out so that amplification and subsequent transition to turbulence cannot occur. At larger Reynolds numbers a range of disturbances is amplified, and transition is possible though not inevitable.

The shape of the laminar velocity profile affects the stability of the laminar layer, and a profile having a point of inflection in it is essentially unstable; this ties in with the effect of a positive pressure gradient, mentioned above.

In spite of the difficulties attached to a theoretical prediction of the position of transition, it is possible to appreciate in a general sense the effects of various conditions on its position. Free-stream turbulence is a cause of early transition and low turbulence is necessary to maintain a laminar layer. Conversely, roughness of the surface will tend to initiate transition in a laminar layer. The position of transition is also influenced by the streamwise pressure gradient, a positive gradient tending to cause early transition and a negative gradient late transition.

There is the additional complication that a positive pressure gradient may cause either separation or transition, depending on how rapidly the amplification of any oscillating disturbances in the laminar layer takes place.

As previously discussed in relation to separation, the positive gradient causes deceleration of the fluid particles in the boundary layer. Provided the particles are all moving in parallel straight lines, this will cause no concern. Suppose, however, that a small lateral disturbance is impressed on a particle so that its path line becomes deflected; the effect of the positive pressure gradient is then, immediately, to tend to increase the deflection of the path line. Since this sort of process will happen throughout the layer, it is evident that general turbulence can rapidly ensue. On the other hand, a negative gradient will tend to urge back towards its original flow direction any particle which starts to stray from its straight path, thus delaying transition.

In any real laminar-boundary-layer flow there are always present, due to some free-stream disturbance or surface irregularity, the small lateral components of pressure which can initiate the onset of turbulence, so that the sign of the pressure gradient exerts a powerful effect on the position of transition.

3.2.3 Flow past cylinders and spheres.

Some of the properties of boundary layers discussed above help in the explanation of the behaviour under certain conditions of a cylinder or sphere immersed in a uniform free stream. Behind bodies of reasonably streamline form, a relatively thin wake is formed; in such cases the drag forces are largely due to surface friction, i.e. shearing stresses at the base of the boundary layer.

When dealing with non-streamlined or 'bluff' bodies, it is found that, because of the adverse effect of a positive pressure gradient on the boundary layer, the latter usually separates somewhere near points at the maximum cross-section, with the formation of a broad wake. As a result, the surface-friction drag is only small, and the major part of the total drag now consists of pressure drag due to the large area at the rear of the body acted upon by a reduced pressure in the wake region.

Experimental observation of the flow past a sphere or cylinder indicates that the drag of the body is markedly influenced by the cross-sectional area of the wake, a broad wake being accompanied by a relatively high drag and vice versa.

The way in which the wake area varies with relative fluid speed may be considered with reference to the flow past a circular cylinder as the relative fluid speed is slowly increased from zero (refer to fig. 3.10). At very low Reynolds numbers (here defined as $U_\infty D/\nu$, where U_∞ is the free stream velocity, ν is the kinematic viscosity in the free stream, and D is the cylinder diameter) — less than unity — the flow behaves as if it were purely viscous (inertial affects negligible) and the boundary layers effectively extend to infinity.

At slightly higher, but still low, Reynolds numbers, true boundary layers form which remain laminar over the whole surface. Separation occurs on either side near the rear of the cylinder, and a narrow turbulent wake develops. With further increase of the Reynolds number (in the region 10 to 60) the laminar separation points on either side of the rear of the streamwise diameter move rapidly outwards and forward to points near the opposite ends of a transverse diameter. This results in a corresponding increase in wake width and consequent form drag.

At some stage, for a value of Reynolds number somewhere between 60 and 140, a pair of symmetrical vortices will begin to develop on either side of the centre line behind the laminar separation points; these will grow with time (at the particular Reynolds number), continuously stretching downstream until a stage is reached when they become un-symmetrical and the system breaks down, one vortex becoming detached and moving away downstream. The subsequent wake motion, which is typical of that within the range $140 < (Re) < 5 \times 10^4$, is oscillatory in character. This motion was investigated by Theodor von Karman in the first decade of this century and he showed that a stable system of vortices will be shed alternately from the laminar separation points on either side of the cylinder. Thus, a standing vortex will generate in the region behind the separation point on one side, while a corresponding

vortex on the other side will break away from the cylinder and move
downstream in the wake. When the attached vortex reaches a particular
strength, it will in turn break away and a new vortex will begin to
develop again on the second side, and so on.

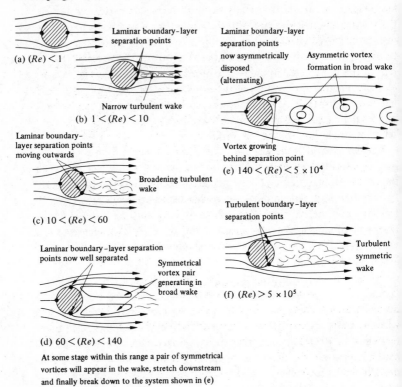

Fig. 3.10 The Reynolds-number limits quoted are only approximate, as
they depend appreciably on the free-stream turbulence level.

The wake thus consists of a procession of vortices of equal strength,
equally spaced but alternating in sign. This type of wake, which can occur
behind all long cylinders of bluff cross-section, including flat plates
normal to the flow direction, is termed a von Karman vortex street or
trail – see fig. 3.11 (a). In a uniform stream flowing past a cylinder, the
vortices move downstream at a speed somewhat less than the free-stream
velocity, the reduction in speed being inversely proportional to the
streamwise distance separating alternate vortices.

It will be appreciated that, during the formation of any single vortex
while it is bound to the cylinder, an increasing circulation will exist about

the cylinder, with the consequent generation of a transverse (lift) force. With the development of each successive vortex, this force will change sign, giving rise to an alternating transverse force on the cylinder at the

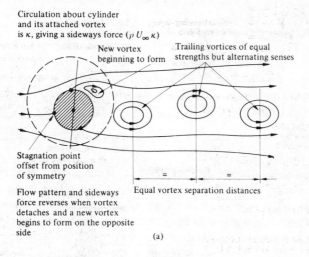

Circulation about cylinder and its attached vortex is κ, giving a sideways force ($\rho\, U_\infty \kappa$)

New vortex beginning to form

Trailing vortices of equal strengths but alternating senses

Stagnation point offset from position of symmetry

Flow pattern and sideways force reverses when vortex detaches and a new vortex begins to form on the opposite side

Equal vortex separation distances

(a)

Approximate relation between Strouhal number and Reynolds number for circular cylinder

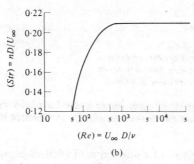

$(Str) = nD/U_\infty$

$(Re) = U_\infty\, D/\nu$

(b)

Fig. 3.11

same frequency as the vortex-shedding frequency. If the frequency happens to coincide with the natural frequency of oscillation of the cylinder (however it may be supported) then appreciable vibration may be caused; this phenomenon is responsible, for example, for the 'singing' of telegraph wires in the wind (Aeolian tones), the ovalling of steel stacks, and the oscillations of many other flexible structures.

The Strouhal number.   A unique relationship is found to exist between
the Reynolds number and a dimensionless parameter involving the shedding
frequency. This parameter, known as the Strouhal number, is defined by
the expression $(Str) = nD/U_\infty$, where n is the frequency of vortex shedding.
Figure 3.11 (b) shows the typical variation of (Str) with (Re) in the vortex-
street range.

During this phase of flow, as the Reynolds number increases, the
separation points move very slowly forward and for values of $(Re) > 700$
the Strouhal number remains constant at about 0·21, so that the oscillation
frequency increases linearly with speed, for a given cylinder size, until at
a Reynolds number of about 5×10^4 the frequency begins to rise very
rapidly and a change in the flow pattern develops, the shedding frequency
becoming random.

The critical Reynolds number.   Throughout all the above changes,
the local laminar-boundary-layer Reynolds number, $(Re)_x$, immediately
upstream of the separation point has been continuously increasing with
speed until a condition is now reached when transition to turbulence
occurs before separation. At this critical stage $(4 \times 10^5 < (Re) < 5 \times 10^5)$
the point of separation, which now takes place in a turbulent layer,
moves suddenly downstream, because of the better 'sticking' property of
the turbulent layer, and the wake width is very appreciably decreased. This
stage is therefore accompanied by a sudden decrease in the total drag of
the cylinder; the wake vorticity remains random with no predominant
frequency. Still further increase in Reynolds number causes no further
dramatic changes, although the wake width will gradually increase to
begin with, as the turbulent separation points slowly move upstream
round the rear surface. The total drag continues to increase steadily in
this stage, due to both pressure and surface-friction drag increases,
although the drag coefficient, defined by

$$C_D = \frac{\text{drag/unit span}}{\frac{1}{2}\rho U_\infty^2 D} \tag{3.19}$$

tends to become constant at about 0·6 for $(Re) > 1\cdot3 \times 10^6$.

The actual value of the Reynolds number at the critical stage when
the sudden drag decrease occurs depends, for a smooth cylinder, on the
small-scale turbulence level existing in the oncoming free stream.
Increased turbulence (or, alternatively, increased surface roughness) will
provoke transition before laminar separation, with its accompanying drag
decrease, at a lower Reynolds number.

The behaviour of a smooth sphere under similarly varying conditions
exhibits the same characteristics as the cylinder, although the Reynolds

numbers corresponding to the changes of flow regime are somewhat
different. One marked difference in behaviour is that the eddying vortex
street, typical of bluff cylinders, does not develop behind a sphere.

Graphs showing the variations of drag coefficient with Reynolds
number for circular cylinders and spheres are given in fig. 3.12.

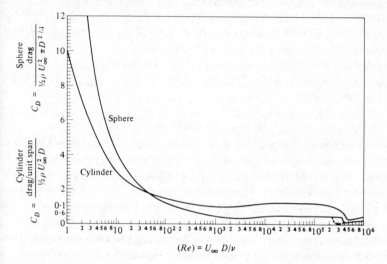

Fig. 3.12 Approximate variations of C_D with (Re) for spheres and
circular cylinders

3.3 The structure of the wind

For many purposes, the characteristics of the natural wind in the
atmosphere near the earth's surface may be considered as being made
up of a mean velocity whose value increases with height in some way,
on which are superimposed turbulent fluctuations as velocity components
along the wind streaming direction and horizontally and vertically
perpendicular to this direction. Thus the surface wind may be treated as
a huge boundary layer, and this model admits the use of statistical and
other methods of analysis used in other problems involving random
phenomena, as well as enabling the properties of the wind to be better
simulated and the results of, say, wind-tunnel tests to be adequately
scaled to full-scale situations in experimental work.

Another model which allows a different interpretation of the
turbulence in the natural wind to be made is to assume the wind to be

a mean streaming flow whose velocity again increases with height but which is 'seeded' with a large number of vortices or eddies of various spinning speeds and of various diameters whose axes are orientated in any direction to the streaming flow. This model allows the visualisation of the elementary growth of vortices 'rolling up' between planes of fluid moving with different relative velocities, and is supported in some measure by common experience of whirls and eddies catching up dust and paper debris, or the billowing smoke from a chimney, on windy days. Further support to this view can be found in 'boiling' of turbulent streams and the elemental spin evident in broken water.

The possibility of giving relative sizes to gusts, by introducing a measurement based on their diameters, and to their rates of spin is inherent in this model and assists to an understanding of 'wavelength' and 'frequency' as applied to the fluctuations superimposed on the mean flow. To extend the simple analogy with streaming water flow further, it is not difficult to think of a mean current speed even though the flow is highly turbulent, or to arrive at a meaningful idea of its magnitude by dividing the measured quantity of water flowing by the cross-sectional area of the stream.

An extension of this notion of a mean flow velocity may be made in the case of the natural wind (although the method employed above in evaluating it can no longer apply), and the concept of a mean wind speed is employed in both of the models for the structure of the wind mentioned above.

3.3.1 The mean or average wind speed.   This is a concept which bears serious and critical examination. Following the first model described above, it is shown on page 81 that a random quantity may be averaged over a given length of time to produce a mean value about which the sum of the fluctuations vanishes. In the case of the random process attributed to the natural wind velocity, this perfectly valuable statistical concept of a temporal mean defined and discussed in detail on page 88 begs one or two questions. These arise from consideration of the instrumentation used to record the variations in wind speed and also the site and height above effective ground level of the sensing head.

3-second and 1-hour means.   In a controlled laboratory experiment using a hot-wire anemometer, variations in velocity at frequencies as high as 20 000 Hz may be recorded, but in the field the anemometers most generally used have a response rate of the order of one or two seconds so that values taken from these instruments are in fact *mean wind speeds averaged over 3 seconds* (or whatever is the response time of the actual instrument used), the averaging process going on within the anemometer. In the UK, for example, the network of anemograph stations of the Meteorological Office uses a standard instrument whose character-istics record a wind speed averaged over about three seconds, and this is the basis of the *basic wind speed* used in the current British Standard Code of Practice on wind loads, CP3: Chapter V: Part 2: 1972.

A typical output plot from such an instrument is shown in fig. 3.13, which traces the variation of horizontal wind speed with time and of wind direction with time. The important thing to remember when extracting information is that the wind speed at any point is the average wind speed over 3 seconds and any maximum values quoted from this chart are themselves strictly the means of fluctuation values which if recorded on an instrument of quicker response would show momentary wind velocities fluctuating around the value recorded. The insert to fig. 3.13 shows the speed-versus-time plot that might appear over a few milliseconds if the meteorological anemometer were instantaneously replaced by a high-response hot-wire anemometer, say.

An averaging process may be adopted to find, from the chart, the mean value for any time longer than 3 seconds, but it is necessary to choose the averaging time with care, bearing in mind, for example, the purpose for which the average value is required. Too long a time interval (one day, say) would produce a mean value of wind speed of little intrinsic value in ordinary affairs: to state that the mean wind speed over 24 hours was 10 km/h would be of little relevance to a day-long experience in which the wind condition changed from flat calm to gale. Too short a time would encroach on the reliable 3-second (gust) value the instrument automatically provides (although it will be seen later that 5-second and 15-second mean values have use in the design of certain sizes of buildings) and would provide little descriptive information of the overall wind behaviour.

A scrutiny of the chart in fig. 3.13 shows that there is a general increase taking place over the first hour or so of the record which would be in keeping with the movement of the air mass under the influence of the pressure gradient. The violent ups and downs indicate the passage of gusts and lulls which are associated with the turbulence induced by roughness of the terrain upstream of the recording instrument. For the value of mean velocity to be meaningful in common usage, it must exclude the 'weather-map' variations on the one hand and the extremes of gustiness due to stirring on the other. It will be shown by other reasoning, page 97, that time averages taken over periods of time between 10 and 60 minutes adequately avoid the two extremes, and the fact that average values taken over 10-minute, 20-minute, and 1-hour intervals are near

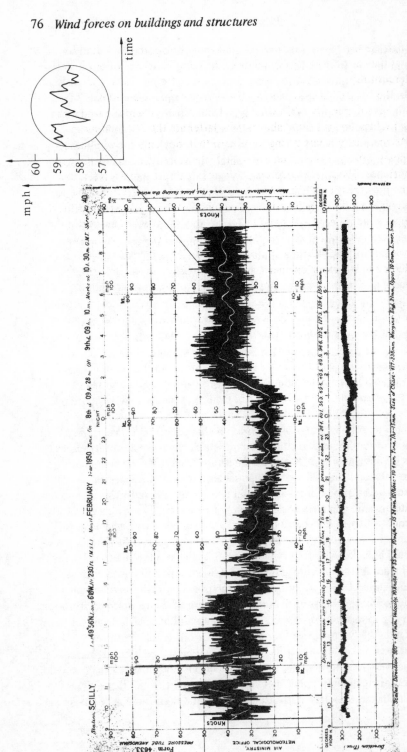

Fig. 3.13 Pressure-tube anemograph record (Meteorological Office, *Meteorological observer's handbook* (805), London, HMSO,

1ough the same goes some way to confirming this, and incidentally
lows the comparison of mean data of different countries who use
ifferent timed means.

In the UK, the data extracted from the anemograph stations as
nutine are the hourly mean wind speed and direction and the maximum
;ust) values, and, as noted above, these latter are the 3-second means.

As an aside, it is interesting to observe that, not only for wind-design
urposes but also in common experience, the wind speed is of secondary
nportance. The wind characteristic of greater direct interest is its force
r the pressure it may exert. Admiral Beaufort had this very much in
iind when he devised his scale of winds shown in fig. 3.14. The Beaufort-
imber scale is linear with wind force; velocity increases in proportion to
ie *square* of the number. Beaufort was concerned with the capacity of
invas sailcloth and ultimately its bursting wind load; in many respects
iilders and structural engineers are also primarily interested in the
·essure a structure sustains and its frequency of occurrence, rather than
ie wind speed (although they are related), and it is somewhat paradoxical
iat the majority of wind-velocity-recording instruments in use actually
·nse the pressure (or a pressure difference).

gnificance of site position on wind mean values.　When considering the
·levance of a particular value quoted as a mean wind speed or direction,
ɔt only the time over which the reading was taken but also the position
f the sensing head of the instrument is important. In well-covered rolling
oodland, or in a town or city centre, a displacement of a few metres
ay have very significant effects on the magnitude of mean wind speeds
gistered, and common experience indicates the sheltering or blanketing
'fects that are found in such situations. For this reason a site away from
imediate obstructions is chosen. Less obviously relevant to the choice
 site are the roughness characteristics of the terrain for several kilometres
ɔund − changes in the nature of the turbulence in the wind and of the
ilue of mean velocity take some time to stabilise after the wind has
ached a surface of different roughness.

The wind blowing in off a large expanse of sea which is relatively
iooth has a different turbulent structure from that experienced at the
ime place if the wind is off shore and has come for any distance over
gged land. Further, a wind coming off the sea, say, and meeting
oken countryside or town or urban development may take several
lometres before the influences of the increased roughnesses at the
rface permeate all the way through the lower atmosphere up to the
adient height.

These considerations alone make comparisons between different

Force	Description	Specifications for use on land	Specifications for use at sea
0	Calm	Calm; smoke rises vertically.	Sea like a mirror.
1	Light air	Direction of wind shown by smoke drift, but not by wind vanes.	Ripples with the appearance of scales are formed, but without foam crests.
2	Light breeze	Wind felt on face; leaves rustle; ordinary vane moved by wind.	Small wavelets, still short but more pronounced. Crests have a glassy appearance and do not break.
3	Gentle breeze	Leaves and small twigs in constant motion; wind extends light flag.	Large wavelets. Crests begin to break. Foam of glassy appearance. Perhaps scattered white horses.
4	Moderate breeze	Raises dust and loose paper; small branches are moved	Small waves, becoming longer; fairly frequent white horses.
5	Fresh breeze	Small trees in leaf begin to sway; crested wavelets form on inland waters.	Moderate waves, taking a more pronounced long form; many white horses are formed. Chance of some spray.
6	Strong breeze	Large branches in motion; whistling heard in telegraph wires; umbrellas used with difficulty.	Large waves begin to form; the white foam crests are more extensive everywhere. Probably some spray.
7	Near gale	Whole trees in motion; inconvenience felt when walking against wind.	Sea heaps up and white foam from breaking waves begins to be blown in streaks along the direction of the wind.
8	Gale	Breaks twigs off trees; generally impedes progress.	Moderately high waves of greater length; edges of crests begin to break into the spindrift. The foam is blown in well-marked streaks along the direction of the wind.
9	Strong gale	Slight structural damage occurs (chimney pots and slates removed).	High waves. Dense streaks of foam along the direction of the wind. Crests of waves begin to topple tumble and roll over. Spray may affect visibility.
10	Storm	Seldom experienced inland; trees uprooted; considerable structural damage occurs.	Very high waves with long overhanging crests. The resulting foam, in great patches, is blown in dense white streaks along the direction of the wind. Of the whole the surface of the sea takes a white appearance. The 'tumbling' of the sea becomes heavy and shock-like. Visibility affected.
11	Violent storm	Very rarely experienced; accompanied by widespread damage.	Exceptionally high waves (small and medium-sized ships might be for a time lost to view behind the waves). The sea is completely covered with long white patches of foam lying along the direction of the wind. Everywhere the edges of the wave crests are blown into froth. Visibility affected.
12	Hurricane –		The air is filled with foam and spray. Sea completely white with driving spray; visibility very seriously affected.

Fig. 3.14 Beaufort scale: specifications and equivalent speeds (Meteorological Office, *Meteorological observer's handbook* (805), London, HMSO, 3rd edn 1969; reproduced with permission of the controller of HMSO)

Force	Specifications for coastal use	Equivalent speed at 10 m above ground					
		Knots		Miles per hour		Metres per second	
		Mean	Limits	Mean	Limits	Mean	Limits
1	Calm.	0	< 1	0	< 1	0·0	0·0–0·2
	Fishing smack* just has steerage way.	2	1–3	2	1–3	0·8	0·3–1·5
2	Wind fills the sails of smacks which then travel at about 1–2 kt.	5	4–6	5	4–7	2·4	1·6–3·3
3	Smacks begin to careen and travel at about 3–4 kt.	9	7–10	10	8–12	4·3	3·4–5·4
4	Good working breeze, smacks carry all canvas with good list.	13	11–16	15	13–18	6·7	5·5–7·9
5	Smacks shorten sail.	19	17–21	21	19–24	9·3	8·0–10·7
6	Smacks have double reef in mainsail. Care required when fishing.	24	22–27	28	25–31	12·3	10·8–13·8
7	Smacks remain in harbour and those at sea lie-to.	30	28–33	35	32–38	15·5	13·9–17·1
8	All smacks make for harbour, if near.	37	34–40	42	39–46	18·9	17·2–20·7
9	–	44	41–47	50	47–54	22·6	20·8–24·4
0	–	52	48–55	59	55–63	26·4	24·5–28·4
1	–	60	56–63	68	64–72	30·5	28·5–32·6
2	–	–	⩾ 64	–	⩾ 73	–	⩾ 32·7

* The fishing smack in this table may be taken as representing a trawler average type and trim. For larger or smaller boats and for special circumstances allowance must be made.

stations difficult, or indeed comparisons of readings from the same instrument if the wind has, in the meantime, shifted direction to blow for long over a surface of different roughness. Ideally, then, all anemographs should be sited away from obstructions in the centre of a large area of open country and at the now standard height of 10 metres. This ideal situation is not always possible, and other sites and/or heights have to be used and the readings corrected to the standard height.

It is the nature of things that if meteorological records are required in a certain area then only local precautions on siting are possible. It is interesting to note that, in the interests of research, an Oceanographic Floating Instrument platform is in operation, and among its other functions is that of measuring wind properties well out of range of possible land-surface influences.[9]

As noted above, the 'standard height' for wind-speed data is 10 metres, and this is 10 metres above the ground at the instrument site, provided it is in fairly level country. The height of the site above sea level is not very critical to the records if this is the general height of the surrounding land, so that if the reverse situation is considered the height above sea level is not a significant quantity in estimating wind: it is height above ground that is important. Special situations such as sites on the edge of an escarpment require particular treatment, and the British Standard Code of Practice CP3: Chapter V: Part 2: 1972, 'Wind loads', allows for special considerations in this and other respects.

Significance of height on wind mean values.   In the discussion of meteorological factors in the previous chapter, it has been shown that in moderate to high winds the wind speed increases with height above the ground. This is in keeping with experience and reasoning. In the British Standard Code of Practice cited above, the mean wind speed is assumed to vary with height according to the power law

$$V_H = V(H/10)^{\alpha}$$
(see eqn 3.1

where V_H is the mean wind speed at height H metres and V is the mean wind speed at the height of 10 m; α is the exponent for the power law and reference back to fig. 2.9 will show the value of α contrived by A. G. Davenport. In the Code of Practice, values of α are quoted which allow for variation not only in ground roughness but also in average time, and, further, allowances may be introduced for the effective height above heavily wooded or built-up surfaces.

Before continuing, it is relevant to consider briefly the origin and effectiveness of a power law for describing the wind variation with height

That there is a variation with height is in no doubt, and some of the factors influencing the magnitude of this variation have been mentioned in Chapter 2. To recapitulate they are firstly the vertical temperature gradient which, for the appropriate local composition of the air, determines the stability or otherwise of the atmosphere, and secondly the mechanical stirring of the lowermost layers by obstructions (roughnesses) standing up from the surface. In other words, the structure of the wind may be affected as much by the buoyancy forces consequent on the temperature variations in the flow as by the nature, frequency, and form of the surface roughness. Generally the effect of buoyancy is to increase the curvature of the 'wind speed *vs* height' profile in unstable air and decrease it in stable conditions. For the admittedly infrequent case of neutral air, the profile would depend mainly on the degree of roughness at the surface, and it is at this point that the classical aeronautical theories of turbulent boundary layers may be involved.

Whether buoyancy is contributory or not, it may be expected that close to the surface in high-wind conditions (which after all are of most relevance here) the effects of ground roughnesses would dominate, gradually giving way to buoyancy effects further away from the surface.

3.2 Observations on the nomenclature for mean wind values, gustiness, and turbulence. References to wind speed, gust values, fluctuating velocity components, etc. are not always precise — values quoted may be instrument readings which contain inbuilt factors which may modify the reading; at other times, values are given to represent situations arising from theoretical predictions in which gross simplifying assumptions have been introduced.

The wind velocity at a particular point in space and at a certain instant in time is a *vector quantity,* having magnitude and direction. The two components of the vector, the magnitude and the direction, are variable, so that at an adjacent point in space and/or at the next instant in time the value of the vector is generally different.

Vector quantities are frequently represented by a straight line whose length is scaled to the size or *magnitude* of the quantity and whose orientation relative to a set of mutually perpendicular axes fixed in space indicates the vector *direction.*

Figure 3.15 shows the vector representation for the velocity felt locally at three separate points in space at two successive instants in time, t and $t + \tau$ respectively. The time difference (τ) between the two sets of values is called the *lag*; the distance of one point from the other the *(spatial) separation.*

Since the wind velocity is a random quantity, all of these values will generally be different from each other and vary in such a way that a statistical approach to the problem of predicting the wind effect is necessary. The elements of such an approach are given in section 3.3.4.

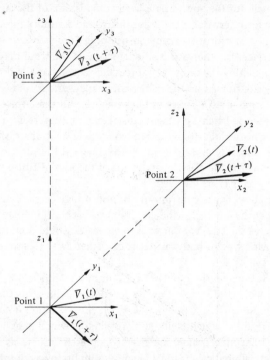

Fig. 3.15 The local velocity vector at three separate points in space at times t and $t + \tau$

Consider the time history of the velocity vector at a single point say, fig. 3.15. As implied above, the wind velocity vector has an instantaneous value $V(t)$. This may conveniently be resolved into its components parallel to the fixed axes ox, oy, oz, fig. 3.16.

Thus the time-dependent vector $\bar{V}(t)$ is the vector sum of the time-dependent components $u(t)$, $v(t)$, $w(t)$ parallel to the ox, oy, oz axes respectively and the magnitude of $\bar{V}(t)$ is given by

$$\bar{V}(t) = \sqrt{\{u(t)^2 + v(t)^2 + w(t)^2\}} \qquad (3.2$$

Now, each of the time-dependent components may be averaged by, for example, the method of section 3.3.3 over a finite length of time to produce a mean value. In the x-wise direction, the instantaneous time-dependent component $u(t)$ can be broken down into the sum of a mean

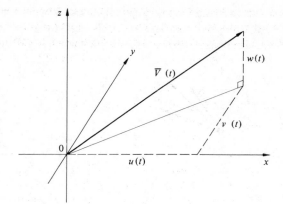

Fig. 3.16

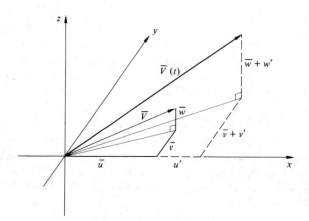

Fig. 3.17

quantity ($\bar{u}$) (independent of time within the finite time over which the averaging process is made) and a fluctuating time-dependent quantity (u').

Thus $u(t) = \bar{u} + u'$
For the other axes,
$\left.\begin{array}{l} v(t) = \bar{v} + v' \\ w(t) = \bar{w} + w' \end{array}\right\}$
$\qquad\qquad\qquad$ (3.21)

It can be seen in fig. 3.17 that the mean components resolve into a mean wind speed $\bar{V}$ which over the short term is invariant with time both in magnitude and direction.

An immediate simplification may be made by reorientating the arbitrary reference axes so that the direction of the mean wind vector $\bar{V}$

is along the x axis (horizontal), say. Figure 3.18 shows the rotation diagrammatically. The perturbation components which are fluctuating with time about the invariant mean speed $\bar{V}$ are respectively u' along the wind, v' across the wind in a transverse (horizontal) sense, and w' across the wind in a vertical sense.

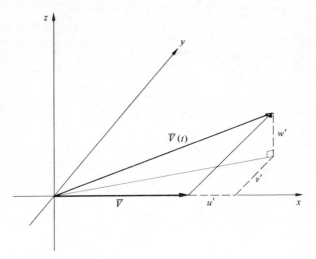

Fig. 3.18

The instantaneous wind velocity $\bar{V}(t)$ is the vector sum of the mean wind speed $\bar{V}$ and the gusting velocity $\bar{v}_g(t)$

i.e. $\bar{V}(t) = \bar{V} + \bar{v}_g(t)$ 　　　　　　　　　　　　　　　　　(3.22)

and the magnitude of the gust speed is the modulus

$$|\bar{v}_g(t)| = \sqrt{\{(u')^2 + (v')^2 + (w')^2\}}$$ 　　　　　　　(3.23)

Note that a minor conflict with general usage arises here in as much as the sum velocity is invariably quoted with reference to gusts. For example, a meteorological station might forecast 'gale force and conditions gusting to strong gale force 9 locally' or report 'the maximum gust speed recorded in the past 24 hours was 80 knots at 17.35 hours'. In each case the maximum speed, $\bar{V}(t)$, was quoted, the implication being that this speed was obtained by a variable addition to a 'steady' mean speed.

Since the mean speed is the average of the total wind velocity, it follows that the gust speed averaged over the same interval of time is zero. A measure of the gustiness is the *variance* (see section 3.3.4).

$$\sigma^2(v_g) = (1/T) \int_0^T \left\{ (u')^2 + (v')^2 + (w')^2 \right\} \, dt$$

$$= \sigma(u)^2 + \sigma(v)^2 + \sigma(w)^2 \tag{3.24}$$

Laboratory instruments are available which record very rapid changes in all three components of air velocity, and the turbulent flow generated in wind tunnels has been thoroughly explored. Only in the last few years, however, have instruments capable of rapid response to all components been designed robust enough for use in the natural wind, and the majority of routine free-wind data are obtained from standard instruments (section 6.1.2) which sense and record the 'instantaneous' magnitude of the wind speed (this is in fact the mean wind speed averaged over the response time of the instrument) and its direction relative to a geographical datum. Figure 3.13 shows the record illustrated in the Observer's handbook[10] and which is typical of the wind data from which estimations of design wind speeds must be made*.

3.3.3 Turbulence (and gustiness in the wind).
Gustiness has long been a recognised feature of the wind, and common experience shows a wide range of gust size and duration. The effects of gusts manifest themselves in changes of wind velocity and wind direction in observations made at a point, but more generally at large they cause dispersion and scattering of air properties, as well as of atmospheric constituents such as smoke and fog. The general name for this sort of unsteady activity in an airstream is *turbulence,* a term used by aerodynamicists to describe that type of flow in which random motion is superimposed on general streaming flow and which has been discussed in the context of boundary-layer flows above (section 3.2.2). It is useful to look at the ways in which the properties of turbulent flows may be described further.

Turbulence can be generated only as a result of a shearing velocity gradient in a viscous fluid. Such *shear flows,* as they are generally termed, will occur in the flow adjacent to any solid boundary, because of the condition of 'no slip' there, and also in the boundary region between streams flowing at different velocities, e.g. at the edges of jets and wakes†.

---

* See, for example, Shellard, H. C., 'The estimation of design wind speeds', *Symposium no. 16, wind effects on buildings and structures,* London, HMSO, 1965.

† Certain passages in what follows form part of the introduction to Chapter 5, 'Turbulent boundary layers', in Houghton, E. L., and Boswell, R. P., *Further aerodynamics for engineering students,* London, Edward Arnold, 1969, to which reference should be made for a fuller exposition.

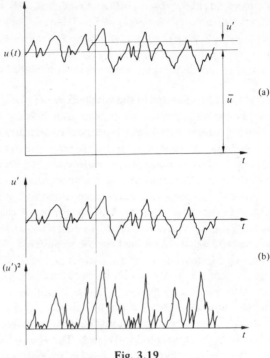

Fig. 3.19

Once generated, the turbulent motion, since it dissipates its kinetic energy into heat by viscous action, must be able to extract energy from the general flow in order to maintain itself. This it does, once again, by virtue of the existence of the shearing velocity gradient. In the absence of such a gradient, a turbulent motion will gradually decay.

A consequence of the above discussion is that any turbulence which may exist in a stream which is without shear gradients can have been generated only in some region upstream where shear gradients did exist; such turbulent motion will eventually disappear unless further shear gradients are in some way imposed on the stream.

In trying to explain the mechanism of turbulence, it is helpful to introduce the ideas of 'size' and 'intensity' of turbulence.

Scale of turbulence. The term 'size' is a relative one which may be taken to specify the average diameter of the rotating mass elements of fluid which constitute the turbulence. For example, the turbulence which occurs in the earth's atmosphere is of large size because the rotating elements or 'eddies' which develop are generally many metres in diameter (the existence of these eddies can be inferred from the patterns which develop in a field of grain when a 'blustery' wind is blowing). At the other extreme, the eddies which will be produced as the result of passing a stream of air through a fine mesh gauze will be very small, and of the same order of size as the mesh size of the gauze itself.

The effect of an eddy or vortex in the wind will depend on the relative size of the building or other object in its path. Smaller eddies within the flow past a large surface may have considerable bearing on the behaviour of the flow, for example in determining whether the boundary layer on the building separates or re-attaches and consequently changes the wind force on the structure. On the other hand, the passage of a large eddy whose scale is considerably greater than that of the building would result in an apparent shift of mean wind direction and magnitude or, in other words, would affect the incidence of the mean wind to the building and hence the overall wind forces.

The intensity of turbulence. The 'intensity' of turbulence is a measure of the amplitude of the velocity fluctuations which occur in the flow and is, to some extent, proportional to the angular velocities of the eddies. Thus eddies of the same size may produce different intensities of turbulence, depending on their rotational speeds. The energy content of a large eddy is much greater than that of a small one for a given intensity, and energy is transferred from larger eddies to smaller ones.

One effect of this is that a string of eddies of varying size which are moving downstream with the flow will tend to interchange their energies to maintain a fairly constant mean size and intensity. However, viscous action tends eventually to damp out the eddies and, unless they can capture energy from the surrounding stream in some way, they will decay. In a shear flow, the eddies in a faster moving level will tend to 'spin up' those in the slower adjacent stream and so re-energise the latter. Because the energy is transferred from larger to smaller eddies, the scale of the turbulence will tend to decrease across the stream from the higher- to the lower-speed regions. At each layer some energy is absorbed by the eddies to maintain their motion. For the large eddies this energy extracted is very small compared with the energy content of the eddies but, as the scale decreases, a stage is reached where the energy extracted is comparable with the energy content of the eddies, i.e. the viscous action in the fluid may become comparable in magnitude with the turbulent action.

It is generally found that the 'size' of the flow affects the size of the turbulence within it; thus the turbulent flow in a large pipe has a larger overall turbulence scale than has a corresponding flow in a small pipe. In some respects this is an advantage, because an overall geometric similarity exists in the two flows, and the characteristics determined for one may be scaled to give the characteristics of the other. While this offers obvious help to investigations in 'closed' flow situations, the eddy size in external flows will be more likely to depend on the size and scale of the obstacles upstream which are 'stirring' up the flow and generating the turbulence. These flows are amenable to scaling techniques, and the ideas of 'size' of flow may be exploited by recognising that the flow below the gradient height is in effect the shear flow of interest in wind problems. An algebraic *definition* of the intensity of turbulence follows below.

The reduction of a turbulent flow to the model of a uniform streaming flow on which random motions are superimposed has already been seen to be valuable in another context, since it leads to the postulation of a mean uniform flow and perturbations from the mean.

Fluctuating velocity components.   One technique which may be employed for the case of turbulent motion is to consider that at any instant the velocity consists of a mean velocity component plus random fluctuating components and thence to investigate the average effect of the fluctuations on the flow. Thus the velocity in the x-direction at any instant may be represented by $u(t) = \bar{u} + u'$, where $\bar{u}$ is the mean value of the velocity and u' is the instantaneous value of the velocity fluctuation about the mean value; similar quantities may be used to describe the y- and z-direction velocity fluctuations (refer back to section 3.3.2).

It must be clearly appreciated at the outset that there are two types of unsteadiness to be considered. The first type is that which is fundamental to turbulent motion, consisting of very rapid fluctuations of local velocity components and fluid properties, while the second is comparable with the type of time-dependent variations which also occur in steady flow, such as, for example, those resulting from a general acceleration of the mean flow. For the former type, it is reasonable to consider the average effects of the rapid fluctuations.

The time or temporal mean velocity.   There are several ways of defining an average quantity, depending upon the particular type of problem being considered.

The most used average quantity is the time or temporal mean which may be used when considering, for example, velocity fluctuations relative to a steady mean motion. In this case, the velocity under investigation is recorded at a fixed point over an appreciable period of time (theoretically approaching an infinite value, but in practice long enough for any further interval of time to make no difference to the mean value

obtained) and the *time* or *temporal mean* value is obtained from a
relationship of the form

$$\bar{u} = \lim_{(t_2 - t_1) \to \infty} \left\{ \frac{1}{t_2 - t_1} \int_{t_1}^{t_2} (\bar{u} + u') \mathrm{d}t \right\} \tag{3.25}$$

for the case of the x-wise mean velocity. t_1 and t_2 are the values of time
at the beginning and end of the record period.

Because it is necessary to average over a finite period of time at the
point considered, it is clear that this method runs into difficulties if the
mean flow varies with time, and other methods of averaging must be
employed to produce other values for mean velocities.

When the various mean values of a random quantity all have the
same value, the quantity is said to be 'stationary'. This simply means that
a stationary random process may be studied either by averaging one
observation over a long period or, for example, by averaging many
instantaneous observations taken at corresponding times and/or points.

When thinking about average quantities, it is usually easier to picture
the continuous variation of a quantity at a point and hence to imagine
the temporal mean value. In what follows it will be assumed that the
random quantities have stationary mean values and, unless otherwise
specifically stated, these mean values will for convenience be discussed
in terms of time averages, on the basis that the conclusions will be the
same whichever method of averaging is used.

The root-mean-square value.   Consider as the randomly fluctuating
quantity the velocity $u(t)$ in the x-direction, which may be represented
as above by a mean value $\bar{u}$ plus the fluctuation value u',

i.e. $u(t) = \bar{u} + u'$ \hfill (3.26)

see fig. 3.19 (a).

The mean quantity (shown with a bar) in each case is simply a
constant. It follows directly that any number of subsequent averaging
processes will produce the same average value so that, for example,

$$\bar{u} = \bar{\bar{u}} = \bar{\bar{\bar{u}}}, \text{ etc.}$$

Also, provided that the mean value is correctly chosen, the fluctuations
on either side of it must on average cancel out, so that

   $\bar{u'} = 0$

However, if for example $(u')^2$ is considered, then, whatever the sign
of u' relative to the mean value, its square will be positive and it is

impossible for the average of the squared value of the fluctuation to be zero, see fig. 3.19 (b), i.e. $\overline{(u')^2} \neq 0$. (Note that the bar includes the index.)

Moreover, the magnitude of $\overline{(u')^2}$ is a measure of the amplitude or 'intensity' of the fluctuating component of the quantity under consideration. The intensity is more usually thought of in terms of the square root of the average value of the square of the fluctuation, i.e. 'the root-mean-square value'. Thus the 'intensity' of the fluctuation is given by the quantity $\sqrt{\{\overline{(u')^2}\}}$, which then has the same dimensions as the original quantity being considered, and which is usually made non-dimensional by division with the mean value $\bar{u}$ (or $\bar{V}$). Thus the intensity of turbulence at wind speed $\bar{V}$ is given by $I = \sqrt{\{\overline{(u')^2}\}}/\bar{V}$.

Correlation coefficient. For a full insight into the turbulent state, information is required on the behaviour of the y-wise and z-wise components of velocity at the same, or some subsequent, instant. A simplification for the present may be made by assuming that the fluid is constrained to flow in two dimensions (or in a plane), and this will be true very close to a solid surface, in which case the z-wise component may be neglected.

Represent the y-wise velocity component by $v(t)$, which again is the sum of a mean value $\bar{v}$ and a fluctuation value v'. Thus $v(t) = \bar{v} + v'$ and all the reasoning applied in the case of the random quantity u above may be reiterated for $v(t)$ so that $\bar{v'} = 0$ and the root-mean-square value of v is $\sqrt{\{\overline{(v')^2}\}}$. In order to discover if any relationship exists between the random variable $u(t)$ and the random variable $v(t)$, it is necessary to consider the product of their fluctuating parts u' and v'. In point of fact it is the mean value of the product of the fluctuations which is of importance, i.e. $\overline{u'v'}$.

Determination of the mean value of the product of u' and v' (i.e. $\overline{u'v'}$) requires rather more thought. If $u(t)$ and $v(t)$ are completely unconnected quantities, then, for every instant of time when u' has a certain value, v' may have any value over its range of fluctuation, either positive or negative, so that the average value of the product of the fixed value of u' with all the values of v' will, over a sufficiently long period, become zero. A similar result will follow for every other fixed value of u' which may be chosen. Finally then, it will be evident that the average value of the product of any two or more fluctuations, where the quantities considered are completely unconnected with each other, is zero. Such fluctuations are said to be 'uncorrelated'.

However, in many physical problems, the two or more quantities may have some connection between them so that, for example, when

u' is positive, v' is positive and vice versa, or v' may always be proportional to u' and so on. When such a state of affairs exists, the quantities are said to be correlated, and the degree of correlation between them affects the mean value of the product $\overline{u'v'}$. Maximum correlation exists when the one quantity depends only on the other, and, in fact, only one of the quantities can then be considered as random.

A dimensionless correlation coefficient ψ may be defined to have a range of values between -1 and $+1$, the two extreme values corresponding to maximum correlation and the central value (0) to zero correlation. The implication of the sign of the correlation factor is simply that if $+v'$ is directly proportional to $+u'$ the sign will be positive, whereas if $+v'$ is directly proportional to $-u'$, or vice versa, the sign will be negative.

The correlation coefficient is defined by

$$\psi = \frac{\overline{u'v'}}{\sqrt{\{\overline{(u')^2}\}} \cdot \sqrt{\{\overline{(v')^2}\}}} \tag{3.27}$$

i.e. it is the mean value of the product of the fluctuating quantities divided by the product of their root mean squares.

In most practical examples of two or more randomly fluctuating quantities — and the velocity components of the natural wind are no exception — some correlation between them is usually present, but it is seldom 100% because almost invariably external factors, other than the first quantity, influence the second quantity.

3.3.4 A statistical method applied to fluctuating wind speeds.

Spectral-analytical techniques have been found to provide the most powerful tools to deal with the hitherto intractable problems posed by the random nature of the turbulent structure of the natural wind. The application of techniques used in the analysis of random processes to wind problems shows promise as a method which is not only of considerable value in generating a solution but which may also go some way to providing a further physical interpretation of turbulence.

Although a complete treatment is beyond the scope of the present book, some value may be taken from a review of the method, even in the absence of the concomitant algebraic manipulation. Undoubtedly more and more literature in the field of wind forces will use the results and references of spectral-analysis methods, and a brief glance at their origins may be of use.

In what follows, take a velocity component of the wind as the (random) variable and time as the independent variable, although the method is applicable to the analysis of many other random phenomena which may be functions of some other physical parameter.

It is useful to recall and build on the concept of Fourier analysis of waveform. Where this is not possible, it is sufficient for the present to observe that a curve of any shape, fig. 3.20 say, may be analysed as a sum of a number of sine (or cosine waves), each of different amplitude and wavelength. The more complicated the original curve, the more harmonics are required in the sum. There are necessary mathematical limitations to, for example, the length of the original curve, and in the simple analysis the curve under analysis is required to be periodic, but an extension of the idea may now be discussed.

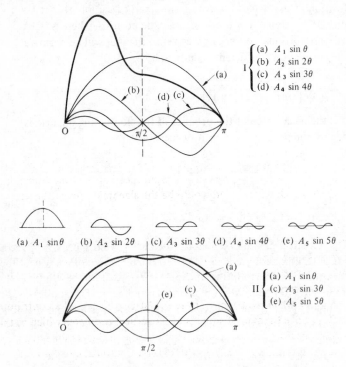

Fig. 3.20 Two different curves made up of selected sine waves

Suppose a change in wind speed felt at a point were sinusoidal, then a graph of wind speed versus time would look like the sine curve of fig. 3.21. The maximum variation in wind speed from the mean wind $\bar{u}$ is the amplitude (a) of the wave. The wavelength λ represents the time (or period) it takes for one complete cycle of speeds to be felt at the point, while the number of times the maximum velocity is experienced per second is the frequency $f = 1/\lambda$.

It is not difficult to imagine that a wind speed felt at any time at a point could be resolved into a number of, say, sinusoidal fluctuations of different frequencies and amplitudes about the mean speed which happened to come together at that point and time to produce the

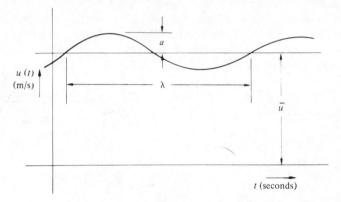

Fig. 3.21

cumulative effect experienced. Figure 3.22 shows six different waves which could contribute to the value of wind speed at the time shown, and the magnitude of the wind would be the algebraic sum of the six values at that instant. The point of consequence in this model is that the six values are fluctuating with different frequencies as well as different amplitudes, and a property of the individual wave may be evaluated and expressed against the wave frequency. Thus the total or cumulative value of the composite fluctuations can be resolved into components according to their frequency.

A property which will demonstrate the 'strength', say, of a contributory wave will require the sum of squares of its vertical ordinate (which in this case is the velocity). It is necessary to square the ordinates since a summation of ordinates alone with time for a sinusoidal curve gives a zero value over a whole period.

The variance (deviation).   The mean-square value of $u(t)$ about the mean value $\bar{u}$ in the general case is called the variance $\sigma^2(u) = \overline{\bar{u}^2} - \overline{u}^2$ and, in so far as the square of the velocity of unit mass of air represents its *kinetic energy,* the variance may represent the average fluctuating 'power' in the wind. (Conventionally most observations of random physical processes are converted to electrical voltages for electronic recording and processing. The *signal* received from the anemometer sensing the component of wind speed would, on conversion to

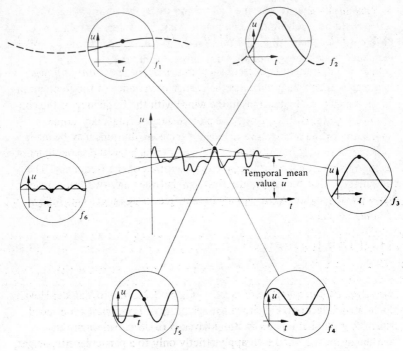

Fig. 3.22

electrical values, possess a variance which in electrical terms would
be the *average a.c. power*; hence the common use of the word power
in this context.) Note also that the positive square root of the variance
is the deviation, $\sigma(u)$ (i.e. r.m.s. value).

The power spectral density. To sum up so far, it seems that the variance
or average power of the time-dependent signal (velocity in this case) can
be decomposed into a number of contributions of different frequency.
As the length of the signal is increased, the number of different frequencies
encompassed by the record will increase so that, instead of the
instantaneous velocity being given as above by

$$u = \bar{u} + A_1 \sin \theta + A_2 \sin 2\theta + A_3 \sin 3\theta +$$
$$A_4 \sin 4\theta + A_5 \sin 5\theta + A_6 \sin 6\theta$$

(i.e. $u = \bar{u}$ + the sum of a limited number of frequencies), the summation
becomes continuous over a wide range of frequencies and is replaced by
an integral.

Thus $u(t) = \bar{u} + \displaystyle\int_0^\infty A_n \sin 2\pi \, nf \mathrm{d}f$ \hfill (3.28)

Now $u(t) = \bar{u} + u'$

and $\quad \sigma^2(u) = \overline{u^2} - \bar{u}^2 = \int_0^\infty S(f)\mathrm{d}f \quad [= \overline{(u')^2}]$ $\hspace{2cm}$ (3.29)

where $S(f)$ is a function of frequency known as the *spectrum* or *power spectral density* which indicates the change of variance of the fluctuations in the signal (i.e. fluctuations in the wind) with the frequency of the contributory wave. If this quantity be plotted against frequency, some indication of the relative size of each of the contributions may be made. It is useful to plot the product of $S(f)$ and f (which has the same dimensions as the variance, i.e. $(\mathrm{m/s})^2$) against the logarithm of the frequency. The advantage is that the area under the curve between any two frequencies gives a true measure of the energy in that frequency range. This follows from the equality

$$\int_0^\infty S(f)\mathrm{d}f = \int_0^\infty fS(f)\mathrm{d}(\ln f) \hspace{2cm} (3.30)$$

Spectrum of horizontal wind speed. Figure 3.23, due to Van der Hoven (following Davenport[11]), shows the spectrum of horizontal wind speed near the ground at a point in Brookhaven NY, USA. Although the particular records used each apply strictly only to a particular site, height, and the time for which the record was made, Van der Hoven pieced together the spectra from numerous records to provide very useful information on the nature of variations in wind speed. The high-frequency range of the spectrum was obtained from measurements taken during a hurricane. The lower-frequency range has peaks at one cycle per 12 hours and at one cycle per 4 days. These are associated, respectively, with the day–night–day changes in wind and the variations due to large-scale movements of air masses (due for example to the passage of a depression).

The major peak in the higher-frequency end is separated from the low-frequency activity by a 'gap' in the spectrum around the 1 cycle/hour frequency.

Bearing in mind that the area under the curve between frequencies represents the energy in the wind, it would seem that the wind has two significant frequency ranges. On the low-frequency side of the gap the variations are due to movements of air masses on a large scale (Davenport refers to these as 'weather-map fluctuations'); on the high-frequency side the variations are due to the gustiness in the wind, which is a consequence of the mechanical stirring of the lower layers of the atmosphere by the roughnesses of the rugged nature of the terrain, buildings, structures, forests, and the like.

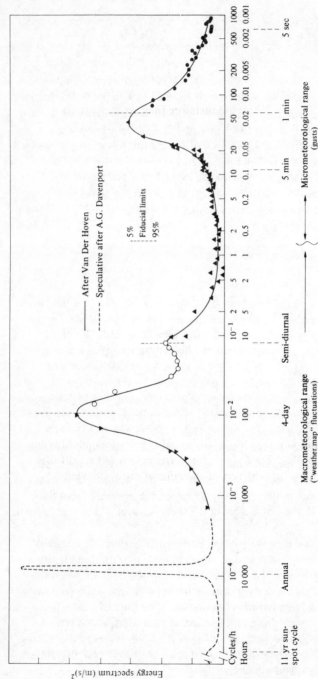

Fig. 3.23 Spectrum of horizontal wind speed near the ground for an extensive frequency range (from measurements at 100 m height by Van der Hoven at Brooklyn, NY, USA)

The consequences of the presence of the gap are as follows.

i) The mean wind-speed value averaged over a period greater than 20 minutes and less than 3 hours is likely to be independent of the length of the record averaged, since any record of longer than 20 minutes or so will encompass all of the significant frequencies of gustiness. One-hour means are therefore fully representative.

ii) The effect of the lower-frequency variations are adequately represented by changes in the (hourly) mean speed.

iii) For a determination of the effects of high winds on structures, it is sufficient if analysis continues on the basis of a gust spectrum whose lower frequency limit is one cycle per 5 minutes. (The high-frequency limitation to the record will depend on the response rate of the measuring system.)

Wind 'waves'.   Before proceeding along the lines suggested by (iii), another useful physical view of the wind fluctuations may be taken. Consider fig. 3.21 again. As implied above, to an observer at rest the maximum wind speed would be felt every λ seconds, or at $f = 1/\lambda$ times per second. If the mean wind speed were $\bar{V}$ m/s, then the distance along the wind between the maximum wind speeds would be $\bar{V}\lambda$ metres ($\bar{V}/f$ metres). For example, the highest values of a fluctuation of $f = 0.2$ (i.e. a 5-second gust) in a wind whose mean speed was 30 m/s would be $30/0.2 = 150$ metres apart. Contributions fluctuating at lower frequencies would have a longer length between peak values, as would those fluctuations immersed in winds of higher mean speed. This allows an analogy to be drawn between sea waves and wind waves[11] where atmospheric motion is seen to be compounded of superimposed trains of wind waves of different frequencies (wavelengths) and amplitudes.

Additionally the introduction of the value of the mean wind speed allows the frequency (or its inverse) to be expressed in the more tangible units of length.

The gust spectra.   From the above discussion, it would seem that the components of a high wind of most significance to the dynamics of structures are contained in the part of the wind spectrum where the period of the contributions is less than an hour.

If the data has been obtained from instruments sensing the horizontal wind component, then, as in the case of Van der Hoven's spectrum of fig. 3.23 above, the resulting spectrum is known as the horizontal gust spectrum. Similar spectra may be obtained from data of the other velocity components.

It has been shown by Davenport[11] and others that for high winds the spectra of horizontal gustiness obtained at numerous sites and under diverse conditions may, after appropriate factoring, reduce to a single non-dimensional curve which can then be 'fitted' by a suitable empirical algebraic expression for further manipulation.

In the *invariant* gust spectrum, as the single curve is called, the product of the spectral density (Sf) and the frequency (f) is made non-dimensional by division with the product of the square of the mean velocity appropriate to the standard height of 10 metres $(\bar{V}_{10}{}^2)$ and a factor (k) representing the drag coefficient of the surface. Thus the reduced spectral density becomes

$$f\, S(f)/k\bar{V}_{10}{}^2 \tag{3.31}$$

This quantity plotted against the inverse wavelength $(f/\bar{V}_{10})$ is called the 'normalised' gust spectrum and is shown in fig. 3.24 as two theoretical versions: the original due to Davenport[11] and a 'modified' expression due to Harris[12]. The figure also shows the experimental points upon which the original curve was based.

The algebraic 'fit' is an expression

$$S(f)\mathrm{d}f = 4k\bar{V}_{10}{}^2\ \phi(fL/\bar{V}_{10}) \tag{3.32}$$

Davenport gave an explicit form for the function ϕ in which the arbitrary length L was 1200 m. Harris improved on the shape of the expression and obtained a better fit for his experimental data with $L = 1800$ m.

A next step is to substitute the expression for $S(f)\mathrm{d}f$ of eqn 3.32 into eqn 3.29 and hence find the *variance,* the square root of which defines the *intensity of turbulence* due to horizontal gustiness. Thus[11]

$$I_{10} = \frac{\sigma_{10}}{\bar{V}_{10}} = \left[\int_0^\infty \frac{S(f)\mathrm{d}f}{V_{10}{}^2} \right]^{1/2}\ (=0{\cdot}735\ k^{1/2}) \tag{3.33}$$

which shows that the intensity of turbulence at the standard height depends solely on the drag coefficient of the ground, that is on parameters which depend on the terrain roughness.

To relate this to the value at any height z other than the standard, the expression for mean wind speed in terms of height must be introduced in eqn 3.32. Then, using the power law

$$\bar{V}_z/\bar{V}_{10} = (z/10)^\alpha \tag{3.34}$$

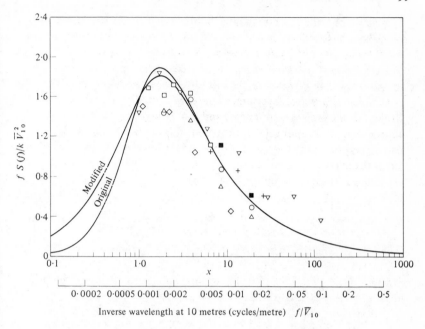

Fig. 3.24 Comparison of the original and modified gust spectra (normalised horizontal gust spectra after R. I. Harris)

a more general form of the eqn 3.32 is

$$S(f)\mathrm{d}f = 4k\bar{V}_z^2 \left(\frac{z}{10}\right)^{-2\alpha} \frac{x\mathrm{d}x}{(1 + x^2)^{4/3}} \qquad (3.32\mathrm{a})$$

and the r.m.s. intensity of turbulence at any height is

$$I_z = \sigma_z/\bar{V}_z = 0.735k^{1/2}(z/10)^{-\alpha} \qquad (3.33\mathrm{a})$$

In general, then, the normalised horizontal gust spectrum and the intensity of turbulence are independent of wind speed and depend only on height above ground and the ground roughness.

Davenport[11] distinguished three noteworthy features of the horizontal gust spectrum. Firstly, the peak in the spectrum corresponds to a wavelength of 600 metres and most of the energy in the wind is confined to wavelengths between 3000 metres and 30 metres, so that in a force-10 wind (30 m/s) significant contributions arise from fluctuations whose periods are greater than 1 second but less than 100 seconds. Secondly, the spectrum is proportional to the quantity $k\bar{V}^2$; that is, as noted above, it is proportional to the shearing forces between the surface and the windstream. Thirdly, the pattern of turbulence is invariant with wind speed as implied by the use of the variable x (or $n/\overline{V}$, the inverse wavelength).

The vertical gust spectrum. The last characteristic immediately above does *not* apply to vertical gust data. In this case an invariant gust spectrum is obtained only when the spectral density is plotted against the ratio of height (z) to wavelength ($\overline{V}/f$), i.e. $x_v = fz/\overline{V}_{10}$.

The suggested empirical curve[11] is shown in fig. 3.25 and a peak is apparent at the value $fz/\overline{V}_{10} = 0.25$, that is for wavelengths about four times the height.

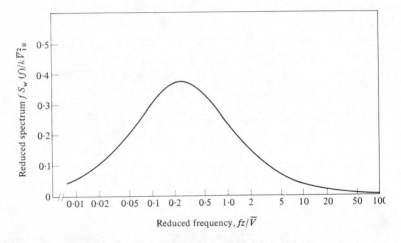

Fig. 3.25 Spectrum of vertical gustiness (after Panofsky)

The major point of significance to emerge here is that vertical gustiness is strongly dependent on height, and a moment's reflection will show that this should not be unexpected, especially near the ground where vertical components are bound to be inhibited by the presence of the surface.

Cross correlation. In what has gone before, the random behaviour of a fluctuating quantity at a particular point in space has been the subject of discussion. For small objects near that point it would be reasonable to assume that the values obtained for wind force, say, due to the gustiness were fairly representative of those experienced over the whole object.

For large constructions, particularly those with one major dimension, such as a long bridge or tall tower, this is no longer the case and there can be no direct relationship between the random behaviour of the wind from place to place along the structure. It is nonetheless necessary to obtain a measure of the distribution of gusts, say, along a bridge, and once again statistical methods must be employed.

If two points A and B along a structure are separated by a distance l, say, then the methods above may be used to find the variance of the wind gustiness at each point, i.e.

$$\sigma(u_A) = \bar{u}^2 - \overline{(u_A)}^2 \quad \text{and} \quad \sigma(u_B) = \bar{u}^2 - \overline{(u_B)}^2$$

This gives no indication of the way in which the gustiness is distributed between points A and B: no information, for example, that when A is in a gust B may be in a lull, or vice versa. For this information it is necessary to utilise the product of the local velocities, $u_A u_B$.

Thus the *covariance* between the velocities at the two *points* is the mean of their product, $\overline{u_A u_B}$, and the non-dimensional *cross-correlation coefficient* is

$$\overline{u_A u_B}/\sqrt{(\bar{u}_A^2 \bar{u}_B^2)} \tag{3.35}$$

4

Steady aerodynamic force and its effect on design

4.1 The elements of hydrostatics

All of our buildings and structures, and we ourselves in the main, exist on the bottom of the immense ocean of air many kilometres deep. Every exposed surface must sustain a static pressure which arises from the weight of the atmosphere above pressing down on and blanketing everything. Under normal still conditions, the pressure inside a ventilated building is the same as that outside, so that no net pressure difference or resultant force is experienced; indeed, we cannot perceive this pressure with our natural senses unless its magnitude changes appreciably from the normal.

When air begins to move, its static pressure is modified accordingly, and, as air flows over obstacles, which in turn change its speed locally, the local static pressure felt on the body differs from that of the ambience at large. It is the *pressure difference* of the local pressure from that of the ambience at large which is 'felt' by a surface as producing a force. In some references, and in particular in the British Standard Code of Practice, this pressure difference is referred to as the 'pressure'. Confusion is unlikely to result from this acceptance of common usage in preference to physical exactitude for it is, after all, only an extension of the engineering practice of the use of 'gauge' pressures which have a zero value at atmospheric pressure. Nevertheless, care must be exercised or the common reference to a 'negative-pressure' pressure coefficient in what follows may cause concern.

Before proceeding to the wider discussion of steady forces induced by the wind, it is helpful to recall the laws of hydrostatics, which are of relevance not only in respect of the atmosphere but also to the measurement of pressure.

4.1.1 Pressure in fluid at rest.
Consider a small cubic element containing fluid at rest in a larger bulk of fluid also at rest. The faces of the cube,

assumed to be made of some thin flexible material, are subject to continual bombardment by the molecules of the fluid, and thus experience a force. The force on any face may be resolved into two components, one acting perpendicular to the face and the other along it, i.e. tangential to it. Consider for the moment the tangential components only; there are three significantly different arrangements possible, fig. 4.1.

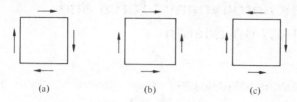

(a)   (b)   (c)

Fig. 4.1 Fictitious systems of tangential forces in static fluid

The system at (a) would cause the element to rotate, and thus the fluid would not be at rest.

System (b) would cause the element to move (upwards and to the right for the case shown) and, once more, the fluid would not be at rest. Since a fluid cannot resist shear stress, but only rate of change of shear strain, system (c) would cause the element to distort, the degree of distortion increasing with time, and the fluid would not remain at rest.

The conclusion is that a fluid at rest cannot sustain tangential pressures, or, conversely, that in a fluid at rest the pressure on a surface must act in the direction perpendicular to that surface.

4.1.2 Pascal's law.   Consider the right prism of width δy and cross-section ABC, the angle ABC being a right-angle (fig. 4.2). The prism is constructed of material of the same density as a bulk of fluid in which the prism floats at rest with the face BCC'B' horizontal.

Pressures p_1, p_2, and p_3 act on the faces shown and, as proved above, these pressures act in the direction perpendicular to the respective face. Other pressures act on the end faces of the prism but are ignored in the present problem. In addition to these pressures, the weight W of the prism acts vertically downwards. Consider the forces acting on the wedge, which is in equilibrium and at rest.

Resolving forces horizontally,

$$p_1(\delta x \tan \alpha)\,\delta y - p_2(\delta x \sec \alpha)\,\delta y \sin \alpha = 0$$

Dividing by $\delta x\,\delta y \tan \alpha$, this becomes

$$p_1 - p_2 = 0$$

i.e.

$$p_1 = p_2 \tag{4.1}$$

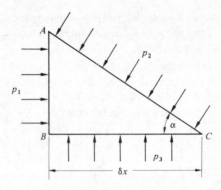

Fig. 4.2 A section of the prism of Pascal's law (note: A'B'C' hidden;
AA' = BB' = CC' = δy)

Resolving forces vertically,

$$p_3\, \delta x\, \delta y - p_2(\delta x \sec \alpha)\, \delta y \cos \alpha - W = 0 \qquad (4.2$$

Now $W = \rho g \tfrac{1}{2}(\delta x)^2 \tan \alpha . \delta y$

therefore, substituting this in eqn 4.2 and dividing by $\delta x\, \delta y$,

$$p_3 - p_2 - \tfrac{1}{2}\rho g \tan \alpha . \delta x = 0$$

If now the prism is imagined to become infinitely small, so that
$\delta x \to 0$, then the third term tends to zero, leaving

$$p_3 - p_2 = 0$$

Thus, finally,

$$p_1 = p_2 = p_3 \qquad (4.3$$

Having become infinitely small, the prism is in effect a point, and
thus the above analysis shows that, at a point, the three pressures considered are equal. In addition, the angle α is purely arbitrary and can
take any value in all the four quadrants, while the whole prism could
be rotated through a complete circle about a vertical axis without
affecting the result. Consequently it may be concluded that the pressure
acting at a point in a fluid at rest is the same in all directions.

4.1.3 The buoyancy equation. Consider a large volume of fluid at rest
and in equilibrium, and imagine a small right cylinder of the fluid, of
cross-sectional area δA and height δh, centred at some point (fig. 4.3).
The forces acting on the cylinder are as shown. There are also pressures
acting on the vertical surface, but these balance out and may be ignored.
It will be seen that there is a pressure p acting on the lower face and a

different pressure $p + \delta p$ acting on the upper face. The weight of fluid contained in the cylinder is equal to the product of density, volume, and g, i.e. $\rho g \delta\, A\, \delta h$

Since the cylinder is in equilibrium,

$$(p + \delta p)\, \delta A + \rho g \delta A\, \delta h - p\, \delta A = 0$$

Dividing by δA and simplifying, this becomes

$$\delta p + \rho g\, \delta h = 0$$

or $\quad \delta p / \delta h = - \rho g$ \hfill (4.4)

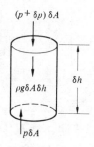

Fig. 4.3

Taking the limit as δh tends to zero, this becomes

$$dp/dh = - \rho g \hfill (4.5)$$

which shows how the pressure varies with height in a bulk of fluid at rest.

4.1.4 Measurement of pressures. Equation 4.5 may be rearranged as

$$dp = - \rho g\, dh$$

To compare the pressures p_1 and p_2 at two points in the fluid at heights h_1 and h_2 respectively, this equation may be integrated between condition 1 and condition 2 as

$$\int_1^2 dp = - \int_1^2 \rho g\, dh$$

In the special case where ρ and g are constant, this may be integrated as

$$p_2 - p_1 = - \rho g (h_2 - h_1)$$

or $\quad p_1 - p_2 = \rho g (h_2 - h_1)$ \hfill (4.6)

If $h_2 - h_1$ is positive (point 2 above point 1), $p_1 - p_2$ is also positive

$(p_2 > p_1)$; thus pressure decreases with height. Also note that $\rho g(h_2 - h_1)$ is the weight of a column of fluid of unit area and height $h_2 - h_1$. It may thus be deduced that the pressure at any point in a fluid at rest is equal to the weight of all the fluid contained in a column of unit area above that point. It should be noted here that most liquids have a density which may be regarded as constant, but this is not true for gases, except over very small height differences.

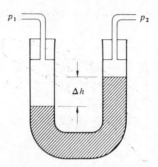

Fig. 4.4 The simple U-tube

This suggests methods for measuring a pressure difference between two points. A pressure difference may be used to support a column of liquid of known density, and can be measured by the height of that column. The mercury barometer is a well-known example of this, and it is common to talk of a pressure difference of, say, 56·1 mm of mercury, which is a pressure difference of 7469 Pa. A practical application of this principle is the U-tube, which forms the basis of several pressure-measuring instruments or 'manometers'. The simplest form is a tube bent into the form of a U and partly filled with liquid (fig. 4.4). The two limbs are connected to the two points between which the pressure difference is to be measured. Equation 4.6 states

$$p_1 - p_2 = \rho g(h_2 - h_1) \tag{4.6}$$

or $\quad \Delta p = \rho g \Delta h \tag{4.7}$

Then by measuring Δh and using the known value of ρ it is possible to calculate the pressure difference Δp, taking care to use consistent units.

4.2 Bernoulli's equation

It was suggested above that the velocity and pressure at a point in a fluid flow are interdependent. Bernoulli's equation connects these two variables.

Consider a fluid in steady flow, and take any small streamtube as in
ig. 4.5. (A streamtube is an imaginary tube formed of adjacent stream-
ines.)

s is distance measured along the axis of the streamtube from some
    arbitrary origin,
A is the cross-sectional area of the streamtube at distance s from the
    arbitrary origin,
p, ρ, and v represent pressure, density, and speed of fluid respectively.

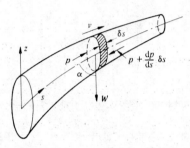

Fig. 4.5 The streamtube and element for Bernoulli's equation

A, p, ρ, and v vary with s, i.e. with position along the streamtube, but
not with time, since the motion is steady.

Now consider a small 'slice' of the fluid in the streamtube, shown
shaded. The first condition to be satisfied is of continuity, i.e. that
matter cannot be created or destroyed. This means that the same mass
of fluid must cross each section of the streamtube in unit time. This
may be expressed as

$$\rho A v = \text{constant} \tag{4.8}$$

Here Av is the volumetric flow per second, and the mass flow is $\rho A v$
(kg/s).

Now consider the small element of fluid shown in fig. 4.6, which
is immersed in fluid of varying pressure. The element is the right
frustum of a cone of length δs, area A at the upstream section, area
$A + \delta A$ at the downstream section.

The pressure acting on one face of the element is p, and on the
other face is $p + (dp/ds)\delta s$. Around the curved surface the pressure
may be taken to be the mean value $p + (dp/ds)\delta s/2$. In addition, the
weight W of the fluid in the element acts vertically as shown.

As a result of these pressures and the weight, there is a resultant
force F acting along the axis of the cylinder, where F is given by

$$F = pA - \left(p + \frac{dp}{ds}\,\delta s\right)(A + \delta A) + \left(p + \frac{dp}{ds}\,\frac{\delta s}{2}\right)\delta A - W\cos\alpha \tag{4.9}$$

where α is the angle between the axis of the streamtube and the vertical.

From eqn 4.9 it is seen that, on neglecting quantities of small order such as $(dp/ds)\,\delta s\delta A$ and cancelling,

$$F = -(dp/ds)A\,\delta s - \rho gA\delta s\cos\alpha \qquad (4.10)$$

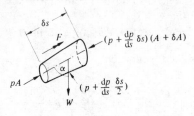

Fig. 4.6 The forces on the element

since the gravitational force on the fluid in the element is $\rho gA\,\delta s$ (volume x density).

Now, by Newton's second law of motion (force = mass x acceleration) applied to the element of fig. 4.6,

$$-\rho gA\,\delta s\cos\alpha - \frac{dp}{ds}A\,\delta s = \rho A\,\delta s\,\frac{dv}{dt} \qquad (4.11)$$

where t represents time.

Dividing by $A\,\delta s$, this becomes

$$-\rho g\cos\alpha - \frac{dp}{ds} = \rho\,\frac{dv}{dt}$$

But $\quad \dfrac{dv}{dt} = \dfrac{dv}{ds}\cdot\dfrac{ds}{dt} = v\,\dfrac{dv}{ds}$

and therefore $\quad \rho v\,\dfrac{dv}{ds} + \dfrac{dp}{ds} + \rho g\cos\alpha = 0$

or $\quad v\,\dfrac{dv}{ds} + \dfrac{1}{\rho}\,\dfrac{dp}{ds} + g\cos\alpha = 0$

Integrating along the streamtube, this becomes

$$\int\frac{dp}{\rho} + \int v\,dv + g\int\cos\alpha\,ds = \text{constant}$$

but since $\displaystyle\int\cos\alpha\,ds = $ increase in vertical co-ordinate z

and $\quad \displaystyle\int v\,dv = \tfrac{1}{2}v^2$

hen $\dfrac{\mathrm{d}p}{\rho} + \tfrac{1}{2}v^2 + gz = \text{constant}$ (4.12)

4.2.1 Bernoulli's equation for an incompressible fluid. Provided velocity and pressure changes are small, density changes will be very small, and it is permissible to assume that the density ρ is constant throughout the flow.

With this assumption, eqn 4.12 may be integrated as

$$\int \mathrm{d}p + \tfrac{1}{2}\rho v^2 + \rho gz = \text{constant}$$

Performing this integration between two conditions represented by suffices 1 and 2 gives

$$(p_2 - p_1) + \tfrac{1}{2}\rho(v_2^2 - v_1^2) + \rho g(z_2 - z_1) = 0$$

i.e. $p_1 + \tfrac{1}{2}\rho v_1^2 + \rho gz_1 = p_2 + \tfrac{1}{2}\rho v_2^2 + \rho gz_2$

In the foregoing analysis 1 and 2 were completely arbitrary choices, and therefore the same equation must apply to conditions at any other points.

Thus finally $p + \tfrac{1}{2}\rho v^2 + \rho gz = \text{constant}$ (4.13)

This is Bernoulli's equation for an incompressible fluid, i.e. a fluid which cannot be compressed or expanded, and for which the density is invariable.

4.2.2 Bernoulli's equation for air. For a full application of Bernoulli's equation to the case of gases whose densities vary with pressure and temperature, it is necessary to return to the differential equation 4.12 above and integrate it with density (ρ) as a variable.

If this be done, the equivalent form of Bernoulli's equation becomes (for adiabatic expansion and compression)

$$\frac{\gamma}{\gamma - 1}\frac{p}{\rho} + \frac{v^2}{2} + gz = \text{constant}$$ (4.14)

It is irrelevant to pursue this line of reasoning in the present case because further manipulation of eqn 4.14 shows* that, for air and gas flows of velocity less than about 15% of the speed of sound, eqn 4.14 reduces to Bernoulli's equation for an incompressible fluid given in eqn 4.13 above. For all practical purposes the relevant wind speeds are less

* See, for example, Houghton, E. L., and Brock, A. E., *Aerodynamics for engineering students,* London, Edward Arnold, 2nd edn 1970.

than 15% of the speed of sound, which is about 192 km/h (105 knots, or force 16 on the Beaufort scale!). (In aeronautics it has been customary to ignore compressibility effects, as they are called, for speeds up to 40% of the speed of sound.)

Bearing this in mind, recall eqn 4.13 as the preferred form of Bernoulli's equation, i.e. $p + \frac{1}{2}\rho v^2 + \rho gz = $ constant (eqn 4.13). It will be observed that if each term is divided by the product of density and gravity, i.e. by the quantity ρg, the form of Bernoulli's equation more familiar in problems in hydraulics appears

i.e. $\quad \dfrac{p}{\rho g} + \dfrac{V^2}{2g} + z = $ constant $\hspace{4cm}$ (4.1

Each term has the dimension of length and in common usage is referred to as a 'head'.

Returning to the preferred form of eqn 4.13 for relatively low-speed air flows, it may be noted that the change in the third term will always be small compared with changes in the first two, since in practical air-flow problems the small magnitude of the density quantity is not compensated for by very large changes in the height term z. In other words, if the variation in the height of the flow above datum is small, as is usually the case in wind problems, the third term may be neglected and the equation becomes

$\quad p = \frac{1}{2}\rho v^2 = $ constant $\hspace{5cm}$ (4.1

It will be observed that the first term (p) is the internal energy of unit volume of air, that is the pressure energy per unit volume attributabl to the molecular 'bombardment' referred to in section 3.11. The second term, $\frac{1}{2}\rho v^2$, is the kinetic energy of mean motion of unit volume of air. (For the general eqn 4.13, the third term, ρgz, is the potential energy of unit volume of air.) Thus Bernoulli's equation is really a statement of the physical principle of conservation of energy. As a corollary it applies only to flows where there is no degradation of the energy into a form not admissible in the equation, such as heat. In aerodynamics, a common form of energy dissipation is viscosity; thus Bernoulli's equation cannot strictly be applied to a flow where the effect of viscosity are appreciable.

Now, energy per unit volume has the dimensions of pressure, as is apparent from the appearance of the first term (p) in eqn 4.16. This first term (p), is called the *static* pressure and is the pressure sensed by an instrument offering no obstruction to the flow. It follows that p is also the pressure felt locally at a point on a surface over which air is flowing smoothly with velocity v.

The second term ($\frac{1}{2}\rho v^2$) is called the *dynamic* pressure of the stream, and is often symbolised by q (see, for example, British Standard Code of Practice CP3: Chapter V: Part 2: 1972). It is an important parameter in air-flow calculations and is used to make many quantities non-dimensional.

Equation 4.16 describes the sum of the *static* and *dynamic* pressures at any point in a smooth flow, and this sum, which is referred to as the constant in the equation above, is more usually called the *total* pressure.

Thus, $\quad p + \frac{1}{2}\rho v^2 = H$ (say) (constant) $\hfill$ (4.16)

or *static pressure + dynamic pressure = total pressure* (constant)

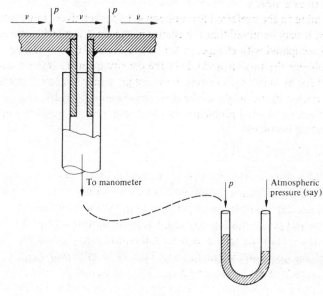

Fig. 4.7

As implied above, the static pressure may be measured by a suitable manometer opening onto, and without obstructing, the flow. This is usually accomplished on a model by making a smooth burr-free hole in the surface at the point required and connecting it hermetically to the manometer. An example is shown in fig. 4.7.

On full-scale buildings, considerable instrumentation is required to take the output from specially designed wind-pressure transducers which are built in to the surface of the building*. These are carefully sited, not only for the necessary wind-pressure observations but also to avoid excessive vibratory interference.

The dynamic pressure cannot be measured directly. If the velocity can be found directly in some way, the quantity q may be obtained, but it is more usual to find q by measuring the *total* pressure directly and using the difference between this and the *static* pressure measurement. This method is the classical one for measuring flow velocity and the instrument most often used to do this in free flows, the Pitot-static tube, takes part of its name from M. Pitot the French scientist who published his 'Description of a machine for the measurement of velocity of flowing water' in 1732. The 'machine' referred to is simply an open tube so arranged that one end opens directly into the stream and the other is connected to a manometer. Figure 4.8 shows the measuring

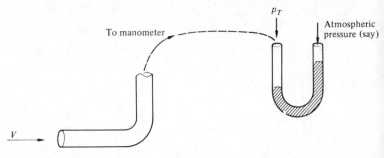

Fig. 4.8

head of a typical Pitot tube which is held pointing into the otherwise free stream. The pressure it will sense is that of the stream when it is brought to rest, i.e. the *total* pressure, which is sometimes referred to as the *stagnation* pressure (but *not* in CP3: Part 2: 1972, 'Wind loads', where 'stagnation pressure' has a slightly different meaning).

4.2.3 The measurement of air speed: the Pitot-static tube. Now

consider the instrument of the form sketched in fig. 4.9, called a Pitot-static tube. It consists of two concentric tubes, A and B. The mouth of A is open and faces directly into the air stream, while the end of B is closed onto A, causing B to be sealed off. Some very fine holes are drilled in the wall of B, as at C, allowing B to com-

* See, for example, Mayne, J. R., 'A wind pressure transducer', *Bldng Res. Stn Curr. Pap.* CP 17/70, 1970, and Eaton, K. J., and Mayne, J. R., 'Instrumentation and analysis of full-scale wind pressure measurements', *Bldng Res. Stn Curr. Pap.* CP1/69, 1969.

municate with the surrounding air. The right-hand ends of A and B
are connected to opposite sides of a manometer. The instrument is
placed into a stream of air, with the mouth of A pointing directly
upstream, the stream being of speed V m/s and of static pressure p Pa.
The air flowing past the holes at C will be moving at a speed very
little different from V; its pressure will therefore be equal to p, and
this pressure will be communicated to the interior of tube B through
the holes C. The pressure in B is therefore the static pressure of the
stream.

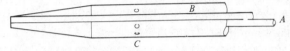

Fig. 4.9 The simple Pitot-static tube

Air entering the mouth of A will, on the other hand, be brought
to rest (in the ultimate analysis by the fluid in the manometer). Its
pressure will therefore be equal to the total head of the stream. As a
result, a pressure difference exists between the air in A and in B, and
this may be measured on the manometer. Denote the pressure in A
by p_A, that in B by p_B, and the difference between them by Δp, then

$$\Delta p = p_A - p_B \tag{4.17}$$

But, by Bernoulli's equation for incompressible flow (eqn 4.16),

$$p_A + \tfrac{1}{2}\rho(0)^2 = p_B + \tfrac{1}{2}\rho V^2 = H$$

and therefore $\quad p_A - p_B = \tfrac{1}{2}\rho V^2 \tag{4.18}$

or $\quad \Delta p = \tfrac{1}{2}\rho V^2$

whence $\quad V = \sqrt{(2\Delta p/\rho)} \tag{4.19}$

The value of ρ (assumed constant as in incompressible flow) may
be calculated from the pressure and the temperature. This, together with
the measured value of Δp, permits calculation of the speed V.

The quantity $\tfrac{1}{2}\rho V^2$ is the *dynamic pressure* of the stream. Since p_A =
total pressure = H and p_B = static pressure = p, then

$$(H - p) = \tfrac{1}{2}\rho V^2 \tag{4.20}$$

which may be expressed in words as

total pressure − static pressure = dynamic pressure

Note also that $\tfrac{1}{2}\rho V^2 = [ML^{-3} . L^2 T^{-2}] \,\hat{=}\, [ML^{-1} T^{-2}] \,\hat{=}\,$ pressure
as is of course essential.

Defining the *stagnation pressure coefficient as*

$$C_{ps} = (H - p)/\tfrac{1}{2}\rho V^2 \tag{4.21}$$

it follows immediately from eqn 4.20 that, for incompressible flow,

$$C_{ps} = 1 \quad \text{(always)} \tag{4.22}$$

4.2.4 The pressure coefficient. It is convenient to express pressures in a non-dimensional form. This is normally done by quoting them as ratios of the *dynamic pressure*. It will be recalled that this has been done immediately above for the stagnation pressure coefficient, but the latter is only a particular case of the general pressure coefficient defined by

$$\text{pressure coefficient } C_p = (p - p_0)/\tfrac{1}{2}\rho V^2 \tag{4.23}$$

where C_p = pressure coefficient;

p = static pressure at some point in the flow (where the velocity is v);

p_0 = static pressure of the undisturbed stream (i.e. where the velocity of flow is V);

ρ = density of the undisturbed stream (effectively constant for low subsonic speed air flows);

V = speed of the undisturbed stream.

Now from Bernoulli's equation (eqn 4.16),

$$p + \tfrac{1}{2}\rho v^2 = p_0 + \tfrac{1}{2}\rho V^2$$

(v is the speed of flow at the point where p is measured).

Then $p - p_0 = \tfrac{1}{2}\rho(V^2 - v^2) = \tfrac{1}{2}\rho V^2 \left\{ 1 - (v/V)^2 \right\}$

and therefore $C_p = (p - p_0)/\tfrac{1}{2}\rho V^2 = 1 - (v/V)^2 \tag{4.24}$

Figure 4.10 (a) shows the pressure at a point on the roof of a barn- or hangar-like building with the wind blowing uniformly over it from the side. The (smooth) wind speed is V and its static pressure p_0 is defined above. The remaining Figs 4.10 (b) to 4.10 (e) represent four different flow conditions.

The negative C_p case [fig. 4.10 (b)] is found at a point (on the roof, say) where the velocity is greater than that of the wind. Here the static pressure is *less than* that of the wind so that if, for the sake of the present example, the pressure inside is that of the wind (p_0), a net upward force (or suction) is felt at this point on the roof.

The zero C_p case [fig. 4.10(c)] occurs at a point on the building

where the local wind speed is *equal* to that of the free wind. The
pressure 'drop' from that at this point to that of the free wind is zero,
and hence the pressure coefficient is also zero.

A positive C_p [fig. 4.10 (d)], i.e. a pressure coefficient greater than
zero, is found wherever the local velocity is *less than* that of the free

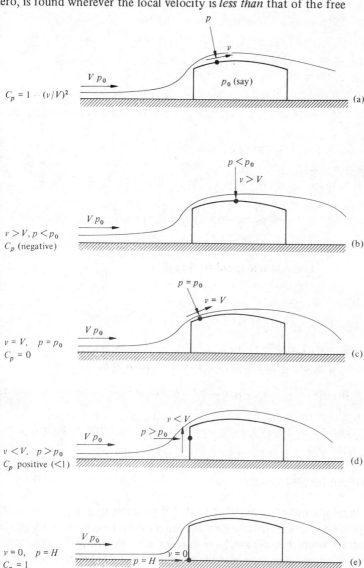

$C_p = 1 - (v/V)^2$ (a)

$v > V, p < p_0$
C_p (negative)   (b)

$v = V, \quad p = p_0$
$C_p = 0$ (c)

$v < V, \quad p > p_0$
C_p positive (<1)   (d)

$v = 0, \quad p = H$
$C_p = 1$ (e)

Fig. 4.10

stream. The least velocity locally is zero velocity, from which it follows that the maximum possible pressure coefficient is unity, as illustrated in fig. 4.10 (e) and quoted as the stagnation pressure coefficient in eqns 4.21 and 4.22.

4.2.5 External and internal pressure coefficients.   As suggested in the section immediately above, the pressure coefficient acting on a surface will give the value of the pressure acting normally on that surface due to the fluid motion in contact with the surface. In order to obtain the net load on that portion of the surface, it is necessary to consider the magnitude and size of the pressure coefficient acting on the other side. Since it is particularly important for the loading on thin cladding material, it is usual (e.g. in CP3: Chapter V: Part 2) to designate the pressure coefficient arising from the streaming flow outside as the external pressure coefficient (C_{p_e}) and the coefficient acting within as the internal pressure coefficient (C_{p_i}). Referring to fig. 4.11, the

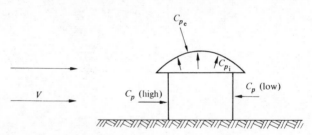

Fig. 4.11

net or total force acting on local area A of the roof cladding will be given by

$$F = (C_{p_e} - C_{p_i})Aq \qquad (4.25$$

the algebraic *difference* of the pressures acting on either side. (Note $q = \frac{1}{2}\rho V^2$.)

The value of the external pressure coefficient may be obtained from the local flow conditions using Bernoulli's equation or from model tests, but the appropriate value of the internal pressure coefficient requires more judgement in its selection. If the roof space shown in fig. 4.11 were vented to the windward side of the building, C_{p_i} would have a positive value; if it were vented to the lee side, C_{p_i} would likely be negative and the force F would be considerably changed in magnitude. It would thus be best in the design situation to assume the worst case for the local force and where C_p was negative to accredit C_{p_i} with the maximum positive value (of unity) and where C_{p_e} was positive to make C_{p_i} negative. In this way the most pessimistic situation would be covered.

4.2.6 Pressure distributions. The external pressure coefficient erected to some scale on an outline sketch of the structure is often very revealing and particularly useful in visualising the effect of the flow in the vicinity of the structure (see, for instance, fig. 4.17).

Some of the subsequent figures show the pressure distribution around some simple shapes. Those around more complex structures are more complicated, so much so in fact that, because of the limited use, in a quantitive sense, of the pressure distribution *erected on an outline of the shape,* it is seldom resorted to except for display purposes. Of much more value is the curve of pressure coefficient erected on certain perpendicular axes, the integration of which gives the aerodynamic force and moment exerted on the body.

4.3 Aerodynamic force and moment (from pressure distribution)

The force felt by a small area of surface A, say, over which a static pressure p is acting is equal in magnitude to the product pA and acts in a direction *normal* to the surface. If a larger surface is flat, the net force acting on it due to pressures will be the simple sum of the products of all the small areas and the local pressures acting, fig. 4.12,

i.e.   total force F (downward as shown) $= p_1 A_1 + p_2 A_2 + p_3 A_3 + p_n A_n$

$$(4.26)$$

or, mathematically,

$$F = \int p \, dA = q \int C_p \, dA \qquad (4.27)$$

the integral being taken over the surface. When the surface is curved, however, the above sum is meaningless since all the contributory pressures act in different directions. Figure 4.13 shows how the contributions from p_1 and p_3 cancel out to a certain extent, and only a small part of each contributes, for example, to the direction of p_2. There will of course be a resultant force arising from the sum of the contributions, and to find its magnitude and direction it is necessary to sum the like components of each contributory product of pressure × area. The following method allows this to be done relatively simply.

Consider a strip AB of the curved surface over which the pressure distribution is as shown in fig. 4.14 (a). The effect of the pressure will be felt as two forces F_x and F_z in the x- and z-directions respectively.

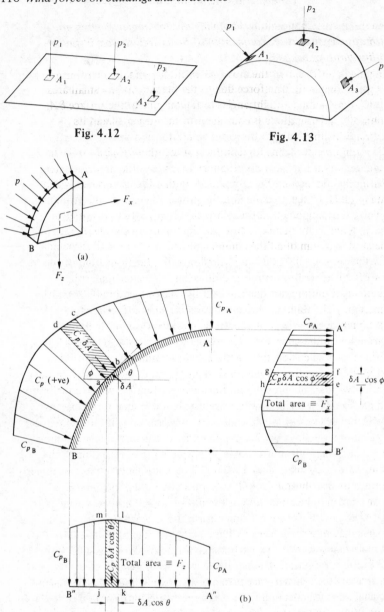

Fig. 4.12

Fig. 4.13

ϕ is the inclination of the pressure to the x-axis
θ is the inclination of the pressure to the z-axis

Fig. 4.14

These forces may be found by *summing the area under the pressure distribution erected over a projection of the curved surface in the x- or z-directions respectively*.

Figure 4.14 (b) shows the curve AB with the pressure distribution $p_A \sim p_B$ acting on it. The force due to the pressure at any small area δA is $C_p q \, \delta A$ acting at right angles to the tangent to the surface δA. Graphically, its magnitude is equivalent to the area abcd and its direction is inclined at ϕ to the x-axis and θ to the y-axis.

The component of this force in the x-direction is $qC_p\delta A \cos \phi$; in the y-direction it is $qC_p\delta A \cos \theta$. Since $\delta A \cos \phi$ is the projected area of δA in the x-direction, the component in that direction is equivalent to the product of the pressure and the projected area, i.e. the strip efgh. Similarly the component in the z-direction is $qC_p\delta A \cos \theta$, which is the strip jklm. Note that ad = eh = jm. The total force in the x-direction is the algebraic sum of all the components $qC_p\delta A \cos \phi$ and is the area under the pressure distribution plotted on A$'$B$'$, the projection of the curve AB. (The total force in the z-direction is the area under the pressure distribution plotted against A$''$B$''$, the projection of AB in the z-direction.) The resultant force is the vector sum of F_x and F_z.

A complication arises when more than one surface of the body is projected onto the same area, but it is easily dealt with. Figures 4.15 (a) and (b) show the curved strip of the previous figure extended to the portion BC. Inspection of the pressure on the total portion ABC in the figure shows that the pressure on the lower portion BC, while contributing to the force F_x , will act upwards against the force, due to the pressure over the upper portion which causes a downward force in the z-direction.

As before, the downward component is equivalent to the area under the pressure distribution from A to B plotted on the projection A$''$B$''$. The upward component shown separately is equivalent to the area under the pressure distribution from B to C plotted on the projection B$''$C$''$. The net force in the z-direction is the difference of these two and, since A$''$B$''$ and B$''$C$''$ are the same, it is usual to erect both curves on the same base, the area *between* them being the algebraic difference and hence equivalent to the net force in the z-direction, fig. 4.15 (c).

A further complication appears when the local pressure on a part of a surface is lower than the ambient pressure and a 'suction' is felt. This state is indicated by a negative pressure coefficient. The integration or summation of 'areas under the curve' will account for this automatically, providing care is taken to observe a simple convention so that negative values of C_p are plotted on the opposite side to positive values. This may be explained by an extension to the previous case.

Suppose the pressure coefficient drops to zero at some point D

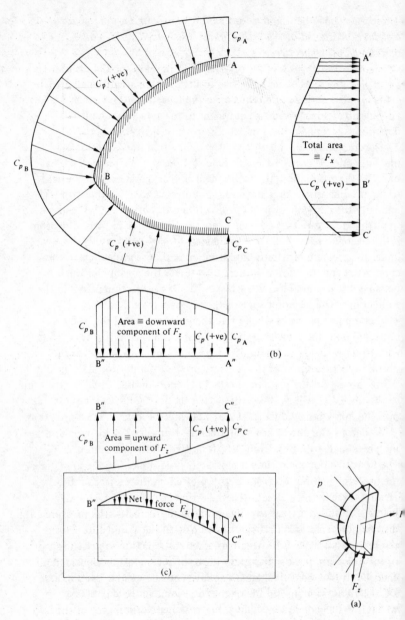

Fig. 4.15

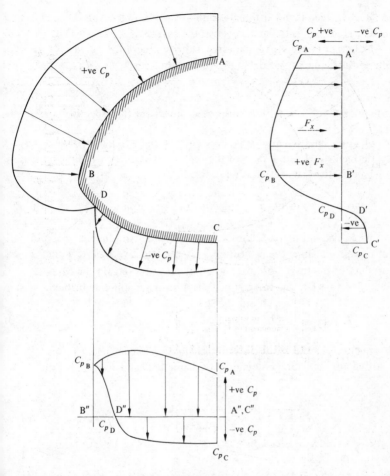

Fig. 4.16

below B and thereafter is negative round to C, fig. 4.16. The pressure
distributions erected on projections of ABC in the *x*- and *z*-directions
respectively will show the negative values plotted on the opposite sides
of the base lines and consequently the shape of the graphs considerably
changed. It is evident that negative pressure gradient over the portion
DC will *reduce* the magnitude of the total force in the *x*-direction,
which is the algebraic sum (that is the arithmetic difference) of the two
areas A′D′ and D′C′.

In the *z*-direction the suction over DC supports the pressure over
AB to increase the downward force. The net force F_z is the algebraic
difference of the pressure distributions on either side of the base line

A″B″C″, which is the arithmetic sum of the two areas A″B″D″ and D″C″, i.e. which is the area between the curves A″B″ and B″D″C″.

Note that in every case the force is the product of the area under the C_p curve and the dynamic pressure,

i.e. force $= q \int C_p ds$ (4.28)

where $ds = dA \cos\phi$ or $dA \cos\theta$ for F_x or F_z respectively.

4.3.1 Force coefficient. It is shown below that a force coefficient may be defined which is the ratio of the force to that of the dynamic pressure on an effective (typical) area (A_e); thus

force coefficient $C_F = F/(qA_e) = (1/A_e) \int C_p ds$ (4.29)

When evaluating the force coefficient from a 'two-dimensional' plot of C_p versus s along the projection base, the effective area A_e is the product of the total z-ordinate and unit thickness (e.g. in the case of a cylinder $A_e = D$). The integral may then be made non-dimensional:

$$C_F = \int_0^1 C_p d(s/D)$$ (4.30)

Figure 4.17 shows the pressure distribution in coefficient form plotted around a circular cylinder of diameter D and also against the

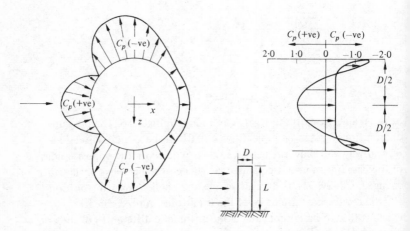

Fig. 4.17 Pressure distribution around a circular cylinder in super-critical flow, for $L/D > 10$ (values-taken from CP3: Chapter V: Part 2: 1972 for the case of a cylinder of smooth surface in supercritical flow with $L/D > 10$

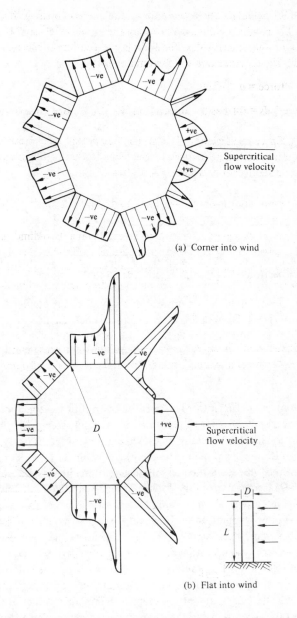

(a) Corner into wind

(b) Flat into wind

Fig. 4.18 Pressure distribution around an octagonal cylinder in super-critical flow, for $L/D > 10$

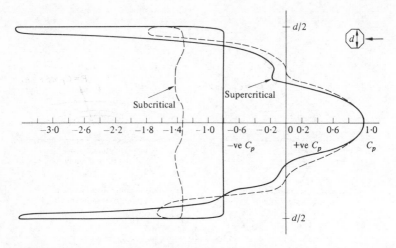

Fig. 4.19 Pressure distribution around an octagonal cylinder plotted on the projection of its frontal area in the wind direction

diameter projected in the streamwise direction. The area under the latter curve gives the streamwise or drag force coefficient.

Figure 4.18 shows similar distributions for octagonal cylinders, and fig. 4.19 shows the area under the curve for estimating the drag coefficient for two flow cases.

4.3.2 Moment coefficient. The pressure distribution acting on the surface of a body produces a resultant aerodynamic force. The line of action of the force is generally unknown and in any case is likely to vary (as indeed is the magnitude of the force) from time to time as the flow over the body alters and the pressure distribution changes. If, as is usual, there is a reaction to the force at a representative fixed (structural) point, the net effect of the pressure distribution is to produce a moment about the point in addition to the direct force now assumed to be acting through the representative point. Figure 4.20 shows the equivalent force—moment systems acting on a curved roof of span L, say, offering an effective area A_e. The resultant aerodynamic force acts at the centre of pressure, and produces an equal reaction plus a moment about any other point, the magnitude of the moment being the product of the force and the eccentricity of the resultant aerodynamic force from the fixed point.

In practice, the position of the centre of pressure is not required, the force through and the moment about a given point being all that is

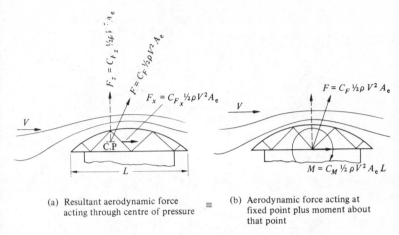

(a) Resultant aerodynamic force
    acting through centre of pressure

≡

(b) Aerodynamic force acting at
    fixed point plus moment about
    that point

Fig. 4.20

necessary. A further simplification is for the aerodynamic force to be
quoted in terms of its components along mutually perpendicular axes
($F_x F_z$, say, as shown in fig. 4.20).

The aerodynamic moment is made non-dimensional and is expressed
in coefficient form as

$$M = C_M \tfrac{1}{2}\rho V^2 A_e L \qquad\qquad (4.31)$$

where L is a typical length measurement of the structure (or the product
$A_e L$ is the cube of an alternative typical length). Both M and C_M may
be obtained directly from the pressure distribution by an extension of the
graphical work.

Figure 4.21 shows the pressure distribution on the two-dimensional
quadrant used in the previous section. A graph of the *product* of C_p and
z is erected on the projection $(A'B')$ of AB in the x-direction and the
area under the curve gives the moment due to the x-wise force component
about P. In a similar manner the area under the graph of $C_p x$ plotted
against the projection $(A'B')$ of AB in the z-direction gives the moment
due to the z-wise force component about P. The resulting total
moment about P is the algebraic sum of the moments arising from the
two force components.

(An alternative method of estimating the value of M_x, say, is to find
the offset of the centroid of the x-force area from P when M_x is given
by the product of this eccentricity and the x force.)

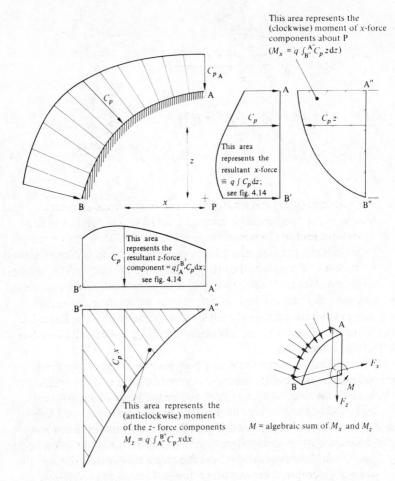

Fig. 4.21

If the line of action of the aerodynamic force is of interest and needs to be found, then the force components F_x and F_z together with the moment M about a known point provide sufficient information for the centre of pressure to be located by the reverse of the process described above; that is, with reference to fig. 4.22, where θ is the inclination of the resultant aerodynamic force to the x-axis and e is the eccentricity of the force from the point P about which the moment acts.

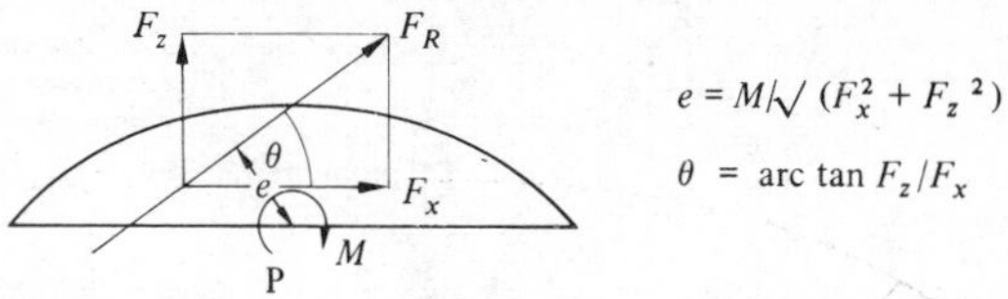

$$e = M/\sqrt{(F_x^2 + F_z^2)}$$

$$\theta = \text{arc tan } F_z/F_x$$

Fig. 4.22

Thus $\quad M = F_R e, \quad F_R = \sqrt{(F_x^2 + F_z^2)}$

and $\quad e = M/\sqrt{(F_x^2 + F_z^2)}, \quad \theta = \arctan(F_z/F_x)$ $\hfill$ (4.32)

4.3.3 Normal (drag) and transverse forces on structural elements. Wind flowing past a body must be diverted from its original path, and such deflections lead to changes in the speed of the air; Bernoulli's equation shows that the pressure exerted by the air on the body is thereby altered from that of the undisturbed stream. Also, the viscosity of the air leads to frictional forces tending locally to reduce the wind speed. As a result of these processes, the body experiences an aerodynamic force and moment and the sections immediately above show how the forces and moments may be obtained from a knowledge of the pressure distribution acting on the body.

In general, the wind force on a body may be resolved into three components along three mutually perpendicular axes about which aerodynamic moments also exist. In the specialised case of aeronautical bodies, all of these forces and moments are of significance and they have acquired a special terminology. Figure 4.23 shows the forces which are conventionally aligned to wind axes; most aeronautical bodies have similar features, and this has encouraged the growth of internationally accepted conventions of nomenclature and symbolism.

In non-aeronautical aerodynamic work, and particularly in the case of wind effects on buildings and structures, it is impossible to relate all features except in the broadest way. It is in the nature of the professions of building construction and civil engineering that most buildings and structures (but not all) are unique in shape and geometry, and a universal convention for wind-force components, say, has so far been denied acceptance. On the other hand for most, but again not all, engineering structures subjected to wind loads, the component axes may be chosen so that forces along or the moment about the third axis are irrelevant. Each case must be treated on its merits, but certain components are acquiring common nomenclature, following the BSI Code of Practice.

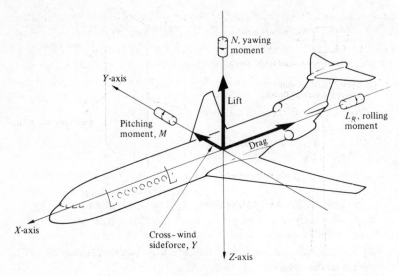

Fig. 4.23

For example, for flows which are essentially two-dimensional in character about symmetrical shapes, fig. 4.24 (a), a *wind (drag) force* may be identified acting in the mean wind direction and a *cross-wind (side) force* acts at right angles to it. No significant component of aerodynamic force exists longitudinally in the case of the chimney, fig. 4.24 (b), i.e. normal to the plane of the flow. For the suspension-bridge section, fig. 4.24 (c), and similar structures with long horizontal spans, the *wind (drag) force* is again predominant but the cross-wind force of greatest significance is in the vertical plane. From structural and stressing considerations, it is more often desired to identify the component of wind force which acts along convenient structural or body axes. Thus in the case of the suspension-bridge section, fig. 4.24 (c), the components in the plane of the section which are parallel and perpendicular respectively to the deck level, say, may be the most appropriate. Neither of these is directly aligned to the wind, which may make some angle α to the x-axis, say. In this and similar cases, the preferred terminology is as shown in fig. 4.24 (c), (d), (e) and (f), where the *normal force* is the wind force along the axis to which the wind is inclined at incidence — this axis is usually the major axis roughly in the wind direction. The corresponding *transverse force,* as it is called, is the component at right angles to this major axis.

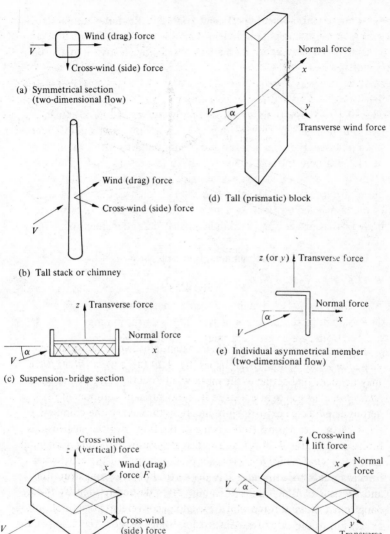

(a) Symmetrical section
(two-dimensional flow)

(b) Tall stack or chimney

(c) Suspension-bridge section

(d) Tall (prismatic) block

(e) Individual asymmetrical member
(two-dimensional flow)

(f)

Fig. 4.24

As for the significant bending or torsional moments induced in the structure by wind loads, these are usually self-evident and are mostly conveniently defined about one or other of the major structural axes as the geometry dictates.

4.3.4 Force and moment coefficient related to Reynolds number.

In the previous discussion on dimensional theory, it was shown in section 1.2.2 that the force exerted on a body by a moving stream of air could be written.

$$F = \rho V^2 D^2 f[(Re)] \qquad\qquad (1.11) \quad (4.33)$$

where $f[(Re)]$ is a function of *Reynolds number* and is, of course, itself non-dimensional, or in other words is a number or a coefficient.

In practice, the equation is not used in quite this form. In place of ρV^2 it is conventional to use the dynamic pressure $\frac{1}{2}\rho V^2$ and, as D^2 is in the form of an area, it is usually preferable to use, in the place of the square of a single typical length, an actual physical area of the body such as the frontal area (or shadow area) for a complete body or the surface area of an individual structural element of cladding.

Using A to denote such an area, it is usual to write

$$C_f = F/(\tfrac{1}{2}\rho V^2 A) = F/(qA) = f_1[(Re)] \qquad\qquad (4.34)$$

in which C_f is the aerodynamic force coefficient and is non-dimensional. Note that the area used in this definition may be variable from case to case and therefore needs to be stated for each case.

Aerodynamic moments are also expressed in the form of non-dimensional coefficients. Since the moment is the product of a force and a length, it follows that a non-dimensional form for a moment (demonstrable by dimensional theory) is

$$M/\rho V^2 D^3 \qquad\qquad (4.35)$$

Here again it is conventional to replace ρV^2 by $q = \frac{1}{2}\rho V^2$. The term D^3 has the dimensions of volume, but this is usually taken as the product of an area (frontal area, say) and a typical length l.

Thus the moment coefficient C_M is defined as

$$C_M = M/(\tfrac{1}{2}\rho V^2 Al) = M/(qAl) = f_2[(Re)] \qquad\qquad (4.36)$$

As implied above, dimensional theory indicates that a relationship *exists* between the coefficients and the Reynolds number but does not indicate what that relationship is. Recourse eventually must be made to experimental data backed by inductive reasoning to explain the form of relationship for any particular body. The physical attribute of the body which controls the form of the relationship is the flow in the boundary layer. This and its impact is discussed above, section 3.2, where the dependence of the drag coefficient, for example, on the Reynolds number — particularly for smooth rounded bodies such as spheres and circular cylinders — is described in detail.

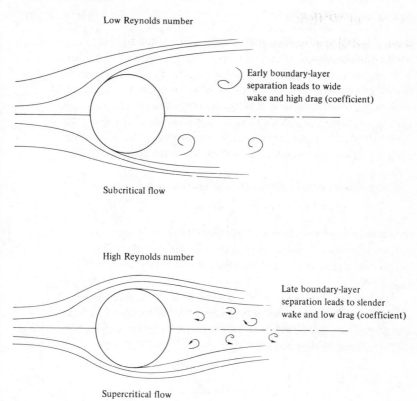

Fig. 4.25

In reducing this for wind-loading-data purposes, the BSI Code of Practice recognises a critical region of flow (a critical value of Reynolds number) which separates the extreme values of drag coefficient, say, which in turn are related to the extreme geometrical limits of movement of the boundary-layer separation points.

Figure 4.25 shows two such extreme positions for the flow breakaway on the surface of a smooth cylinder. It will be recalled that the higher drag coefficient which arises from the wider wake is a consequence of early boundary-layer separation, while the lower drag is because of the smaller wake due to delayed separation

4.3.5 The origin of the wind force (components).   It is necessary now
to look at the origin of the wind force and the relationship of its
magnitude and direction to the wind direction. To do this it is convenient
to refer to the force components about axes fixed in the body, and the
definitions of the preceding section may be recalled. For the present
purpose, consider a two-dimensional flow situation about a typical
bluff shape, say, fig. 4.26 (a).

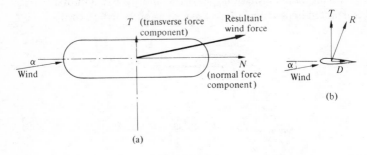

Fig. 4.26

The wind may be aligned at some angle α to the major axis of
the structural element. The resulting wind force will in general be in
a direction different from that of the wind, the normal and transverse
force components being as shown. In this event it is clear that some
mechanism other than drags directly opposing the wind direction must
exist, and it does exist in the form of an additionally generated
transverse force.

The transverse force (T).   The fact that a large transverse (or lift) force
may be obtained from a small deviation in wind direction is exploited in
the design of aerofoil shapes, fig. 4.26 (b), and, although not so predominant, the same mechanism exists to produce a transverse force
component on all shapes (other than circular) in a steady wind.

The transverse force arises directly from and is proportional to the
rotation (or 'circulation' as it is called) induced in the flow streaming
past the body by the shape the body offers to the flow. To understand
how this comes about, consider the case of wind streaming about a
symmetrical body aligned to the wind direction. The stream splits at
the nose, each half travelling the same distance to join up at the rear,
fig. 4.27 (a). Now, if the wind direction changes, or if the body is
asymmetrical, the distance each half of the stream travels to reach the
rear is different, fig. 4.27 (b). The consequences of this are twofold.

Firstly the farthest travelling stream must move faster on the average and, partly for this and partly for other reasons, the wake is deflected towards the slower side. The flow as a whole thus has the same characteristics as if, in place of the body, an element of rotation had been superimposed on the stream; that is, the average velocity on one side is higher than on the other.

It will be remembered from elementary fluid mechanics that the flow type which exhibits rotation is a vortex, and the strength of a vortex is denoted by its circulation (K) or rotation, which in turn

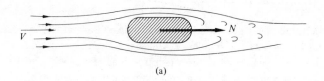

(a)

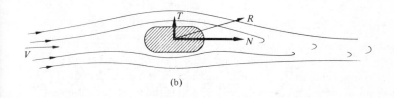

(b)

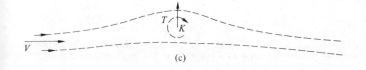

(c)

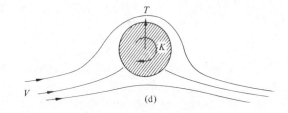

(d)

Fig. 4.27

depends on the rate of spin (vorticity) and the size of the vortex.

Now a vortex, or the flow associated with a vortex (such as that in the vicinity of a spinning object held in a steady stream, fig. 4.27 (c) and (d)) produces a sideways force, a phenomenon readily observed and sometimes used in ball games. It is precisely this mechanism of rotation induced in the stream by the body shape which results in the sideways or additional transverse force.

The exact value of the transverse force is found* from the formula

$$T = \rho V K \tag{4.37}$$

Now, the value of K, and hence the magnitude of the transverse force, is dependent on the angle of incidence (which is sometimes referred to as the angle of attack), and the way in which this dependence varies is of considerable importance in deciding the possible aerodynamic stability of the body, since instability can arise when the slope of the transverse force ▸ incidence curve is negative.

As is usual, the transverse force is made non-dimensional for comparison purposes and, when plotted against angle of incidence, produces a curve of which some part has in general a negative slope.

All bodies produce their own characteristic curves, and two extreme shapes are shown in fig. 4.28.

Curve (a) is a plot of incidence against the (lift) transverse force coefficient of a typical low-speed aerofoil section. Beyond the stalling point (shown for this aerofoil section at $\alpha = 17°$) the slope has a high negative value. When operated at these high incidences, the aerofoil exhibits marked instability which results in the phenomenon known as autorotation. These incidences are of course well beyond the normal operating angles of normal aircraft wing sections. Most slender plate-like sections have similar C_{F_t} versus α curves whose major feature is a strong positive slope at low angles of attack.

Curve (b) is typical of the C_{F_t} versus α curve of rectangular prisms and is in fact that obtained from tests on a model of the Empire State Building by Dryden and Hill. In this case, marked instability occurs at small angles of incidence; in other words, small changes in wind direction from the normal produce significant *into-wind* components of transverse force. It will be seen in the next chapter that this characteristic

* For a fuller exposition of circulation and vorticity and the development of this and related formulae, see, for example, Houghton, E. L., and Brock, A. E., *Aerodynamics for engineering students,* London, Edward Arnold, 2nd edn 1970.

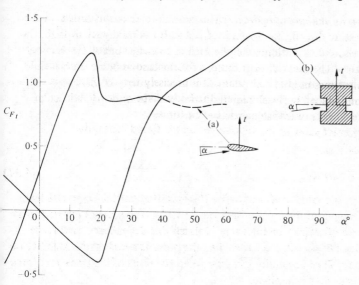

Fig. 4.28 (Davenport, A. G., *The treatment of wind loading on tall buildings*, Oxford, Pergamon, 1966 (after Dryden and Hill))

major contribution to the phenomenon of galloping and related oblems of aeroelastic stability—see section 5.2.2.

e normal force (N). The normal force is more familiarly known in id mechanics and more common usage by the word 'drag'. It is the al force tending to *drag* the body in the direction of the wind (or ding to resist the motion of the body through the bulk of the air). The total drag may be separated into a number of components which e different mechanisms, but all of them of consequence here, luding vortex drag which may exist theoretically even in an inviscid id, may be put down ultimately to the fluid property 'viscosity'. A convenient sub-division of total drag is into contributions from surface friction and (ii) normal pressures.

Surface-friction drag arises from the resolved components of the gential stresses on the surface of the body.

It has been shown in previous chapters that shear stresses exist at surface—boundary-layer interface, and these acting over the ropriate surface area aggregate in the wind direction to form the *tion drag.* This component of drag is directly attributable to osity, the contributory shears having a higher value under a bulent boundary layer than under a laminar layer.

(Normal) pressure drag.   This normal force has its origins in the pressure distribution around the body. If the fluid were inviscid, the pressure distribution would be such as to cancel out all streamwise forces. The pressure distributions for the case of bodies in real fluid streams — that is, fluids that exhibit the property of viscosity — differ markedly from those predicted from ideal-fluid theory, particularly over the rearward facing parts of the bodies.

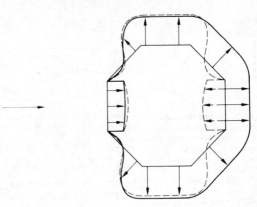

Fig. 4.29 Pressure distribution on an octagonal prism with flat face normal to the stream in viscous (real) flow (full line) and in inviscid flow (dotted line)

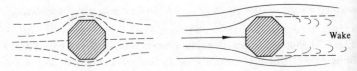

Fig. 4.30

Consider fig. 4.29, which shows the pressure distribution on an octagonal section when the stream is normal to a flat face. If the stream were inviscid, the velocity over the rear face would return to zero at a stagnation point; the streamlines (fig. 4.30) would be symmetrical in shape over the front and rear halves of the body — the pressure distribution likewise — and the net force in the streamwise direction would be zero.

In real flow, the boundary layers over the forward-facing parts distort the flow slightly from the inviscid streamline shape, which makes a small change in the pressure distribution in this region. Over the rearward parts, the stream and flow in the boundary layers separate to form the wake, and the pressure over these parts does

recover and remains low. The increased pressures near the nose
d to push the section backwards; the decreased pressures behind
d to pull the section backwards. The net effect is a drag force in the
eamwise direction. It will be noted that the difference in pressure
tribution is due entirely to viscosity. The essential difference in the
w patterns between ideal and real flow about bodies is that the latter
s no fore-and-aft symmetry and a *wake* is generated.

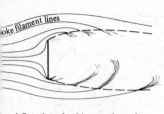

rmal flat plate. In this case the wake
illates up and down at several cycles
second. Half a cycle later the picture
uld be reversed, with the upper
ments curving back as do the lower
ments in this sketch.

(b)

Flat plate at fairly high incidence

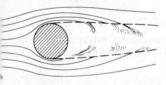

rcular cylinder at low (*Re*)

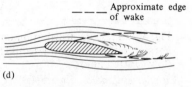

_ _ _ _ Approximate edge
of wake

(d)

Aerofoil section at moderate incidence
and low (*Re*)

Fig. 4.31 The behaviour of smoke filaments in the flows past various
bodies, showing the wakes

In fact, the total drag of a body appears as a loss of momentum and
increase of energy in the wake. The loss of momentum appears as a
uction in average streamwise fluid speed, while the increase of energy
een as violent eddying (vorticity) in the wake. The size and intensity
motion in the wake is therefore an indication of the normal force or
g force of the body. Figure 4.31, together with fig. 4.30, gives an in-
ation of the comparative widths of wakes behind a few body shapes.

ag comparison on four different bodies.

Normal flat plate, fig. 4.32 (a).   This is a flat plate set broadside in a
eam. In this case, the drag is entirely boundary-layer normal pressure
ag, coming mostly from the large negative pressure coefficients over the
r face. Although viscous tractions exist, they act along the surface of the

plate and therefore have no rearwards component to produce surface-friction drag.

Parallel flat plate, fig. 4.32(b).   In this case the drag is entirely surface-friction drag. Whatever the distribution of normal pressure may be, it can have no rearward component, and therefore the boundary-layer normal pressure drag must be zero.

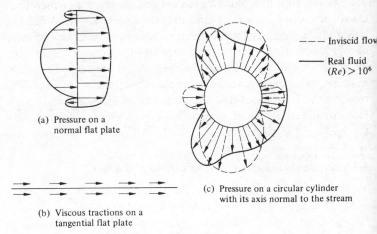

(a) Pressure on a
    normal flat plate

- - - - Inviscid flow

———— Real fluid
$(Re) > 10^6$

(c) Pressure on a circular cylinder
    with its axis normal to the stream

(b) Viscous tractions on a
    tangential flat plate

Fig. 4.32

Circular cylinder.   Figure 4.32 (c) is a sketch of the distribution of normal pressure round a circular cylinder in inviscid flow (dotted lines) and in a viscous fluid (full lines). The perfect symmetry in the inviscid case shows that there is no resultant force on the cylinder. The drastic modification of the pressure distribution due to viscosity is apparent, the result being a large boundary-layer normal pressure drag. In this case, some 5% of the drag is surface-friction drag, the remaining 95% being normal pressure drag, though these proportions depend on the Reynolds number.

Aerofoil or streamline strut.   The effect of viscosity on the pressure distribution is much less than for the circular cylinder, and the boundary-layer normal pressure drag is much lower as a result. The percentage of the total drag represented by surface-friction drag depends on the Reynolds number, the thickness/chord ratio, and a number of other factors, but between 40% and 80% is a fairly typical range.

Transverse force-dependent drag.   For completeness, it is necessary to mention the final mechanism that can produce a drag or normal force in

low-speed flow, although its effects are less relevant to general building
or structural aerodynamics.

All finite bodies which generate a lift or transverse (side) force
generate at the same time and as a consequence an induced or vortex drag
force. As its name implies, the drag is due to the continual generation of
the circulation or vorticity which goes to produce the lift (or side) force
described on page 134. This drag can exist in the absence of viscosity,
always provided some way of generating the lift is available. A full account
is available in the aeronautical literature, where the prediction of this type
of drag (and indeed others) is of considerable importance. Where it is
likely to be significant as a normal wind force on a high building — say, for
example, on a highly curved suspended roof — it will be absorbed in the
total normal-force values. This itself is unremarkable unless scaling is
introduced, because the lift-dependent drag is no longer proportional to
the square of the wind velocity as are all other forms of low-speed drag.

4.4 Some steady aerodynamic considerations in design

4.4.1 Criteria for buildings.
The criteria which have to be satisfied for
a safe building are that there should be no local or overall structural
failure due to fatigue, buckling, or plastic failure. Further, the joints in
the fabric should not open due to excessive deflections, and sway
accelerations should not cause discomfort to occupants. In addition to
the structural requirements of a building, the atmospheric environment
around the building must be tolerable for pedestrians and others in most
normal weather conditions. This implies that the wind speed at
pedestrian level should be acceptable and that any effluent from chimneys
or stacks should be sent well clear of, and not cause undue pollution in,
the vicinity. A further requirement is that the level of noise within the
building should always be tolerable in the worst wind conditions, and not
distracting in normal conditions.

4.4.2 Requirements for pedestrians.
Since the shape of the building
or structure should not produce unacceptable wind conditions for
pedestrians at ground level, research has been conducted into those wind
conditions that cause discomfort and inconvenience[1]. These investigations
have shown that at wind speeds above 5 m/s (Beaufort scale 3) considerable
cooling of the body can occur, and unpleasant disturbance of hair and
clothing is experienced while at the same time the eyes may be irritated.
At Beaufort scale 4 (5–8 m/s) dust is raised from the ground by the wind,
the greater vertical velocities in a highly turbulent wind aggravating the
problem of eye irritation.

Tests have also shown that the expenditure of energy while walking against the wind is hardly affected by wind speeds up to 5 m/s. This indicates that 'acceptable' wind speeds will be determined by 'comfort' rather than by 'performance' considerations.

Turbulence makes the adverse wind effects worse, increasing the disturbance to clothing and hair and irritation to the eyes. Further, gusty conditions make those occasions in which physical stability is reduced from the normal — such as when riding a bicycle or carrying a shopping basket, or the perambulations of the frail or infirm — especially difficult. Other activities may be adversely influenced by gusty conditions, for example reading bus timetables, putting on a raincoat, holding an umbrella, or writing a parking ticket.

It is probable that a wind speed of 5 m/s, although acceptable for most outdoor activities, is too high for recreational areas, parks, or similar places. For these areas, additional wind breaks may be necessary. Acceptable wind speeds depend not only on the activity of the person subjected to the wind, but also on his age. White[2] has suggested that wind speeds of 8–11 m/s or above are undoubtedly uncomfortable for a fit person, while 5–8 m/s is the highest acceptable wind speed for the young in push-chairs or for the elderly.

The effect of ambient temperature on the comfort of pedestrians can be shown graphically. A typical plot of comfort conditions for strolling in full sun is shown in fig. 4.33. It is apparent that if an area

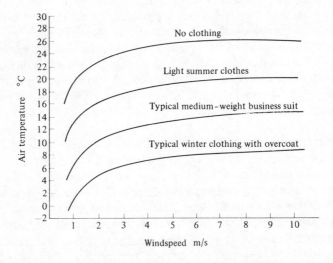

Fig. 4.33 Comfort conditions: lines of maximum comfort for strolling in full sun (after Penwarden[1]) (Crown Copyright)

s to be used only in summer time, then the wind speeds which are
icceptable can be higher than in an area which is to be used throughout
he year.

.4.3 Effect of the sheared flow. The effect of the sheared flow, caused
•y the atmospheric boundary layer, is to modify significantly the pattern
•f flow on the windward side of a high-rise block. When the building is
quare to the wind, a vortex forms in front of the building below the
tagnation point. This vortex is shed on each side of the building (fig.
1.34 (a)) and can produce excessively high winds at ground level, causing
liscomfort or even danger.

It is convenient to express wind speeds around buildings as a ratio:

$$R_p = \frac{\text{wind speed at pedestrian height near a building}}{\text{free wind speed at the same height with no building present}}$$

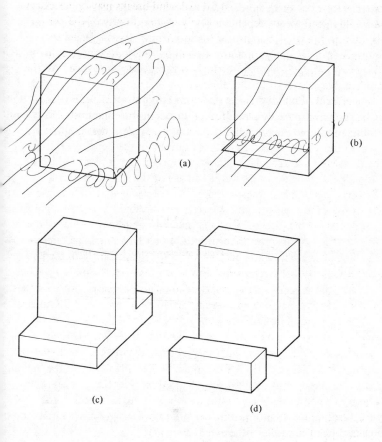

In older areas of towns where buildings are relatively low, R_p has a value of about 0·5–0·7, indicating that pedestrian areas are reasonably sheltered by low buildings. Around a high-rise building which is considerably taller than its neighbours, however, R_p on the windward side may reach 1·5 and on the leeward side 2·0.

In the vicinity of doors on the front of the building, the effect can be reduced by a canopy, see fig. 4.34 (b), or by building the tower on a plinth, fig. 4.34 (c).

The strength of the vortex, and hence the magnitude of the local R_p value, is always increased if a low building is positioned immediately to the windward, and such a layout, fig. 4.34 (d), should be avoided if possible.

If the region downstream of the tall building is to be enclosed by low buildings and used intensively as a shopping precinct or similar public place, serious consideration should be given to the possibility of roofing over the area. Wind speeds in the absence of roofing may well be 2·5 times the free-wind-speed value (i.e. $R_p = 2·5$) if the main building is 50 m or more in height; but if the principal building is less than 25 m high it is unlikely to produce significantly undesirable effects.

4.4.4 Effect of building shape on forces and moments. The proportions of a rectangular building modify the force coefficients substantially, and these effects have been well established for steady wind conditions by wind-tunnel tests. Typical values are quoted in the Code of Practice for a wide range of rectangular building proportions. If, however, the building is not of rectangular cross-section or one of the simpler polygonal shapes but has rounded end walls, the flow may not separate at the corners as it does for a rectangular building (see fig. 4.35). One of the results of this tendency for the flow to remain attached to buildings with curved ends it so to modify the pressure distribution that large torsional moments may be generated. With a building of rectangular plan form, torsional moments are small because the flow separates from the building at the corners and remains detached throughout the complete range of angles. Two plots of torsional moment coefficient, shown in fig. 4.36 for a rectangular building and a building of the same frontal area with a curved planform and rounded ends, illustrate this effect. If the shearing forces on the building are carried by shear walls there is usually no difficulty in dealing with the torsional moment. However, if the building is constructed with the shear force carried on a central core and the floors are cantilevered from this, there is very little resistance to torsional moment, and with such a structural design rounded ends and curved planforms are best avoided.

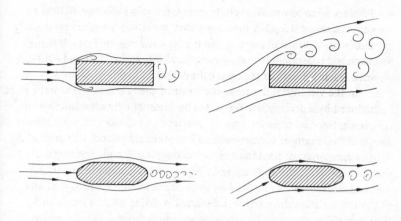

Fig. 4.35

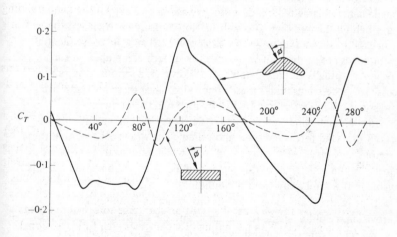

Fig. 4.36 Variation of torsional moment coefficient with wind direction

For most buildings their rigidity is such that the shape of the structure is little changed by the wind loads to which it is subjected, unless damage occurs. Such damage was reported to have caused the loss of the roof of a block of flats in Glasgow in 1968[3], when tiles blown from neighbouring blocks broke the upper floor windows. This allowed the full total pressure to be applied to the underside of the roof, which had not been designed for such an increased loading and consequently failed.

4.4.5 Effect of corner radii. The corner radii on a building can modify the peak suction pressures which are generated at the corners. It is extremely difficult on the small-scale model buildings normally tested in wind tunnels accurately to model corner radii: the 'sharp' model corner represents a well-rounded corner on the full-scale building. There is some evidence to suggest that the peak suction pressures measured on model buildings may underestimate the full-scale pressure coefficients. For this reason, caution has to be exercised when using wind-tunnel results for the design of, for example, a high-rise block in which the window frames go right to the corner of the building. If the building is made with well-rounded corners, caution must again be exercised in interpreting local pressure coefficients, since the Reynolds numbers of the test model and of the full-scale building will be substantially different, and hence the flow separation patterns for the flows may well differ.

4.4.6 Effect of roadways beneath buildings. Roadways are sometimes made beneath large tall buildings to give access to a car park or similar area behind the building. The high suction-pressure coefficients which can exist in such a roadway are well appreciated and the consequential wind loads are easily dealt with since the structural members in such a region are usually of considerable size. However, a serious situation can arise for pedestrians under these conditions, since these high negative pressures are in fact caused by locally high wind velocities.

In such high winds, elderly pedestrians may well be unable to withstand the wind forces imposed upon them. The wind-speed ratio in these regions may give an R_p value of up to 3, which implies that the wind force on the pedestrian in this region will be increased nine-fold over its value in the wind away from the building.

If pedestrians are to be allowed through an underbuilding access, provision should be made for handrails and possibly shielding screens.

Particular care is needed if cyclists and motorists are likely to be subjected to this high velocity wind as a cross wind which is likely to cause a significant deviation in path, especially for cyclists. Road users should be warned of the danger, and again screens should be considered as ameliorating devices.

4.4.7 Effect of shielding. Tall buildings are frequently constructed in groups, with the result that a downstream building may be shielded by an upstream one (see fig. 4.37). The dynamic results of this arrangement will be considered later (section 5.4.1) but the static result, considered here, may be equally important.

The steady shearing forces and overturning moment are usually reduced by the presence of a building to windward, since the leeward building is no longer subjected to the full dynamic pressure of the wind over its entire face. Local wind velocities may be increased, with the consequent reduction in pressure, especially on a corner exposed to the wind, but the general result of an upstream building will be to produce a reduction of loading on the leeward building. The exception to this is that the turning moment about the vertical axis may not be reduced.

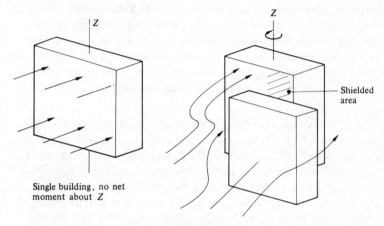

Fig. 4.37

In general it is no embarrassment to have a vertical turning moment on a building if it is caused by a reduction on the force on one half of the building, since the moment can easily be carried on the shear walls at the end of the structure. However, as indicated above, for a building constructed on a central core with cantilever floors, such a moment could present difficulties. It should be noted that this situation is likely to occur with any building constructed in this way: although the building may initially be isolated, neighbouring buildings may be constructed later.

4.4.8 Layout of buildings. The basic flow pattern around a single tall building in a sheared flow has been sketched above in fig. 4.36. The vortex which forms on the windward side of the building and streams behind it is strengthened by a low building positioned to windward (fig. 4.34 (d)). If two tall buildings are to be constructed separately but close together, one of the least desirable layouts for pedestrians is with one building at right angles to the other, as sketched in fig. 4.38: wind velocities 80% higher than the free-stream velocity can be expected in the gap between the two buildings. The wind velocity is little altered by the gap size or the block width but, as would be expected, is significantly increased by increase of the building height.

Some effects of building layout have been discussed in section 4.4.7 above, where one building shields another, and certain dynamic effects are considered in the next chapter. It is apparent, for example, that the flow around a single block may be significantly modified if a secondary block is butted up to it at right angles, fig. 4.39. The result will be an increase in the force coefficient in the windward direction and some considerable increase in the torsional moment about the vertical axis. Wind-tunnel tests have indicated that the maximum change in torsional moment will be of the order of 400%[4].

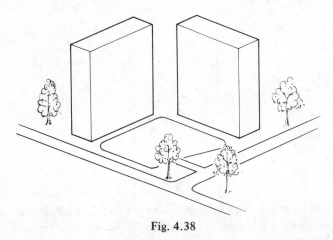

Fig. 4.38

If two blocks are aligned side by side with a small gap between, certain wind directions on the pair may be critical and the result of this juxta-positioning would be to increase the negative pressure coefficients on the abutting corners, indicating a need for improved fixing for windows and cladding in this region.

4.4.9 Effect of building 'permeability'.   The pressure distribution around a building can be modified by the 'permeability' of the building, i.e. the number of window and door apertures in its surface. It is unusual in an occupied building for all the windows and doors to be closed even in windy weather unless full air-conditioning is available. In full-scale tests conducted by the Building Research Establishment[5], substantial discrepancies were shown to exist between 'non-permeable' model results and the 'permeable' full-scale results. Although the overall forces on the building were found to be much as predicted, the effect of permeability

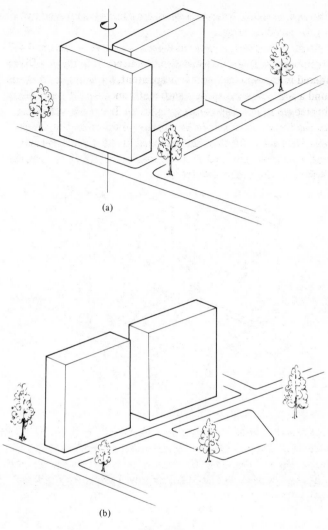

(a)

(b)

Fig. 4.39

was, in fact, to increase the loading on the windward side of the building and decrease it on the leeward side.

The degree of permeability is also significant in the design of internal partitions. If partitions are made to go from floor to ceiling then, when an outside window is left open to one side of the partition, a large force which may cause failure can be developed across the partition. If full-depth lightweight, partially fixed partitions are to be used, some

form of permanent ventilation should be incorporated if one or both
sides of the light structure is to be subject to external pressure in this
way.

A particularly severe situation which can arise is as sketched in
fig. 4.40. The pressures on the windward side of the building will be
high, especially if the windows are recessed. The vented corridor will
be subjected to the low pressures which exist at the sides of the building.

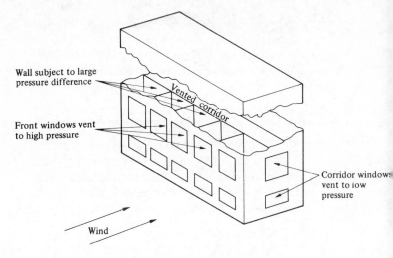

Fig. 4.40

Consider typical values in such a situation. Assume a C_p value of 1·6
(i.e. + 0·8 on the windward face and − 0·8 on the face aligned with the
wind) then at 40 m above ground in the edge of a town in the south
east of the UK, say, the design pressure for a 5-second gust would be
about 500 Pa. A partition suffering this load would require substantial
fixing if damage were to be avoided.

4.4.10 Load alleviation.   It is found that with certain structural
shapes the wind loads alleviate other structural loads. This situation has
been recognised for cooling towers, but it also applies to other
structures. Figure 4.41 shows a possible water-tower design in which
this could occur. The tower base is subject to compressive loads from
the weight of the structure and the water. In a high wind, the compressive
loads on the leeward side would be increased by the overturning moment
and alleviated by the lift forces generated on the upper part of the
structure. If the lift force and overturning moment had been evaluated
from wind-tunnel tests, the result might be that a factor of safety of 2

applied to the tower structure in the absence of wind-tunnel data might become equivalent to a factor of 1·5 if the wind-tunnel lift data were used. Now, suppose that the tower were so positioned that for some wind directions, due to the local topography, say, the wind blows slightly downwards on the structure, then the predicted upload could well become a download which would be added to the overturning

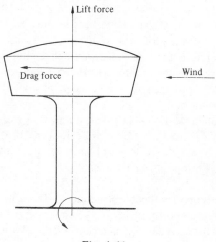

Fig. 4.41

moment. In this situation the factor of safety would be dangerously low. Moral: caution must be exercised when interpreting wind-tunnel results which seem especially favourable.

4.4.11 The shielding provided by screens. It has been shown that pedestrians in the vicinity of tall buildings are likely to be subjected to quite high wind speeds on windy days. To provide shelter, screens can be erected, either singly or in groups.

The characteristics of the wake downstream of a perforated screen depend on the screen porosity. Investigations of the conditions downstream of the screen have shown that if the porosity — i.e. the ratio of hole to screen area — is greater than 38% there will be no appreciable eddying. This is an important consideration, as an eddying flow causes far more discomfort than does a steady one. If the screen porosity is made greater than 38%, the degree of shelter is decreased. It is recommended, therefore, that screens should have between 35% and 40% porosity.

It might be supposed that if two or more screens were spaced one behind the other the effects would be cumulative and downstream of the rearmost screen a substantial region of shelter would exist. On the contrary, it is found that, unless the space between the screens is less than twice the screen height, no additional shelter is gained.

A typical application for porous screens is in a shopping precinct where high localised winds can deter shoppers. In this situation, adequate screening may well present an alternative to erecting roofing over a large area.

In agricultural and horticultural work, adequately screened areas may be necessary for the protection of livestock or plants. From a shielding consideration, the traditional wattle sheep hurdle may well be too dense to provide the optimum shelter. Similarly, better protection against wind will be provided by a good hedge than will be given by a solid woven fence or wall.

It will be recalled (section 4.4.2) that, for areas of recreation and relaxation, wind velocities must be kept below 5 m/s if pedestrian discomfort is to be avoided. The use of hedges and porous screens can well provide the appropriate environment.

4.4.12 Wind loads on very flexible structures. Tents, marquees, and pneumatically supported structures can be expected to change their external shape considerably under the action of wind loads. Structures of this type are manufactured in a wide range of shapes and sizes, constructed of materials of varying porosity, and restrained by guy ropes of different elasticity. Each year in the UK approximately three incidents of serious damage to marquees are reported, and many more failures with tents occur. It is fortunate that such structures are not usually used during the months of most severe winds.

No design procedure for canvas structures is given in the Code of Practice. Some small tents could be tested full-scale in wind tunnels, but for larger structures models must be made and care taken to scale all the relevant parameters to ensure that full-scale deflections and model deflections are the same.

There are two types of pneumatically supported structures — single-skin structures ('air-supported'), which are supported by the general internal air pressure, and double-skin types ('air-inflated'), where all or part of the structure has pressurised panels. Both types of structure have been made in a wide range of sizes, from the 'igloo' tent to complete exhibition halls.

Wind-tunnel tests[6] have shown that, for air-supported structures, the internal pressure must not be less than the dynamic wind pressure (q) if the structure is spherical or $0.6q$ if the structure is semi-cylindrical with quarter-sphere ends. At lower internal pressures the structure folds.

When an air-supported structure deforms under sudden gust loads, the small volume reduction involved results in an increase in pressure which is normally sufficient to stabilise it again.

The failures of air-supported and air-inflated structures that have occurred have been caused either by chafing or by damage due to flying debris, although the usual internal pressures used (250–500 Pa, 25–30 mm H_2O) correspond to a 'folding' wind speed in the range 26–28 m/s (58–63 mile/h) if the 0·6q criterion is assumed.

5

Unsteady aerodynamic forces

It is convenient when discussing wind problems to group the unsteady aerodynamic forces which may arise on structures into two broad subdivisions:

a) those due to the flow of a steady airstream over a structure, at rest or in motion relative to the same datum, and which depend on the shape of the structure; or

b) those due to unsteadiness or turbulence in the air flow which manifests itself as fluctuating loads or pressures on an otherwise unresponsive structure.

It is unlikely in practice for either of the two subdivisions to be singly representative of the unsteady aerodynamic forces experienced by a particular structure, since each is likely to give rise to the other; for example turbulence in the stream corresponding to (a) above may modify its effects considerably. However these subdivisions are convenient for the description below of the various mechanisms by which unsteady aerodynamic forces arise.

The existence of an unsteady force on a structure inevitably implies an unsteady response from the structure, so it will be useful to review the basic notions of vibration mechanics before considering the origin of the forces in more detail.

5.1 The elements of vibration mechanics

5.1.1 Natural frequency of vibration.   Engineering structures possess *mass* and *elasticity* and consequently are capable of exhibiting motion of one part relative to another. If a structure is displaced from a mean shape or position so that the elastic forces are out of balance, and is then released, a motion ensues. In the absence of other forces or effects, the motion will be repetitive or vibratory, the structure moving through the original displacement once during each cycle. The time the structure takes to go through one complete vibration cycle (or oscillation) is called the *period,* and the number of periods repeated in unit time is the frequency of the vibration.

In the simple system mentioned above, in which the structure oscillates under the elastic (spring) and mass (inertia) forces only, the resulting motion is known as a *free vibration* and its frequency is termed the *natural frequency* (of free vibration).

5.1.2 Damping. All real structures or systems possess positive damping characteristics which act against the motion and are dissipative of energy in effects such as friction or viscous resistance, internal deformation in the material, and the like, all of which inhibit the motion. Thus usually a real free vibration eventually decays away and, as a consequence, is often called a *transient* motion. The magnitude of the damping is significant. Light damping will allow many oscillations to occur but they will gradually lessen in amplitude. The amount of decay can be judged by the rate at which successive amplitudes decrease, that is by the steepness of the curve which envelopes the time—displacement graph. Increasing the damping beyond a critical level will inhibit oscillation altogether, the structure returning to the mean position and not passing through it. This motion is said to be '*dead beat*'.

5.1.3 Aerodynamic damping. Whereas in common experience friction, hysteresis, viscous effects, and other retarding actions act against motion, situations can arise where the motion itself creates a force which actually supports the motion. When this happens on a structure due to its movement relative to the wind, it is known as *aerodynamic instability* or negative aerodynamic damping. Positive aerodynamic damping creates the situation already described, the forces generated by the motion of the structure acting against the motion trying to retard it. This can arise either in a disordered way, as a consequence of the stirring or turbulence-making action of the structure on the fluid (air), or in an ordered way, in which case it is usually designed in and contributes to the stability of the structure. For example, the righting force on the down-going wing of an aeroplane due to a small displacement from the normal straight and level flight is immediate and a consequence of the aerodynamic characteristics of the wing. In other circumstances the aerodynamic characteristics of the structure may be such that the displacement produces an aerodynamic force which acts in the direction of the displacement and tends to increase it. This is the classical case of instability, and in the absence of other forces these structures would always diverge away to failure. In real situations some magnitude of positive (structural) damping exists, and a conflict develops between the positive and negative damping for control of the motion. The origins of aerodynamic instability are described in more detail below (section 5.2.2); until then, consider further the vibration of a simple structure in the presence of positive damping only.

5.1.4 Forced vibrations. In the absence of aerodynamic excitation, a structure may be displaced from its mean position by an external force which does not then disappear but continues its application in some unsteady way so that the structure is forced into a periodic oscillation of a type which will depend on both the free characteristics of the structure *and* the characteristics of the forcing system. The resulting motion is known as *forced vibration*. During the initial stages of the motion the free-vibration behaviour is present, but, as the positive damping takes over, this decays away (is *transient* in fact) leaving the steady-state forced vibration.

The various possibilities are illustrated in fig. 5.1, which shows a simple cantilevered beam displaced under a steady load W which is suddenly removed from its free end. The subsequent motion of the end of the beam is displayed as a plot of vertical displacement of the tip of the beam (y) against time (t) in seconds. In the case of no damping, fig. 5.1 (a), the natural vibration continues with the beam moving through its maximum displacement every p seconds. The natural frequency of the vibration is $f = 1/p$. Sometimes the frequency is quoted as a circular frequency, that is the steady angular velocity of a particle moving in a circular path whose radius is the amplitude of the motion and whose projection on a (vertical) diameter is the vibratory motion. Thus if ω is the angular velocity,

$$p = 2\pi/\omega \quad \text{and} \quad f = 1/p = \omega/2\pi \tag{5.1}$$

The next case, fig. 5.1 (b), shows the real beam in which some light damping exists, due probably to the stirring of the surrounding air or to the hysteresis in the stress of the material of the beam. The period of the vibration is slightly less than that of the undamped system but remains constant until near the end of the motion. The rate of decay can be seen in the shape of the dotted curves which mark the successive upper and lower limits of displacement. These curves are exponential in form and the decay found thereby leads to a method of defining the magnitude of the damping. The expression universally quoted for this parameter is the logarithmic decrement (δ): the motion defined as

$$\delta = \ln (y_n/y_{n+1}) \tag{5.2}$$

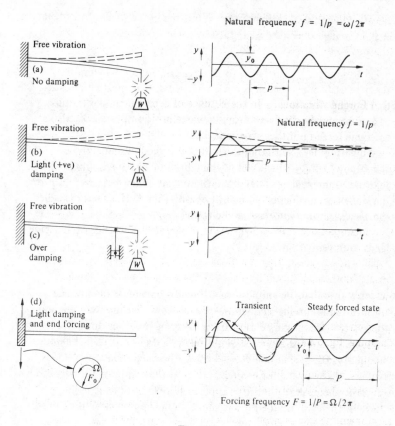

Fig. 5.1

where y_n is the amplitude of the nth oscillation.

As fig. 5.1. (c) implies, the damping is now so severe that the beam never crosses the equilibrium position. A critical amount of damping is possible which just prevents the beam swinging through the null position and is the boundary between underdamped and overdamped systems. The magnitude of the critical damping forms a useful parameter for the system.

Figure 5.1 (d) shows the beam subject to an external oscillating forcing motion impressed through the end fixing, say. The forcing motion is itself assumed to be sinusoidal with a circular frequency Ω and hence a frequency (F) and period (P) given by

$$F = 1/P = \Omega/2\pi \tag{5.3}$$

After the few initial vibrations of the beam, the transient (free

vibration) vanishes, leaving the beam moving in the steady forced state
at the frequency of the exciting force.

5.1.5 Resonance.   Turn now to the steady-state forced vibration,
fig. 5.1 (d). The excitation is due to a force of magnitude $W_0 \cos \Omega t$,
that is equivalent to a force vector W_0 rotating at a circular frequency
of Ω. The steady-state response is a vibration of amplitude Y_0 also at
the same forced (circular) frequency Ω.

Now, if under static conditions the beam were to deflect y_s under
the steady load W_0, the effect of the vibration on the amplitude Y_0
that the beam reaches under excitation might be quoted as a factor of
the static displacement — a quantity easily found. This factor is called
the *amplification factor* and is the ratio Y_0/y_s.

One-dimensional forced-vibration theory in the absence of damping
leads to the equation

$$Y_0/y_s \propto 1/(\omega^2 - \Omega^2) \tag{5.4}$$

which shows that the amplitude of forced vibration tends towards
infinity as the forcing frequency approaches the natural frequency of
the system. The presence of positive damping modifies this extreme
frequency-response curve (of amplitude (Y_0)) plotted against excitation
frequency, fig. 5.2, in two ways. Firstly, the maximum amplitude is
reduced to lower and lower finite values as the damping increases, and
secondly the peak of the curve appears at a frequency increasingly
below the natural frequency. As the damping approaches the critical
value, the amplification factor is seen not to rise above unity, which
implies that the forcing excitation can make no headway against the
system and the beam never reaches the static load deflection.

For a physical understanding of the important phenomenon of
resonance, without recourse to the differential calculus, appeal is made
to the transfer of energy between the spring, inertia, and excitation
forces as well as to the degradation and eventual dissipation of energy
through positive damping.

Consider the components of the vibrating beam 'system' and refer
them to the neutral position of the end of the beam.

i)   The acceleration of the beam is always towards the neutral position,
thus the inertia forces which oppose the acceleration act *away* from
the neutral position.

ii) The elastic forces are always *towards* the neutral position.

iii) Positive damping is opposed to the motion and thus is not unidirectional.

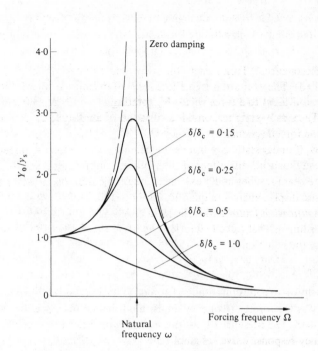

Fig. 5.2 Frequency-response curves

It is apparent that (i) and (ii) oppose each other, and it is instructive to see in what manner.

At very low frequencies of motion, the elastic forces will dominate since the accelerations and hence the inertia forces are small.

At very high frequencies the reversals are so rapid that the inertia of the system will dominate, the inertia in effect preventing a full deflection taking place before the reversal tries to bend the beam back, and so on.

At a frequency near that of the natural frequency of the structure, the elastic and inertia forces balance and the motion proceeds as if it were due entirely to spring and mass forces, i.e. in the absence of excitation and damping, which is precisely the first case considered above: that of free frictionless vibration. This being so, the only demand on the excitation force is to overcome the positive damping which, if the damping is small, it soon does, leaving the remainder to maintain a free motion of much higher amplitude. Under such circumstances the degree of damping has a significant effect on the subsequent motion near the resonant frequencies, which are in fact frequencies of motion to be avoided.

[It is useful at this point to anticipate the later discussion by noting that near the resonance frequencies where the elastic and inertia forces balance, the negative aerodynamic damping (i.e. the aerodynamic excitation) may take the role of the external force mentioned above, in which case the motion of the structure will reach a steady state only when the negative (aerodynamic) and positive (structural) damping balance. This may well not happen until large amplitudes and accelerations unacceptable for civil-engineering structures occur.]

5.1.6 Beats. Although the free vibration should generally die away, its importance to the subsequent motion may be overriding. The forcing excitation first generates the free vibration. Now, if there were no damping, the free vibration would persist and be summed to the forcing excitation. Generally being of different frequencies, the two rhythms would overtake each other and come to a point where their maximum amplitudes both coincide to add together to form the largest amplitude possible and then die away to a point where they would subtract to give the minimum amplitude, and so on. This phenomenon is known as *beating*, see fig. 5.3. When positive damping is present it can be readily

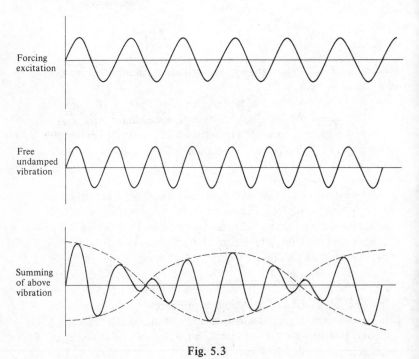

Fig. 5.3

seen that, for the case of light damping, if the exciting force were commenced at a point in which the first movement of the free vibration were additive to that of the first effects of the excitation, the subsequent amplitudes might be so large as to overstrain the system. Equally, if the first impact of the excitation were to coincide with the first movement of the transient in such a way that they annulled each other, the damping might well take over before the beat continued to prominence. To sum up, although the natural rhythm of the structure is overtaken and damped out at the expense of the forcing rhythm, the transient motion may be capable of contributing to early overstrain.

5.1.7 Multi-degrees of freedom and coupling. So far in this brief introduction to vibration, the structure (the end of the cantilevered beam) has been assumed to move in one sense only, that is up and down in the vertical direction. Additionally, the impressed external excitation has been applied in the same sense. In the general case, engineering structures are capable of displacement in more than one of the six degrees of freedom, and fig. 5.4 shows some of the possible

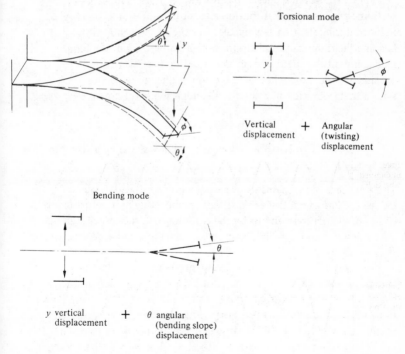

Fig. 5.4

modes of movement of the end of the simple cantilever beam of the previous example. Even without twisting there will usually be an angular displacement (θ) of the elements in the sense of accommodating the changing spanwise slope of the beam, and, if the beam twists in addition to bending, a further rotation (ϕ) takes place in the plane normal to that of the span. Additionally, if the fixed end of the cantilever is itself part of an elastic structure, further movements — linear, sideways or in and out, or angular in a yawing sense — may be superimposed. Equally, particular sections may be found to move only in one of the possible freedoms, and in a generally vibrating structure these forms of motion are called *modes*.

For a first approach to the general problem, it is sufficient to consider only those displacements which are significant in magnitude and to disregard the remainder, but care must be taken to identify the predominant modes correctly. It does not follow, for example, that because a cantilever beam such as that of fig. 5.1 has its free end displaced vertically and then released the subsequent motion will involve the bending mode only. Indeed, common engineering and everyday experience suggests that for beams of irregular cross-sectional area or mass distribution a torsional vibration is quickly induced during the first few cycles after the release, and this may become the dominant mode even though no twisting or torsional load is initially applied. The reverse situation may also arise.

This phenomenon whereby a motion in one mode creates a sympathetic vibration in a totally dissimilar mode is known as *coupling*.

5.2 Unsteady aerodynamic forces due to body shape on a structure in a steady wind

There are several mechanisms of aerodynamic excitation which induce oscillatory motions in a structure. Buffeting by the turbulent eddies in the natural wind or by the turbulence in the wake of an upstream body is an immediate and obvious example and is dealt with more fully in section 5.3.1.

For many structures — beams, suspension bridges, columns, chimneys — the natural wind may not have sufficient energy (due to gusts) near to their natural frequencies for excitation due to this cause to be initiated, and mechanisms other than turbulence are involved when such structures oscillate. It is reasonable, therefore, to discount the presence of turbulence in the natural wind in what follows, except in so far as its presence changes the boundary-layer flow conditions, and to ascribe the aerodynamic excitation to the body shape.

Three ways in which a body may become excited into a vibratory motion due to a steady wind blowing over it may be identified as having their origins in separate aerodynamic phenomena, although they are not always mutually independent. These motions are (i) due primarily to vortex generation and separation, sometimes known as *strumming*; (ii) due to excess negative aerodynamic damping, known as *galloping* or *plunging*; and (iii) *flutter,* a motion which relies on the aerodynamic and inertial coupling between two degrees of freedom. As a rule the first two occur on bluff bodies while the last named arises on structures which are flexible as well as possessing shapes with pronounced lifting (transverse) or side-force aerodynamic characteristics.

5.2.1 Vortex generation and excitation (strumming).

Although the phenomenon of vortex generation is not yet fully understood, sufficient evidence is available and adequate theoretical models exist to explain the

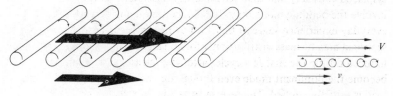

Fig. 5.5

occurrence of discrete vortices in fluid flows. A simplified view is as follows. The prerequisite for the growth of a vortex is a surface of velocity discontinuity in the flow, that is a thin layer or zone (idealised in theory as a sheet) between two streams moving at different velocities. The presence of viscosity causes the particles of fluid in the zone to spin so that the separation region becomes a sheet of vorticity (a sheet of vortex filaments) which can be thought of as behaving as a sheet of roller bearings between the streams of differing velocities, fig. 5.5.

Vortex sheets are unstable and cannot remain plane, for example, but roll up to form discrete vortices, fig. 5.6. In this form they are extremely stable and may remain at the point of discontinuity as a form of standing vortex or, on having reached a certain size, they may be washed off and flow on downstream as free vortices. It is in the latter form that they constitute the major present interest, although it will be seen below that the standing vortex can also present problems to civil and structural engineers.

It would seem reasonable, then, to expect vortices to be present whenever a velocity discontinuity exists in a flow, and it is evident from previous chapters that large areas of flow exist where the velocity changes across the flow direction. Such layers are liberally endowed with vorticity

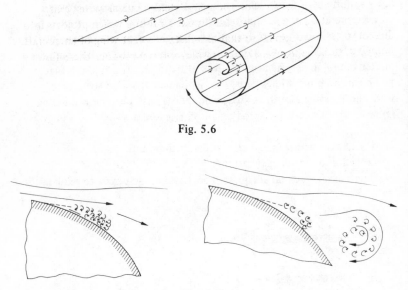

Fig. 5.6

Fig. 5.7

as a consequence; in particular, the boundary-layer region of flow generates the vortices of present interest.

The phenomenon of boundary-layer separation was described in Chapter 3. Downstream of the separation point (point S in fig. 3.9) conditions exist approximating to those described above, in that the upstream boundary-layer flow has moved off the surface of the body and/or past an adjacent 'dead-water' region of fluid moving at a different velocity. The vortex sheet so formed rolls up into the thickened stagnant region of fluid against the body and grows as it is continually fed and gradually moves down the dead-fluid region. At a particular stage in its growth it is washed away from the body and goes into the wake, while the formation of its successor starts the process all over again,* fig. 5.7.

For sharp-edged shapes, a sharp projection into the boundary layer or the abrupt change in surface inclination will force the flow to separate from the body, when the conditions will become once again

* Classical photographs of vortex generation by Prandtl show these phenomena in graphic detail, see for example, Prandtl, L., Tietjens, O., *Applied hydro and aerodynamics*, New York, McGraw-Hill, 1934.

conducive to the growth of a vortex, fig. 5.8.

When the vortex remains attached to the body, its pressure field may produce loading conditions unanticipated by the structural engineer, particularly if the vortex remains stationary, i.e. rolled up on the surface of the body. For example, a stable conical vortex exists over the surface of any triangular fin-like structure which projects into the flow in a way similar to that of a delta or swept wing of an aircraft, fig. 5.9. Many modern architectural features can produce these flow

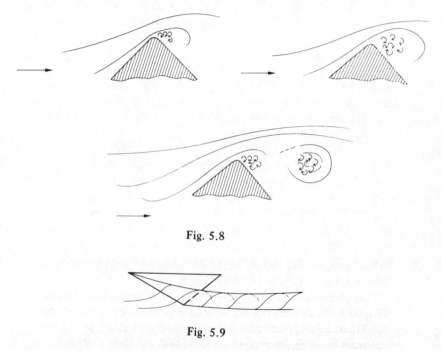

Fig. 5.8

Fig. 5.9

conditions, an example being when the wind blows cornerwise onto a rectangular building with a single sloping roof, fig. 5.10. The tip of the vortex attaches to the upstream corner, the cone lying roughly along (and being generated by) the leading edge of the roof. If the slope of the roof is large, the vortex sheet is tightly spiralled into a strong conical vortex whose pressure field may be severe. Further, if the vortex swings or changes in intensity (i.e. pulsates), as it may do in a natural wind, a pulsating load may be experienced on local cladding materials, windows, or doors — to their detriment. Such vortex configurations are very well exploited in aerodynamics and have been observed and measured in connection with building aerodynamics[1].

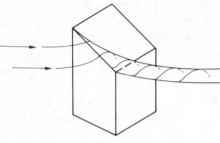

Fig. 5.10

Vortex excitation.   Bluff bodies are subject to a periodic force normal to the wind direction over a wide range of Reynolds number. The periodic force is a direct consequence of the alternate generation and shedding into the wake of vortices from either side of the body. The mechanism has been described in section 3.2.3 for the classical case of smooth flow about rigid circular cylinders.

Aerodynamic excitation by vortex shedding is probably the most common of all wind-induced vibrations and has been known and observed since ancient times. Aeronautical interest had largely confined itself to the behaviour of the flow in the vicinity of rounded bluff bodies at near-critical Reynolds numbers. More recently, interest has been extended to include prismatic and non rounded sections, 'three-dimensional' end effects, the effects of shear layers and turbulence in the stream, and that of the motion (oscillation) of the body. Historically, even in the case of the vortex excitation on a circular cylinder, theoretical analysis and practical data have mostly been available only on the relationship between the frequency of excitation and the wind (or flow) speed and on the time-average (drag) forces generated.

More recently, a few quantitative data and some tentative theoretical work have appeared aimed at the origins and magnitude of the fluctuating forces experienced by the cylinder both when at rest and when in oscillatory motion.

There seems little doubt that the growth and shedding of an individual vortex changes the symmetry of the boundary layer and gives rise to a concomitant growth of circulation. This manifests itself as a changing asymmetrical pressure distribution whose integrated effect is a swinging force vector. This is illustrated in fig. 5.11[2]. The range of wind speeds during which the separated flow in the wake of a cylinder induces nearly periodic unsteady aerodynamic forces is outlined in section 3.2.3. These unsteady aerodynamic forces may induce aeroelastic oscillations (or aeroelastic deformations, such as the ovalling or breathing of the

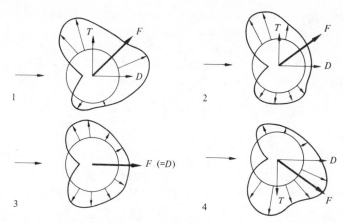

Fig. 5.11 Progressive change in pressure distribution and development of forces

open end of a stack or chimney)[3,4] particularly as the frequency of the unsteady force approaches the resonant frequency of deflection of the structure.

Account must be taken of the movement of the cylinder. If the shape exposed to the airstream is stationary, there can be no interchange of energy between the wind and the body, the total effect of the vortex generation going into the eddying of the wake. On the other hand, if the body is subjected to a forced or self-sustained oscillation of a frequency near that of the induced aerodynamic force, then the wind will do work on the body through the transverse components of the force, and an energy transfer takes place.

The sequence of events as the normal air speed past a circular cylinder was gradually increased was described (following Ferguson) by Parkinson and Modi[5] and is enumerated below (fig. 5.12).

1. As the wind speed is increased from low values, the frequency of vortex formation f_v increases proportionately to the shedding frequency of a rigid cylinder f_{vs}.
2. When the frequency of vortex formation nears the natural frequency of transverse oscillation of the cylinder (F_n) the cylinder begins to oscillate at a frequency f_c $(f_c < F_n)$.
3. At a small increase in speed, $f_c = F_n$ and so remains thereafter. During the subsequent interval, the frequency of vortex shedding (f_v) is 'locked on' to the natural frequency (F_n) for a considerable wind speed increase $(f_v = f_c)$. During this time the amplitude of oscillation increases to a maximum and then decreases again.

4. At the upper end of this wind-speed interval, the frequency of vortex shedding reverts to that found on the stationary cylinder.
5. The cylinder continues to oscillate at lower and lower amplitudes but with $f_c = F_n$ until a wind speed is reached at which the oscillation stops.

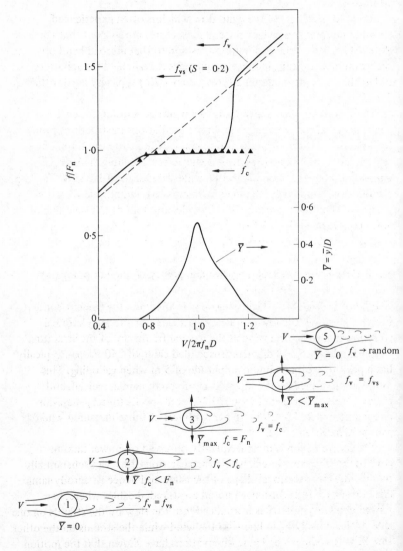

Fig. 5.12 Oscillation phenomena for circular cylinder (low transverse damping). Data after Parkinson et al.[5]

At higher wind speeds (Reynolds numbers), the shedding loses its periodicity. Note that for rigid cylinders and prisms, for an increase in Reynolds number well beyond these higher Reynolds numbers, strongly periodic vortex shedding recurs at slightly higher Strouhal numbers, but if the cylinder is free to oscillate the higher Strouhal numbers are not attained.

Reynolds numbers of the wind flow which is often experienced around buildings and civil-engineering structures are so great that vortices are shed into the wake in a random fashion so that a broad band or spectrum of significant induced frequencies is available for excitation rather than a single predominant frequency ((Re) typically greater than 3×10^6).

The work described above leads to a major conclusion for civil engineers: that, to avoid high-amplitude oscillations in structures prone to vortex excitation, the natural frequency of the structure should be remote from the frequencies of periodic vortex shedding. This is corroborated by, for example, work at the UK National Physical Laboratory[6,7] where in related experiments large-amplitude vibration occurred when the frequency of the model and that of the shedding of vortices coincided.

5.2.2 Motion due to excess negative damping (galloping or plunging)

The galloping motion. Galloping, as it is known in the present context, is the large-amplitude low-frequency oscillation of a long cylindrical structure in a transverse wind at the natural frequency of the structure. For example, a 25 mm diameter suspended cable of 250 m span typically has a peak-to-peak maximum amplitude of 5 m when galloping. This motion is sustained by the interaction of aerodynamic, inertial, and elastic forces and does not require high wind speeds for its generation and maintenance, 12−25 km/h being typical of those measured when galloping has been noted.

The phenomenon is most frequently observed on power lines in countries with cold winters, where the accretion of ice can substantially modify the cross-sectional shape of the cable and hence its aerodynamic characteristics. It has also been noted on stranded cables where, in a yawed wind, asymmetry is introduced into the flow by the strands on one side of the cable lying in line with the wind while the strands on the other side lie across the wind. These observations have shown that the motion of the power lines is basically simple harmonic, with the wave form modified by travelling waves, and also that the frequency of the galloping

168 *Wind forces on buildings and structures*

coincides with the fundamental or first-harmonic natural frequency of the line.

Galloping is not, however, limited to cables. Many cylindrical structures are subject to this form of oscillation. Usually, as with oscillations induced by vortex shedding, the structure moves across the wind, the first bending mode being excited. With most structures moving in this fashion it is unusual for there to be any substantial twisting, and each point effectively moves in one degree of freedom. When the term 'galloping' is applied to cables, however, a much more complex motion may be being described in which the cable both twists and moves laterally, although the motion is predominantly a cross-wind oscillation.

The mechanism of galloping. The mechanism of galloping is deduced by considering both the observations of galloping and the lift-curve slope of the sections which exhibit this behaviour. Observations show that the amplitude of a galloping oscillation increases continuously with increasing speed, and the mechanism of excitation is not therefore entirely one of vortex shedding. Further, the transverse motion of most galloping structures is not accompanied by twisting, as would be the case if the oscillation were caused by flutter. The process therefore appears to be caused by the change in wind direction due to the motion of the structure.

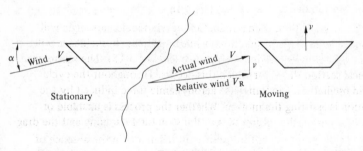

Fig. 5.13

When the structure is stationary, the wind meets it at an angle α, say (see fig. 5.13). If the structure is disturbed so that it moves sideways at velocity v, in a wind of velocity V, then the relative wind direction becomes $\alpha - v/V$. Now, for many shapes the side-force coefficient C_F increases with wind incidence (see fig. 5.14) so that, as the structure moves, the aerodynamic force in the direction of motion is reduced. This is clearly a stabilising effect, since the aerodynamic force induced by the motion opposes that motion. It is apparent that if, however,

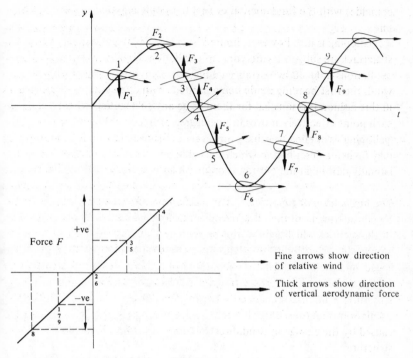

Fig. 5.14

C_F decreases with α, then a reduction of wind incidence angle will
produce an increase in side force while an increase in incidence will
be associated with a reduction in force (see fig. 5.15). The square is a
typical section shape for which this occurs. Throughout the cycle
of an oscillation, the transverse aerodynamic force induced by the
motion is assisting the motion. Whether the process is unstable or
not depends on the magnitudes of the structural damping and the drag
force. The conditions for instability in this mode, in the absence of

$$(\mathrm{d}C_F/\mathrm{d}\alpha)(\mathrm{d}C_L/\mathrm{d}\alpha + C_D) < 0. \tag{5.5}$$

In the investigation into the Severn crossing conductor oscillations[8],
a more complex form of galloping was revealed. It was found that over
parts of the Reynolds-number range applicable to the conductors, the
drag force decreased with increasing speed. This occurred in the speed
range 10–15 m/s and depended on the yaw angle, the larger yaw angles
being associated with higher critical speeds. A substantial reduction of
side (lift) force with increasing speed was noted to occur over the same
range, and again the critical speed depended on yaw angle. The

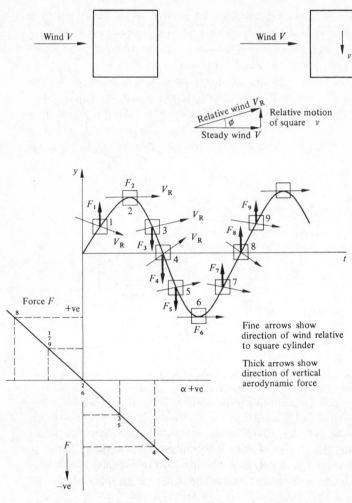

Fig. 5.15

oscillations of the conductors in the windward direction therefore induced transverse oscillations, and over the critical speed range the characteristics of both the normal (drag) and the side (lift) force variations with wind velocity produced negative aerodynamic damping.

Potentially unstable shapes. For vertical cylindrical structures, the initial value of incidence is determined only by the direction from which the wind blows. The slope of the side-force curve for many structural shapes is likely to be negative for some wind directions. Fortunately, for many sections the drag-force coefficient is high, but the stability condition must nevertheless be checked over the complete incidence range if a tall flexible structure is to be erected.

The amplitude of motion of many structures is limited both by the non-linear aerodynamic characteristics and by non-linear damping. In many cases lateral motions are quite acceptable — this is so, for instance, with street lamps — but for some structures such as microwave towers, or remote television camera masts, where movements may be critical to

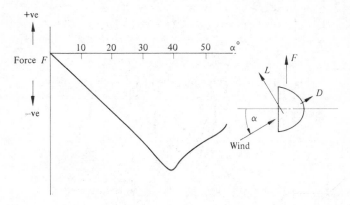

Fig. 5.16 'D' section

their function, care should be taken in the selection of a suitable section. It is found, for example, that polygons with up to twelve sides exhibit the unstable side-force characteristic over some of the incidence range. The greater the number of sides of the polygon, the weaker is the galloping tendency, so polygons with less than twelve sides should be avoided if lateral movement is undesirable for a given application.

A selection of shapes which produce the unstable side-force characteristic over part of the incidence cycle is sketched in figs 5.16 to 5.20; in each case, F is the cross-wind force, L is the lift force, and D is the drag force. It is seen that the modified circle, the 'D' section, and the 'pear' section are shapes which might be formed by ice on circular-section cables, while the square section and the 'H' section are shapes used for buildings and stacks.

The 'pear' section has a side-force curve which is stable over the range $\alpha = 0\text{--}15°$ and is then extremely unstable from $\alpha = 15°$ to $\alpha = 30°$. This characteristic is similar to that exhibited by an aerofoil at the low-speed stall, and the effect of this on early aircraft was an uncontrollable roll which acquired the name 'autorotation'.

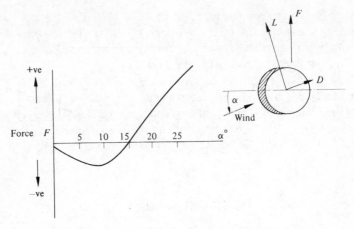

Fig. 5.17 Circle shape modified by ice accretion, say

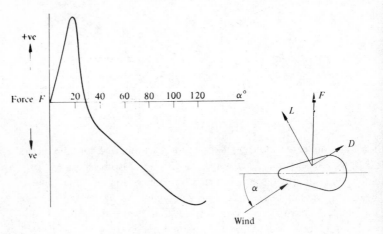

Fig. 5.18 'Pear' section

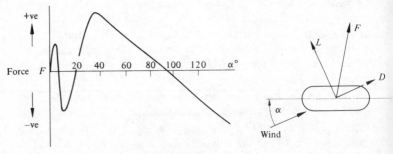

Fig. 5.19 Oval section

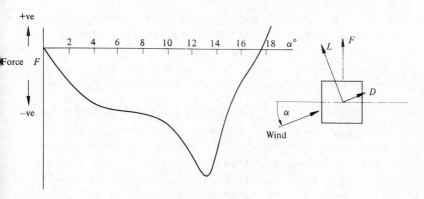

Fig. 5.20 Square section

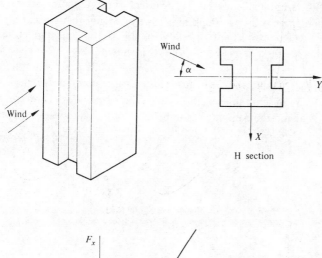

H section

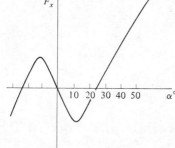

Fig. 5.21 'H' section

The 'H' section (see fig. 5.21) is similar to the cross-sectional shape of the Empire State building in New York. It can be seen that this section is potentially unstable for wind directions between $\alpha = -10°$ and $\alpha = +10°$. The observed fact that the building is stable indicates that the drag forces and the structural damping overcome the destabilising effect of the side force.

It should be noted that many civil-engineering structures, both in the uncompleted and completed stages, possess negative aerodynamic characteristics and are capable of contributing negative aerodynamic damping. Caution should be exercised when structures are being erected in a windy environment, as the rigidity and damping of the partially complete structure may be substantially less than that in the complete form.

The stability diagram. It will be seen from previous comments that the structural damping is important on many structures over at least part of the wind incidence range. The effect of this damping can be presented graphically by establishing experimentally that structural damping which gives a neutrally stable oscillation. A typical graph for the stability of a square-section cylinder is shown in fig. 5.22. The area to the left of the curve is a region of divergent oscillations while that on the right is a stable region. There are two distinct parts to the curve. The lower line represents an oscillation where the frequency depends on the wind speed and the damping has to be increased as the speed is increased.

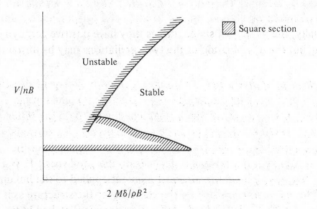

Fig. 5.22 Stability diagram for square-section prism (V = free-stream mean velocity, n = frequency of oscillation, B = characteristic length, M = mass per unit length of structure, δ = structural damping (logarithmic decrement), ρ = air density)

is situation corresponds to a vortex-shedding oscillation. The upper
e represents a region where the frequency is constant with increasing
nd speed. This corresponds to a galloping oscillation. The slope of this
rt of the diagram is equal to $-2dC_F/d\alpha$, which indicates how the
mping δ has to be increased as the slope of the force–incidence curve
comes more negative.

The stability may be estimated by summing the aerodynamic and the
uctural damping. Oscillations are undamped when

$$k_a + k_s = 0 \qquad (5.6)$$

The structural coefficient k_s is defined by

$$k_s = 2M\delta_s/\rho B^2 \qquad (5.7)$$

The aerodynamic damping coefficient is given by

$$k_a = \frac{v_r^2}{4\pi^2 \zeta_0} \int_0^{2\pi} C_F(1 + \tan^2 \alpha) \cos \omega t \, d(\omega t) \qquad (5.8)$$

ere $v_r = v/nB$, $\zeta_0 = Z_0/B$, Z_0 = amplitude of oscillation.

2.3 Divergence and flutter. Two forms of aerodynamic instability
ich become more likely as structures are made more flexible are
vergence and flutter. A divergent motion is a non-oscillatory one in
ich the deflection, caused by either a bending or a torsional loading
uation, produces a load which deflects the structure more than the
tial load. In contrast, flutter is an oscillatory motion in which two
more modes of oscillation, usually bending and torsion, are combined.
dividually, the modes are stable, that is they have positive aerodynamic
mping, but the combination of the two oscillations may be unstable.

e mechanism of divergence. Consider first a non-divergent situation
which a torsional load is applied to the structure sketched in fig. 5.23,
e load–incidence graph of which is sketched in fig. 5.25 (a). When the
nd blows on the building at an angle of incidence ϕ, the torsional
oment applied can be read from this graph. The magnitude of the
plied moment for this incidence depends on the wind speed V. If a
eed V_1 is assumed, then the torsional moment applied to the building
T_{A1}. This moment is resisted by the elasticity of the structure as it
flects under the load. The load–deflection graph is sketched in fig.
25 (b). From this it is seen that the applied torque T_{A1} produces a
an deflection α_1, (see fig. 5.24). Neglecting the influence of wind
ear, which makes deflections at the top of the structure more

significant from wind-loading considerations than those lower down, the mean wind incidence is now $\phi + \alpha_1$, and reference to the applied-torque graph shows this to be associated with T'_{A1}. This new torsional moment again increases the mean deflection to α'_1 but this increase is seen to be small compared to α_1 and the process converges on a value little greater than α'_1. This is the normal situation and no divergence has occurred.

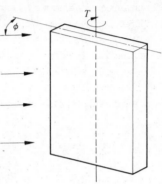

Fig. 5.23

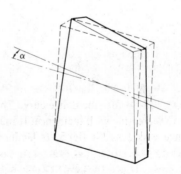

Fig. 5.24

Now, suppose the wind speed increases to V_2 from a direction ϕ_2. Again, by reference to figs. 5.25 (a) and (b) it is seen that the mean deflection angle α_2 produces a modified applied torque T'_{A2}. This is again resisted by the structure but, because of the shape of the load—deflection curve, the increase in α to α'_2 is larger than the initial mean deflection α_2 and the process is seen to be divergent. It will be appreciated that divergence is associated with high wind speeds and elastic structures working in the high-stress region. Caution must be exercised especially when using new high-strength materials.

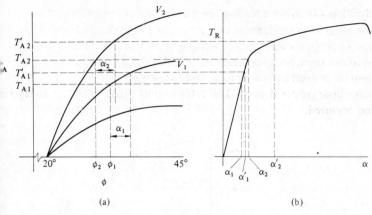

Fig. 5.25

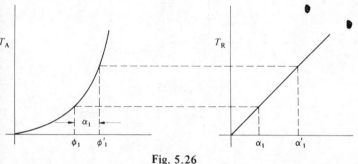

Fig. 5.26

An alternative way in which divergence can be initiated depends
on the shape of the applied-torque–incidence curve. In fig. 5.25 (a)
the torque is shown as decreasing with incidence. It may, however,
increase with incidence as sketched in fig. 5.26. Under these circumstances
divergence is again likely to occur in high winds. As can be seen,
divergence can occur when $dT_A/d\phi > dT_2/d\alpha$ if the effects of wind
shear are neglected.

Structures liable to divergence. A range of structures liable to
divergence is sketched in figs. 5.27 to 5.31. The first three examples
of tower structures (a look-out tower, a hose tower, and a lamp
standard) exhibit an increase in drag force with bending deflection.
This drag force acts well above the ground level, causing a substantial
bending moment. It is seen that the frontal area increases with bending
deflection for shapes of this type. Figure 5.30 shows a horizontal
cantilever whose frontal area increases substantially with deflection,

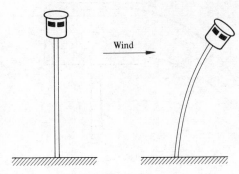

Fig. 5.27

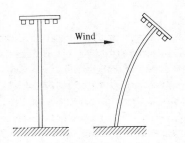

Fig. 5.28

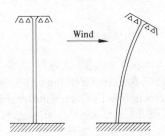

Fig. 5.29

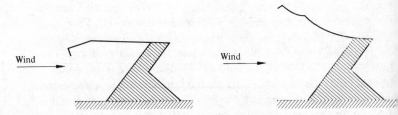

Fig. 5.30

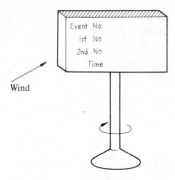

Wind

Fig. 5.31

while fig. 5.31 shows the type of sign used at an athletics meeting. The divergent failure of the latter structure, if it occurred, would be in torsion. It should be noted that the bending moments at the base of the three tower structures are increased by the weight of the top of the structure when offset from the centre line in the deflected position. *The mechanism of flutter.* The movement of a section of a long structure in torsional oscillation is sketched in fig. 5.32 (a). It is seen that, as the wind blows on the structure, if the aerodynamic centre is aft of the shear centre then the aerodynamic force is a stabilising influence, tending to reduce the angular deflection throughout the entire cycle. The greater the deflection, the greater is the restoring moment. Since the centre of the structure does not move laterally, the wind direction is not influenced by the rotation of the structure.

Figure 5.32 (b) shows the motion of the section of the same structure restricted to bending. The lateral movement sketched changes the relative direction of the wind throughout the cycle. The aerodynamic force generated by the section can be seen to act in a direction which opposes the motion throughout the cycle. When the two motions are combined, fig. 5.32 (c), and the torsion cycle is 90° in advance of the bending cycle, the resultant aerodynamic force on the section acts in the direction of the bending motion throughout the cycle. This force is therefore a destabilising force, supplying energy from the air to the structure throughout the cycle. It can be seen, however, that the aerodynamic forces are assisting the torsional motion during only half the cycle. In respect of both motions, therefore, the aerodynamic damping has been changed. The stabilising effect of the aerodynamic forces in the bending mode has become destabilising, and the stabilising influence in the torsional mode has become neutrally stable.

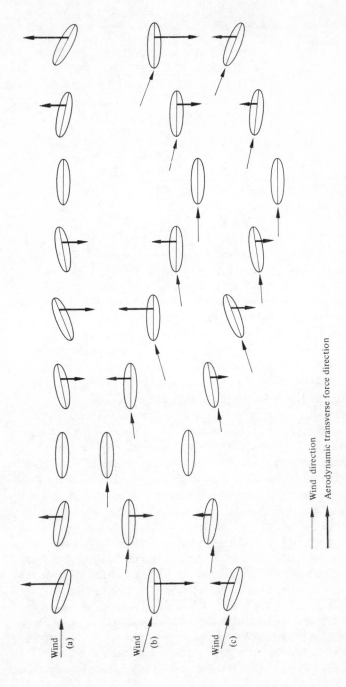

→ Wind direction

⟶ Aerodynamic transverse force direction

Fig. 5.32 (a) Torsional oscillation (b) Bending oscillation (c) Torsional and bending oscillation

If the air flow separates suddenly from the curved surface of a structure, having previously remained attached as the incidence was increased, the air flow is said to be 'stalled'. Decreasing the angle of incidence again does not immediately cause re-attachment; this is achieved at some incidence below the stalling angle (see fig. 5.33). With some bowl-shape structures, such as are used for radio telescopes, 'stalling flutter' can be experienced due to this hysteresis, with the bowl oscillating about the stalling angle as the flow alternately separates from and re-attaches to the curved surface.

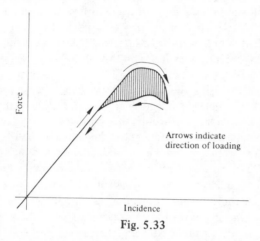

Arrows indicate direction of loading

Fig. 5.33

Structures liable to flutter.   Structures liable to flutter are those in which substantial bending and torsional deflections can be established. One such structure is a suspension bridge, especially one in which a clean shape has been chosen to reduce the transverse wind loading. Another possibly susceptible structure is a tall stack of non-circular section, and flutter oscillations have been observed during model tests on bowl-shaped structures.

5.3 Unsteady aerodynamic forces due to body shape in unsteady and turbulent winds

5.3.1 Buffeting.   Buffeting oscillations are induced in a structure subjected to a disturbed air flow. Gusts occurring in the natural wind produce structural deflections which, because of the random nature of such turbulence, do not build up. Because of this random nature, it is usual to design buildings to withstand gust loads rather than to estimate structural deflections. The estimation of such structural deflection is a complex process, and detailed information has to be known about the structure and the wind. A procedure for doing this is given below (section 5.3.2).

Many buildings, however, do not always lie in a region of random gusting. They lie, instead, in the wake of neighbouring bluff structures, and in a steady wind this wake may exhibit a regular pattern of eddy formation and shedding. In consequence, the gusting in this region is not completely random but has a regular pattern of flow speed and direction superimposed on it. This periodicity may be significant enough to build up a large oscillation in the leeward structure if the natural structure frequency of this building coincides with that of the shedding frequency.

The eddy-shedding frequency behind a flat plate is given approximately by $f = 0.15 \, V/B$, where V is the mean wind speed and B is the projected depth of the plate in a plane perpendicular to the direction of the stream. For a structure of circular cross-section the constant is 0.20.

It might be supposed that buffeting would be more severe the closer the two structures were together, but in wind-tunnel tests[9] on a model of the Runcorn–Widnes bridge complex (where a suspension road bridge was planned to be built adjacent to an existing railway bridge) it was found that the maximum buffet amplitudes on the leeward bridge (the suspension bridge) increased linearly as the horizontal separation was increased up to 40 m. However, it is clear that buffet amplitudes must decrease and eventually disappear as separation is further increased.

Wind-loading problems may still arise for a building in the wake of another structure even if the natural frequency is well removed from the vortex-shedding frequency. Scruton[10] has reported that, with the models of two tower blocks in line, local pressure fluctuations up to five times larger than the corresponding time-averaged pressures were recorded in wind-tunnel tests, while the pressure amplitudes on the windward tower were similar to the time-averaged pressures.

For many shapes the influence of turbulence in the air stream is to reduce the drag forces. This has been shown to be the case with a flat plate normal to the stream, square and rectangular prisms, and circular cylinders. The magnitude of the effect depends on aspect ratio and is caused by flow re-attachment induced by the turbulence.

5.3.2 The response of a structure to turbulence. The likely maximum deflection of a structure in the turbulent wind is of interest to the structural engineer whether he be concerned with tall buildings, cantilever roofs, or tall towers. The processes involved for establishing this have been presented by Davenport[11], from whose work the diagrammatic representation reproduced in fig. 5.34 is taken. The procedure outlined below is described more fully by Anthony[12]. For design purposes, reference should be made to Davenport's report, where appropriate graphs will be found.

The first information needed in the response estimation is a description of the wind. This will depend on the site of the structure. The hourly mean wind magnitude can be obtained from data published by the appropriate meteorological office, as has already been discussed, while the turbulence can be presented as a gust spectrum. Although the mean wind speed will be in one direction, gusts will be experienced in three orthogonal directions. Most practical wind-loading problems, however, can be dealt with by considering only the longitudinal component of the gust vector.

A description of the longitudinal gust spectrum has been obtained by full-scale measurements, and a mathematical expression which fits the spectrum for strong winds is

$$nS^v(n) = 4k\bar{V}_{10}^2 \, \tilde{n}/(2 + \tilde{n}^2)^{5/6} \quad \text{(Harris)} \tag{5.9}$$

or

$$nS^v(n) = 4k\bar{V}_{10}^2 \, \tilde{n}^2/(1 + \tilde{n}^2)^{4/3} \quad \text{(Davenport)} \tag{5.10}$$

where $\tilde{n} = nL/\bar{V}_{10}$ and k is a surface drag coefficient. (See fig. 6.5 and recall section 3.3.4, but note that the symbol in common usage for frequency is n in spectral analysis and hereafter replaces the symbol f used previously.)

The structure is subjected to fluctuating loads over a range of frequencies and, just as the deflection of a spring—mass system depends on the frequency of excitation, so does the response of the structure in the wind. A typical graph of the resulting response of a structure to a simple harmonic force is sketched in fig. 5.35. On the vertical axis, the mechanical admittance $|X_m(n)|^2$ is the ratio of the mean-square amplitude of the output to the mean-square amplitude of the input. The product of the force spectrum and the mechanical admittance gives the deflection spectrum:

$$S^y(n)/\bar{Y}^2 = |X_m(n)|^2 S^f(n)/\bar{F}^2 \tag{5.11}$$

where $\bar{Y}$ is the mean deflection due to the mean wind load and $\bar{F}$ is the mean force.

Reference to fig. 5.34 shows that this is the latter part of the response calculation. This must be preceeded by a technique which gives

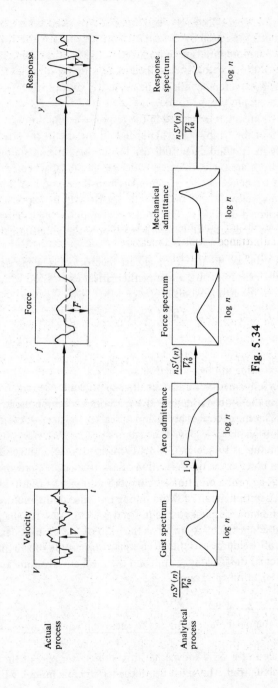

Fig. 5.34

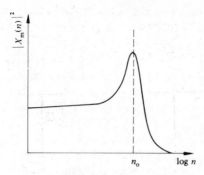

Fig. 5.35 Mechanical admittance

the force spectrum from the gust spectrum and which involves the aerodynamic admittance – this is a measure of the effect that the turbulence
has on the drag forces in relation to those which occur in steady flow,
i.e. it is the ratio $C_{F\,\text{steady}}/C_{F\,\text{unsteady}}$. Two features cause this
variation: firstly, the separation and re-attachment of the flow at the
corners of the structure changes as the gust size varies, and secondly the
distribution of gusts over the structure depends on the relative size of
the structure and the gusts – a large gust, totally enveloping the
structure, will act in the same direction all over the structure, while
small gusts acting in the x-direction, say, at the top of the structure,
may be accompanied by similar small gusts acting in the negative x-
direction at the bottom. In general, the lower the frequency the closer
the admittance approaches unity.

A typical graph of aerodynamic admittance is sketched in fig. 5.36.
Usually a value of 1·0 can be assigned to admittance, as the reduction in
value from unity often occurs well above the natural frequency of the
structure. The problem is further complicated by the variation of the
mean speed with height (i.e. wind shear) and also by the building
dimensions, some buildings being tall and narrow, others being long
and low, etc.

The relationship between the force spectrum and the velocity
spectrum can be written

$$S^f(n)/\overline{F}^2 = 4\,|X_a(n)|^2 S^v(n)/\overline{V}_{10}^2 \tag{5.12}$$

where $|X_a(n)|^2$ is the aerodynamic admittance if the wind shear and
the shape effects are neglected.

The response to this force spectrum then becomes

$$S^y(n)/\overline{Y}^2 = 4\,|X_a(n)|^2\,|X_m(n)|^2\,S^v(n)/\overline{V}_{10}^2 \tag{5.13}$$

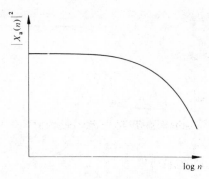

Fig. 5.36 Aerodynamic admittance

Comparing this with Davenport's expression,

$$nS^y(n)/\overline{Y}^2 = (16/3)(1 + \alpha)^2 |X_m(n)|^2 \, |J_z(n)|^2 \, |J_h(n)|^2 \, nS^v(n)/\overline{V}_1^{\,2} \tag{5.14}$$

where α is the wind-shear power index, and $\overline{V}_1^{\,2}$ is the mean velocity at the top of the structure, it is seen that the aerodynamic admittance has been replaced by 'acceptances' $|J_z(n)|^2$ and $|J_h(n)|^2$ in the vertical and horizontal sense. Approximate values for $|J_z(n)|^2$ and $|J_h(n)|^2$ can be gained from

$$|J_z(n)|^2 = [1/(1 + \alpha)^2] \; [1/(1 + c/3)] \tag{5.15}$$

and

$$|J_h(n)|^2 = 1/(1 + c'/2) \tag{5.16}$$

where $c \approx 8 \, hn/V_1$ and $c' \approx 20 \, nb/\overline{V}$ (b = breadth of structure, h = height of structure).

Having obtained the spectrum of the displacement, the maximum deflection, Y_{max}, is given by

$$Y_{max} = \overline{Y}(1 + g\sigma_y/\overline{Y}) \tag{5.17}$$

where σ_y is the r.m.s. response.

The value of g is given by

$$g = \sqrt{(2 \ln vT)} + 0 \cdot 57/\sqrt{(2 \ln vT)} \tag{5.18}$$

The effective frequency, v, for a structure is the number of times the displacement trace crosses the mean-value line in unit time, and T is the sample time, usually 3600 seconds. In a lightly damped system, $v \approx n_0$, the natural frequency of the structure.

A typical graph of the response is sketched in fig. 5.37, the area under the curve being σ_y^2. The value of $\sigma_y/\overline{Y}$ can be determined from the relationship

$$\sigma_y/\overline{Y} = r\sqrt{(B + sF/\beta)} \tag{5.19}$$

where

$$r = 4\sqrt{K}(30/h)^\alpha$$

($k = 0.005$ for open country, 0.05 for a city centre)

$$B = 2 \left\{ \frac{1}{[1 + (1\,500/h)^2]^{1/3}} - 1 \right\}$$

$$s = \frac{\pi}{3} \left(\frac{1}{1 + 8/3\xi_0} \frac{1}{1 + 10\,b/h\xi_0} \right)$$

where

$$\xi_0 = hn_0/\overline{V}_1$$

$$F = \frac{(Ln_0/\overline{V}_{10})^2}{[1 + (Ln_0/\overline{V}_{10})^2]^{4\beta}}$$

if Davenport's spectrum is assumed.

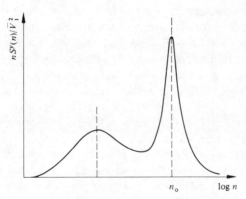

Fig. 5.37

The length of scale L is approximately 1300 m (4000 ft). The damping term β has a value which lies between 0.005 and 0.01 for steel structures and 0.01 and 0.02 for concrete structures.

The values of $g, r, B, s,$ and F can be presented graphically, covering a wide range of conditions, so that the process of obtaining the gust factor $G = 1 + \sigma_y g/\overline{Y}$ is greatly simplified.

Note: In the above equations, the physical significance of the terms is as follows:

g is the 'peak factor', since peak deflections not r.m.s. values are of interest to the designer;

r is a ground roughness factor;

B is the excitation by background turbulence;

sF/β is the excitation by turbulence resonant with the structure;

β is the damping factor.

5.4 Some 'unsteady' aerodynamic considerations

Wind forces on buildings and structures are always unsteady. Sometimes the unsteadiness is due to the gustiness of the wind, sometimes to vortex shedding, and on other occasions to the interaction between inertial, elastic, and aerodynamic forces on the structure. These various forms of loading produce deflections of the structure which can be estimated when the loads are known.

The most potentially dangerous unsteady forces are those which are cylic and can be written in the form

$$F = F_0 + F_1 \sin \omega t \tag{5.20}$$

since the frequency ω of the fluctuating part of the applied force F may coincide with the natural frequency of the structure. The frequency of the vortex shedding, for example, depends on the size and shape of the structure and also on the wind speed. It is often found that the frequency of the fundamental mode of the structure matches the vortex-shedding frequency at a low wind speed. The energy available to force the structural oscillation is then limited, as the aerodynamic forces depend on the square of the wind speed. At first sight it would appear that the structural deflections would be greater at higher wind speeds when the vortex-shedding frequency coincides with the frequency of the higher modes of oscillation. It is found, however, that the motion of parts of the structure under these conditions is opposed by the aerodynamic forces. The vortex-shedding forces act in the same direction over the entire length of the structure but, apart from the fundamental mode, the motion of the structure is not unidirectional at any given time, and the structural deflections are consequently limited.

It is usually found that failures under unsteady conditions are local failures resulting in the destruction of tiles, panels, or cladding, rather than that of the entire structure. These failures are frequently caused by local vortices, shed by small parts of the structure, which are difficult to predict analytically and almost impossible to model accurately on a small-scale wind-tunnel model. Experience with similar designs is the best guide to likely sources of trouble.

The manner in which unsteady forces affect various types of structure is considered below. The list is not exhaustive but is intended to cover the most likely sources of difficulty.

5.4.1 High-rise blocks.

The 'time-averaged' results of having one building situated in the wake of another have been discussed in section 4.4.7. It is apparent that the vortices shed from an upstream structure could excite an oscillation of a downstream structure if the shedding frequency of the upstream structure and the natural frequency of the downstream structure coincide. Similarly, if the frequency of the gusts in the wind approaching an isolated structure matches the shedding frequency of the vortices from the building, it may be supposed that these vortices could be strengthened and hence the magnitude of the lateral forces increased.

The effects of vortex shedding from an upstream structure on a downstream structure have been reported by Eaton[13] and by Scruton, Woodgate, and Alexander[9]. In the first case, tiles were stripped from a roof downstream of a substantial chimney stack. A similar effect was observed during wind-tunnel tests on models of the Runcorn—Widnes bridge (see section 5.3.1 above).

Excitation of the second type has been reported by Hunt[14]. During tests intended for measuring the effects of wind on people, gustiness in the wind was generated by oscillating aerofoil-shaped vanes. In the absence of gustiness, regular sideways oscillations were observed on a large rectangular prism set in the airflow. When the frequency of the vanes (and hence gusts) coincided with the frequency of the sideways oscillations, a large increase in amplitude was observed. It is possible that the gust spectrum was not representative of that of the lower atmosphere, but the test illustrates that large-amplitude and potentially unpleasant swaying of a tall building may occur if the predominant gust frequencies coincide with the shedding frequency. If both these frequencies coincide with the building's natural frequency of vibration then the effects may become severe.

At first sight it would appear that there is little likelihood of these three frequencies — gust, shedding, and natural — coinciding. It must be remembered, however, that shedding frequency varies with wind speed so that a range of shedding-frequency values is normally applicable. Similarly, the gustiness of the wind is not all of the same frequency at any given wind speed. There is always a range of frequencies which contain substantial energy (see fig. 6.5) and it is values in this range which must be checked for comparison with the range of shedding frequency and the magnitude of the structural natural frequency.

In discussing the time-averaged wind loads on high-rise blocks with rounded ends (section 4.4.4), it was noted that the flow may remain attached to such a building over a small range of wind incidence. This effect has implications for the dynamic forces as well as for the static loads. When the wind blows at a small incidence to the long face (fig. 5.38), the building will deflect about its longer horizontal axis. A sudden gust of wind or change in wind direction will cause a sudden

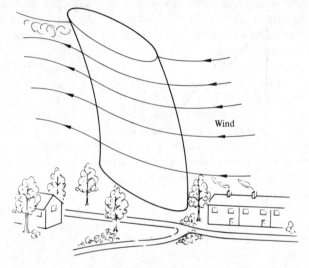

Fig. 5.38

deflection. The change in wind direction may be sufficient to cause the flow to separate, with a consequent sudden change in flow pattern and loading. A sudden change in loads will excite the building at its natural frequency. For a tall flexible structure the change in relative wind direction due to the motion at the top of the building may be sufficient to allow the flow to re-attach. A forced oscillation could then result from the flow alternately separating and re-attaching. The sudden change in force coefficient that can be developed on a building with rounded ends is shown in fig. 5.39. These coefficients were measured in a wind-tunnel on a model building whose horizontal section was bean-shaped, set next to a similar building of lower height.

The swaying of high-rise blocks can influence both the structural integrity of the building and the comfort of the occupiers. Davenport[15] suggests that human response to lateral accelerations has a threshold in

the range 0·01−0·1 m/s, which indicates sway amplitudes of 4 to 40 mm
for a forty-storey building with a four-second sway period.

To minimise sway amplitudes, building shapes which are known to
have negative aerodynamic damping should be avoided. The mechanical
damping of the structure should always exceed any negative aerodynamic
damping, and the use of sectional shapes which encourage conditions in
which the attached flow is followed rapidly by flow separations for small
wind changes should be treated with caution.

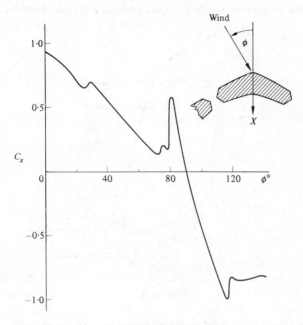

Fig. 5.39

5.4.2 Towers and chimneys. In the design of tall slender structures of
any cross-sectional shape, it is essential that the natural frequencies of the
structure in bending and torsion and the vortex-shedding frequency should
be well separated. As the diameter which determines the vortex-shedding
frequency for a given wind speed will usually be determined by non-
aerodynamic considerations, a means must be found for modifying the
vortex-shedding frequency, modifying the natural frequency, or ensuring
substantial damping. If this is not done a plastic failure (the tensile
strength being exceeded locally by excessive deflections), or a fatigue
failure, or at the least an inferior electronic performance (if the tower
is being used as a transmitter) may result.

It is usual to try to modify the vortex-shedding frequency for chimneys, and this is done by adding strakes to the top 25% of the structure. The effect of the strakes is to prevent periodic shedding of vortices at this top section. Although the shedding will be periodic for the rest of the chimney, the bending moments applied to the chimney are greatly reduced. In the absence of strakes, the shedding frequency usually 'locks on' to that of the top third of the chimney. Also, the damping of a stack of riveted steel construction is greater than that of one of welded construction and it should not be assumed therefore that, because a riveted stack is stable, it can be safely replaced by a similar welded stack.

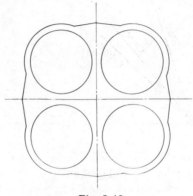

Fig. 5.40

The damping of a steel stack may be increased by the addition of an internal coating of suitable material. Hydraulic dampers may be used if the stack or mast is guyed.

Tall chimneys frequently contain several flues as architects improve the appearance of factories, power stations, and similar buildings. An investigation into such a multi-flue stack by Vickery and Walshe[16] showed that one which contained four flues and had a cross-section as sketched in fig. 5.40 was less stable than the corresponding circular stack. However, since the stack contained four flues, it was possible to perforate it, allowing air to flow from the high-pressure windward side to the low-pressure leeward. With the top 20% of the stack perforated to give 28% porosity, based on overall surface area, the amplitudes of oscillation were lower than those of the corresponding circular section for all wind directions. For the most adverse wind direction tested, the amplitudes were approximately 30% of those for the unperforated stack and 75% of those for the corresponding circular cylinder (see fig. 5.41).

Little can be done to modify the damping of concrete structures such as those that may be used in multi-flue applications. Typically the damping, as given by the logarithmic decrement, has a value[17] of not less than 0·06. The damping of a prestressed concrete stack, however, increases dramatically as soon as cracking of the concrete begins.

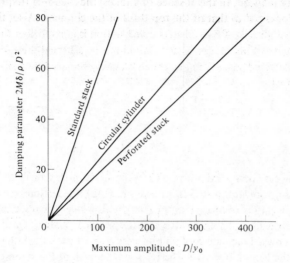

Fig. 5.41

Although it is difficult to change the damping significantly, the addition of a mass to the stack can reduce the natural bending frequency. The natural frequency and the vortex-shedding frequency may then coincide at a lower wind speed but are then in a region where the structural damping may be greater than the aerodynamic excitation.

In the design of tall stacks on exposed sites, consideration must be given to the formation of ice on the top and along the length of the stack. This can change the natural frequency of the structure, the vortex-shedding frequency, and, because of the change in cross-section, the aerodynamic characteristics of the stack. In the case of tall steelwork masts, such as may be used at transmitting stations, the formation of ice can substantially change the frontal area presented to the wind, producing high time-averaged loads as well as dynamic loads.

5.4.3 Cantilever structures. Cantilever structures, such as roofs of grandstands and of sheltered loading bays, are less liable to dynamic excitation than are chimneys or bridges. This is because, with the wind blowing directly into the stand, the air flow comes over one side of the roof only — unless the grandstand has no back to it. The mechanism of excitation, if any, depends on the roof shape and the wind direction. The roof is excited either by the gustiness in the wind or by the turbulence in the airstream as it separates at the sharp corners of the structure.

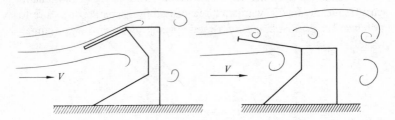

Fig. 5.42

For the case of a wind blowing onto the front of stand whose roof is inclined downwards at the front (see fig. 5.42), the gustiness is the most likely source of roof vibrations, as the flow over the upper surface of the stand will probably be attached to the upper surface. On the other hand, an upward inclined roof will be excited by vortex shedding whether the wind blows from the front or the back of the stand.

Although the grandstand designer must be concerned with deflections of the complete roof, cantilevered or stayed, and it is these which are usually investigated in wind-tunnel tests, the excitation of the individual cladding panels should also be considered. This local effect has become especially significant with the increased use of light-weight translucent roofing panels. The panels can be easily excited by vortices shed from projections of the main structure, and the low modulus of elasticity of such materials and their thinness means that deflections can be large and lead to destruction. Further, they are likely to respond to gusts of much shorter duration then the 3-second ones for which data are available. Translucent cladding panels are therefore particularly susceptible to wind damage.

5.4.4 Bridges.   Much research has been done on the wind loads on bridges because they are frequently built on exposed sites and are subject to very severe wind conditions. The long span and lightweight construction of suspension bridges has made these bridges particularly susceptible to wind-induced oscillations. Classic failures of similar bridges have greatly publicised the problems and have alerted designers to their severity.[18,19]

Wind-induced oscillations are caused either by aerodynamic instability or by buffeting. The oscillations caused by aerodynamic instability are set up in a steady wind by the interaction of the structure with the airstream (see 'Vortex generation', 'Galloping', and 'Flutter', sections 5.2.1, 5.2.2, and 5.2.3). The oscillations caused by buffeting are due to the bridge being immersed in an unsteady wind with a predominant gust frequency. Such a wind could be caused by a separate structure to windward or by shedding from the supporting towers in a longitudinal wind.

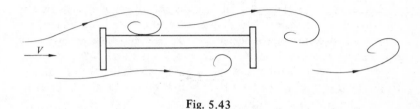

Fig. 5.43

To the designer, the oscillations due to aerodynamic instability are the more important of the two types and were responsible for the failure of the Tacoma Narrows bridge in 1940[20]. The magnitude of the oscillations depends on the structure shape, natural frequency, and damping. The oscillations are caused by the periodic shedding of vortices on the leeward side of the structure, a vortex being shed first from the upper section and then from the lower section (see fig. 5.43). These asymmetric flows induce corresponding asymmetric forces on the bridge. Because the oscillations induced depend on the bridge characteristics, they can be reduced in magnitude by changing the bridge shape, frequency, or damping. In the investigation into the aerodynamic characteristics of the Severn Bridge, at the National Physical Laboratory, Frazer and Scruton[21] drew the following conclusions about the design of suspension bridges in general.

stiffened bridges.
2. Truss-stiffened bridges do not suffer from vertical bending oscillations. Any torsional oscillations can be reduced by incorporating features which break up the continuity of the flow pattern, e.g. castellated parapets, slots or gratings between roadways, side tracks mounted outboard of stiffening trusses, lattice-type lateral bracing fitted near deck level, etc.
3. Coupling between vertical and torsional oscillations should be avoided unless the ratios of the natural frequencies concerned are close to unity.

Conditions which produce buffeting on bridges are very rare. The gusts in the natural wind will cause displacement of a bridge, but, as the gusts are aperiodic, the displacements do not build up. If a large bluff body exists upstream, then the vortices from this may be periodic, and, if their frequency coincides with the natural frequency of the bridge, very-large-amplitude displacements may be expected. It is unusual for an existing upwind bridge to be positioned near to a proposed bridge such that problems of this type are caused, although it may be expected to become an increasingly frequent occurrence as more urban bridges are constructed.

As remarked above, the possibility of the end towers of a suspension bridge shedding vortices and exciting the structure when the wind blows along the bridge must be considered. For example, the shedding frequency for a circular tower of diameter D is given by $f = 0.2 \ V/D$. If the two towers are joined by a deep portal structure, depth P, then the shedding frequency from this will be $f = 0.15 \ V/P$. The vortices shed from the portal structure will usually be of a lower frequency than those shed from the towers and hence closer to the bridge natural frequency at wind speeds which have a reasonable energy content. Suppose, to continue the example, the bridge had a natural bending frequency of 0.4 Hz and was supported by towers of 4 m diameter stiffened with a portal of 5 m depth. The vortex-shedding frequency of the towers and the natural frequency of the bridge would coincide at a wind speed of 8 m/s. The portal and bridge frequencies would coincide at 13 m/s. Both speeds are likely to occur, but the structural damping of the bridge would more readily overcome the oscillations induced at the lower speed.

5.4.5 Cables. Cables are used both as electrical conductors, supporting only their own weight and wind loads, and as stays for towers or suspended structures, when they carry additional loads. Like other structures, cables may be excited by vortex shedding or by aerodynamic instability (see section 5.2).

In general, cables will behave like rough cylinders when the wind blows on them at right angles. It will be recalled that the shedding frequency from a long cylinder is given by $f = 0.20 \ V/D$. This frequency is usually too high to coincide with the natural frequency of the suspended cable, but this should be checked. A further possible source of excitation occurs if the strands are untwisted. It may then be found that the strands oscillate as they move into and out of the wake of neighbouring upstream strands. This is unlikely to cause structural damage, but the noise of one cable striking another can be very annoying, and, if the cable is an electrical conductor and the insulation breaks down, electrical loss may result. The problem can be overcome by bunching the strands together at mid-span or by separating them at mid-span with a block.

Oscillations also occur in cables supporting tall masts. This problem has been overcome by fitting hydraulic dampers. In certain cases this solution might result in unacceptably large movements of the mast, and it would then be preferable to modify the natural frequency of the cable, by adding mass dampers to them or by tying the cables to the tower at some intermediate point.

Not all cables are circular in section. Cables formed by twisting a number of strands of circular section provide a cross-section shape which may induce aerodynamic instability. Also, the accretion of snow or ice to the cable can considerably alter its aerodynamic characteristics. Little can be done to modify ice formation on cables, though in temperate climates it is usually a minor problem. In countries which experience severe winters, galloping oscillations of power lines can occur (see section 5.2.2). Devices have been designed to dampen the motion of a galloping power line, and one such is described by Richardson, Martuccelli, and Price[22]. An interesting case of excitation due to the former problem did, however, arise on the Severn crossing conductor[23] — see page 169. This has a crossing span of 5319 ft (1620 m) with a minimum height above the river of 135 ft (41 m). The stranding on the cable produced a flow which differed from that around a rough circular cylinder. With the wind blowing at a small yaw angle to the cable, the strands could be aligned with the flow on the upper surface and lying across the flow on the lower surface. This resulted in substantial lift forces which varied very rapidly with wind and caused significant swaying. The problem was overcome by wrapping the conductors in tape, thus presenting a similar surface to the wind at all yaw angles.

6

Experimental and testing techniques

6.1 Meteorological measurements

Meteorological measurements are made continuously to establish the understanding of atmospheric conditions around the world. These measurements are of some interest to architects and civil-engineering designers, since they provide a statistical basis for design. The principal records of interest are those of wind speed, wind direction, and atmospheric pressure. In the UK, the Meteorological Office publishes atmospheric data daily, but these data, although extrapolated, are in fact a representative record only of the sites where the instruments are mounted.

Where any doubt exists, or local topography or local knowledge would indicate marked differences in wind data from those obtaining at the nearest meteorological station or site, wind records should be taken for as long as possible prior to the commencement of construction and, if possible, should be correlated against those of the Meteorological Office.

6.1.1 Measurement of ambient pressure.
Atmospheric pressure is recorded continuously on a barograph, which consists of an aneroid capsule, a rotating paper drum, and a marker-pen. The pen moves vertically as the atmospheric pressure changes, while the paper rotates horizontally on the drum. One complete revolution takes seven days, so the recording paper has to be replaced weekly. The instruments in common use can record over a pressure range of 70 cm mercury to 78 cm mercury.

Atmospheric pressure is of interest to the civil engineer as sudden changes in pressure are often followed by high winds. Such information could indicate, for example, the need to protect a partially constructed building or to delay the erection of a cantilever roof.

6.1.2 Measurement of wind speed and direction. The usual meteorological devices for measuring wind speed are the cup anemometer and the pressure-tube anemometer*. The cup anemometer operates by the rotation of a system of three hemispherical or conical cups mounted on a vertical spindle. The dimensions and design of the devices are such that the rate of rotation is directly proportional to the speed of the wind. The signal from the anemometer is in the form of either a counter reading or a generated voltage, presented on a dial as a wind speed in knots. The counter anemometers are designed primarily for measuring the run of wind over a period of hours rather than the short periods needed for most immediate observations. The generator anemometer is more satisfactory for short periods and is ideally suited for driving a recorder.

The pressure-tube anemometer operates as a Pitot-static tube, sensing the difference between the total and static pressures of the air stream. To keep the device heading into the wind, the anemometer is mounted on a spindle, together with a vane. The pressure difference generated is used to drive a pen up a chart wrapped around a rotating drum, and the vane position is recorded on the same chart, its pen being driven by a helix. The limitation of the device is that, if the recorder unit cannot be mounted directly below the 'head', the fluctuating signal will be unduly attenuated by the pressure lines.

An electrical anemograph consisting of a cup-generator anemometer and a remote-indicating wind vane provides an instrument in which the recorder may be housed well away from the sensor. The standard speed range for this equipment is 0–90 kt (0–165 km/h), but the cup assembly is specially strengthened so that a 0–180 kt (0–330 km/h) range may be covered. Each strip chart takes a continuous record for 31 days, but timing marks have to be put on at regular intervals. The size and robustness of these cup anemometers mean that they cannot respond to gusts of less than 3-seconds duration. Smaller and lighter anemometers which do respond to short-duration gusts are less robust than the standard types and are only now becoming more generally used.

The choice of site for an anemometer is an important consideration. For standard data and reference, the wind speeds are required at a standard height of 10 metres, but if the site is unduly sheltered by trees or buildings the standard-height records of both wind speed and direction may be completely unreliable. Where such conditions exist, the anemometer has to be mounted well above the surrounding obstacles

* These devices are fully described in Meteorological Office, *Meteorological observer's handbook* (·805), London, HMSO, 3rd edn 1969, to which reference should be made for completeness.

to obtain conditions free from disturbance. The anemometer is then allotted an 'effective height' which is the height over open level terrain, in the vicinity, which would have the same mean wind speed as that recorded by the anemometer. A correction is then applied to reduce the measurements to the standard height.

More sophisticated anemometers have been constructed by the Electrical Research Association (ERA)[1] for research into the structure of the wind. These are designed to respond to short-duration gusts. One such anemometer consists of a perforated hollow sphere, about the size of a golf ball, mounted on a strain-gauged support. Since the rod is strain-gauged for one direction only, two anemometers are usually mounted close together so that the resultant velocity can be established. The readings from an array of mast-mounted instruments can be sampled simultaneously to show the variation of wind speed over a height of 100 m.

6.2 Measurements on full-scale buildings

Measurements of wind speed, air pressure, structural deflections, sway accelerations, and wind-induced strains can be made on full-scale buildings. The results of one such investigation[2] in which the Building Research Establishment studied wind pressures and their resultant strains on the Post Office Tower in London are given by C. W. Newberry, K. J. Eaton, and J. R. Mayne.

Research is being conducted on full-scale structures in at least ten countries, and interest is not confined to tall buildings. Low-rise buildings in Japan, the UK, and the USA have been instrumented, and in other tests measurements have been made on bridges, towers, chimneys, and hyperbolic cooling towers[3].

Full-scale measurements are particularly important as they allow comparison with wind-tunnel predictions and a consequent improvement in wind-tunnel techniques.

Since a large number of channels of information are normally recorded, it is usual only to take a record of the behaviour of a building, say, in high-wind conditions.

6.2.1 Measurement of wind speed. As noted above, wind speed may be measured by cup anemometers as used in meteorological measurements. To prevent excessive interference with the air flow, the anemometers can be mounted on a temporary lattice mast close to the building or on a mobile mast mounted on a vehicle which can be moved around the building. Wind speeds should be measured at several heights to allow a proper interpretation of the pressure data.

6.2.2 Measurement of pressure. The technique of pressure measurement on full-scale buildings has been pioneered in the UK at the Building Research Establishment. They have developed a strain-gauged transducer[4] of 140 mm diameter having a measuring range of ± 1200 Pa. A schematic view of this type of device is sketched in fig. 6.1.

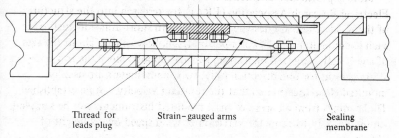

        Thread for   Strain–gauged arms   Sealing
        leads plug   membrane

Fig. 6.1 Section through pressure transducer. Note: two strain-gauged arms have been sketched for clarity; in fact the diaphragm is supported on three equispaced arms.

The transducer was developed because no suitable equipment existed for the measurement of pressures on the sides of full-scale buildings. The device has an accuracy of ± 10 Pa and can measure transients whose period is of the order of 0·1 s. The size of the instrument is such that the pressures measured are representative of those over a panel and are not influenced by very small or local irregularities. It was designed to be fitted into 'curtain-walling' components with the pressure plate flush with the surface of the building.

Another pressure-measuring device adapted for fullscale use by the B.R.E gives the free-stream static pressure. The static pressure is important if the accurate distribution of pressure is to be obtained, rather than the assessment of overall forces. Suppose, for example, that one side of a pressure-transducer diaphragm records pressures on the front of a panel and the other side of the diaphragm is vented to the back of the panel. The force on the panel can be obtained from these results, but, unless data is available to show how the pressure behind the panel compares with the ambient pressure (say) or some standard value, no absolute assessment can be made. To get a meaningful pressure value, all the transducers are vented to some still-air region, usually in the building basement. By using the free-stream static pressure as a reference, true pressure coefficients can be established all over the building.

$$C_p = (p - p_0)/\tfrac{1}{2}\rho V^2 \qquad\qquad (4.23) \quad (6.1)$$

where p = pressure at observation point, p_0 = free-stream static pressure.

The instrument consists of a vertical cylinder pressure-tapped at eight stations spaced equally around the circumference. A sleeve with a skirt is fitted over the cylinder and is positioned so that the tappings are shielded by the skirt (see fig. 6.2). The sleeve is adjusted under controlled conditions until the mean pressure reading shown by the tappings corresponds to the ambient static pressure.

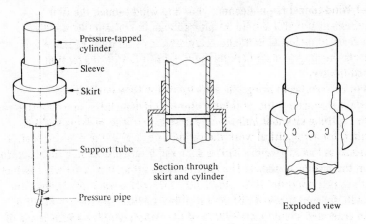

Fig. 6.2 Static pressure device (not to scale)

6.2.3 Measurement of strain. Strain measurements due to wind loads can be made by attaching strain-gauges to the steel reinforcing in a building under construction or directly onto the smooth concrete surface. Wire or film gauges can be used, and are normally attached to the structure by a fast-setting cement. If the gauges are to be used over a lengthy period, they must be regularly checked for temperature drift, and those attached to concrete may well drift as this material dries.

To establish dynamic loads in the structure, the gauge is set in the arm of a Wheatstone-bridge network and the bridge is balanced in the absence of any wind loads. The out-of-balance galvanometer reading is then recorded in windy conditions.

The recording of the strain measurements may be either as a continuous reading on paper or magnetic tape, or the gauges may be scanned in turn and records taken at a fixed time interval. This was the technique adopted by Newberry, Eaton, and Mayne on the Post Office Tower[2].

6.3 Wind-tunnel design for aerodynamic testing of structures

The majority of wind tunnels in use today were designed for testing aircraft models, and many of the tests conducted on building models are made in these tunnels. Such is the importance now attributed to wind effects that there is a growing number of purpose-designed and built wind tunnels specifically for testing models of buildings and structures. These tunnels have their own special requirements as outlined below.

6.3.1 Wind-tunnel requirements. For any wind tunnel, the first requirement is that it should be large enough to contain the models which are to be tested in it, and adequate provision must be made for putting the models in and taking them out of the working section expeditiously.

For aeronautical testing, the velocity of the flow needs to be constant throughout the working section. This demands a short contraction from a settling chamber immediately upstream of the working section. Further, for aeronautical work the turbulence level in the working section has to be as low as possible. This is achieved by the use of fine mesh screens set in the settling chamber. The requirements for an industrial wind tunnel are the exact opposite: it should be possible, over a wide speed range, to generate sheared flows of different profiles; further, the spectra of turbulence generated should match those of the atmosphere for a wide range of model scale sizes.

An industrial wind tunnel is likely to be used for force measurement, pressure measurement, local-velocity measurement, flow-visualisation tests on static models, and oscillating tests on dynamic models. The tunnel should be made so that at least two force components can be measured simultaneously, and it is desirable that at least one moment, either the torsional or the overturning moment, should be recorded as well.

Provision must also be made for the model to be rotated in the wind tunnel so that the influences of shift of wind direction can be investigated. At the same time, it must be possible to lead the pressure tubing and other instrument conduits from the inside to the outside of the tunnel without influencing the air flow. For local-velocity measurements a traversing arrangement is necessary, and for flow visualisation provision must be made for admitting smoke and for photographing or otherwise recording the results.

6.3.2 Working-section size. There is no ideal working-section size for an industrial wind tunnel since a wide variety of tasks can be included under the heading of industrial aerodynamic testing. However, if scale models of tall buildings are to be tested, a tunnel of at least 2 m^2 cross-sectional area is needed, otherwise the test models become so small that it is impossible to model detail accurately.

Hunt has suggested[5] that the optimum industrial aerodynamics tunnel is an open-return type with a flexible roof having a working section of about 1·5–2 m by 2–3 m and a fetch of 10–20 m. The tunnel model should not occupy more than 10% of the cross-sectional area, although models giving more blockage have been tested.

Typical working-section sizes of wind tunnels used for industrial aerodynamics are given below.

Colorado State University	1·9 m x 1·9 m x 28 m
Central Electricity Generating Board (Marchwood UK)	9·1 m x 2·7 m x 21 m
Central Electrical Research Laboratory (Leatherhead UK)	4·6 m x 1·5 m x 11 m
Building Research Establishment (Garston UK)	1 m x 2 m x 6 m
Lyngby (Denmark)	1·1 m x 1·1 m x 13 m
Marseilles (France)	3·2 m x 1·5 m x 40 m
Hanover (German Federal Republic)	2·4 m x 2·4 m x 24 m
Zurich (Switzerland)	3 m x 2·1 m x 9 m
University of Western Ontario	2·5 m x 2·5 m x 30 m

For the dynamic wind-tunnel testing of the Severn Bridge model, the scaling problems were such that the National Physical Laboratory built a temporary wind tunnel. No existing available tunnel was large enough to test the very large model that had to be constructed to model accurately the full-scale conditions.

6.3.3 Speed range. The speed range for an industrial wind tunnel should allow a wide range of testing techniques to be employed. If smoke flow filaments are to be photographed, wind speeds as low as 1–2 m/s will be necessary, while for pressure measurements much higher speeds, usually in the range of 25–30 m/s, are required if a reasonable accuracy is to be achieved. The scales of building models usually used are too small for the full-scale Reynolds numbers to be attained, even if the largest wind tunnels are used. A wide speed range, however, does give the opportunity to match the dynamic similarity parameters (see section 6.4.1) when oscillating effects are being investigated.

In selecting the motor size to give the desired speed range, the large resistance of bluff models must be taken into account as must be the resistance of the devices used for developing the shear flow.

This last point has been found to be most significant where a wind-tunnel originally designed for aeronautical work has been converted to try to simulate the natural wind for non-aeronautical test work.

6.3.4 Sheared-flow velocity profile.   Full-scale measurements have shown that the natural wind speed varies with height. This variation, it will be recalled, is known as the vertical wind gradient and can be represented by the relationship

$$V_z/V_{z_0} = (z/z_0)^{1/\alpha} \tag{6.2}$$

where V_z is the wind speed at any height z and V_{z_0} is the wind speed at the reference height z_0 (see page 32).

The value of the index $1/\alpha$ depends on the terrain upwind of the measuring point, varying from 0·13 (i.e. $\alpha = 7\cdot5$) for open grassland to 0·25 (i.e. $\alpha = 4$) for heavily built-up areas. These values apply to mean hourly wind speeds and the value of $1/\alpha$ is decreased if a shorter averaging time of, say, 10 minutes is used. Typical values then become 0·16 for open grasslands to 0·40 for heavily built-up areas[7].

Two basic techniques exist which produce the type of profile required. Either the velocity can be non-uniformly reduced across the entire depth of the tunnel, by placing rods or similar obstacles close together near the floor and further apart near the roof, or a very thick boundary layer can be grown by roughening the floor ahead of the working section. The first technique is more suitable for ex-aeronautical wind tunnels where the working section is close behind the contraction. The second technique is preferred where the wind tunnel has been specially designed or suitably modified for industrial testing and a long fetch exists upstream of the working section.

Since a range of profiles will be needed to cover the range of conditions that may be experienced in practice, any system employing velocity-profile grids must be readily changeable. The grids should be far enough upstream of the model for the wakes from the individual rods to merge and form a stable profile. The technique for designing such grids is given by, for example, Cowdrey[8]. He shows that the height, y, of the centre line of a cylindrical rod, diameter d, in a tunnel of depth δ is given by

$$\frac{y}{\delta} = \left(\frac{\alpha}{1+\alpha}\right)^{\alpha} \left[\frac{1+k}{1+\{(d/l)/(1-d/l)\}^2}\right]^{\alpha/2} \tag{6.3}$$

In this expression α is the reciprocal of the power-law index, l is the spacing of the axes of the rods at height y, and k is the overall pressure-drop coefficient for the grid. The value of k chosen determines the rod spacings. If it is too small the upper part of the grid will have widely spaced rods from which the slow-velocity wakes will persist downstream. Too close spacing gives very high local resistance which causes the boundary layer to separate. In practice k is chosen to be between 0·2 and 1·0.

An alternative technique uses a wire-mesh screen, bent so that it is vertical at the tunnel roof and almost horizontal at the floor, instead of vertically spaced rods. The curvature of the screen determines the profile attained. This technique is used less often than the rod grids, probably because it occupies more space in the tunnel and is more difficult to set up.

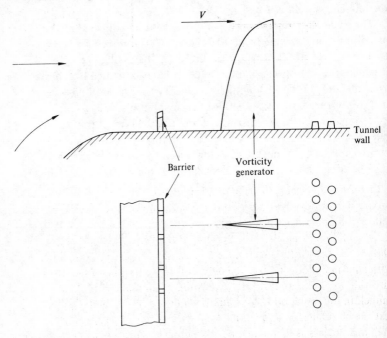

Fig. 6.3

The thick-boundary-layer technique is the preferred method for obtaining the required profile, provided sufficient length of tunnel ('fetch') is available upstream of the working section. Such a boundary layer is usually grown by having a castellated (transverse) board placed across the tunnel at floor level, the depth of the board being about 10% of the tunnel depth, followed downstream first by vorticity generators and then by a series of small obstacles, e.g. blocks or inverted cups, glued to boards and set on the tunnel floor (fig. 6.3). The sizes of the transverse board, vorticity generators, and roughness elements determine the profile achieved and also modify the turbulence.

If an ex-aeronautical wind tunnel is being used, the velocity distribution can be improved by a board as sketched in fig. 6.4. The holes in the board placed horizontally across the contraction encourage a high-velocity flow in the upper half of the tunnel and permit the required profile to be attained in a shorter fetch. With this arrangement, vorticity generators are not used, but the profile near the ground is again obtained by a castellated board and small obstacles.

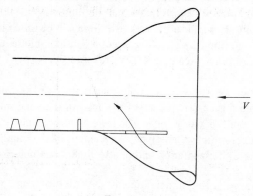

Fig. 6.4

A further method is to generate most of the turbulence from a very coarse wooden mesh, perhaps consisting of as few as five slats, followed by the small obstacles glued to the floor.

In some wind tunnels – for example at the University of Western Ontario[9] – the working sections are made of the order of 30 m long, with adjustable roofs to vary the depth of the section in a streamwise direction to ensure uniform static pressure down the length of the tunnel. In this situation the terrain to windward of the model under test can be simulated, and a thick boundary layer can be grown by the same process as that which occurs full scale. This has the advantage that the turbulence characteristics of the wind are correctly scaled also.

In any particular wind tunnel, the choice will depend on the use to which it is to be put and the desired accuracy of the results. If it has been exclusively assigned to industrial aerodynamics, then the thick-boundary-layer technique is to be much preferred to the velocity-profile grid, provided the working section can be moved sufficiently far downstream to allow the profile to develop. If the tunnel is to be used for aeronautical as well as industrial testing, the barrier (with the addition of vortex generators to modify the turbulence) may be preferred as it can be easily removed from the tunnel.

When the proposed tests are concerned with the qualitative assessment of the flow, around a given structure, then the simple grid is a satisfactory way of obtaining the required velocity gradient as the level of turbulence would be of limited interest. But when a wind tunnel is in permanent use f industrial aerodynamics there is little point in using a grid if a satisfactory boundary layer can be grown.

At first sight the wind tunnel with very long fetch and thick 'natural' boundary layer appears to be the ideal solution. It does, however, suffer from the disadvantage that boundary layers will also grow on the long sides and roof. Although these will be much thinner than on the rough floor, they still represent a considerable reduction in useful cross-sectional area unless they are removed.

6.3.5 Turbulence spectra. If a complete simulation of the wind is to be obtained, the size and frequency of the gusts in the wind must be correctly scaled in the wind tunnel. The level of turbulence in the full-scale situation determines the dynamic movement of the building in the wind and also the separation and re-attachment characteristics of the flow.

As stated above, if the tunnel boundary layer is grown in a very long fetch, the correct scale of turbulence is automatically grown. If a sheared flow is generated by a grid of rods, the wavelength of the predominant gusts will be much shorter than that in the natural wind. Again, if a thick boundary layer is grown using a barrier and distributed roughness, vorticity generators are needed to produce a graded distribution of additional turbulence.

It will be recalled from section 3.3.4 that the spectrum of horizontal gustiness has been shown graphically by Davenport[9] and a curve has been fitted to experimental data from a variety of sites. This curve is shown in fig. 6.5. The reduced spectral function $nS^v(n)/k\bar{V}_{10}^2$ is a function of the 'reduced frequency' $\tilde{n} = nL/\bar{V}_{10}$, where $S^v(n)$ is the power per unit frequency interval at frequency $\bar{n}$, $\bar{V}_{10}$ is the mean velocity at 10 m above ground, L is a length scale, and k is the surface drag coefficient, which depends on roughness.

In the foregoing paragraphs, turbulence has been considered in the longitudinal sense only. If a complete simulation of the wind is to be obtained, the gust components in three orthogonal directions must be considered. Counihan[10] has summarised empirical expressions for the power spectral densities, and reference should be made to his report for a comprehensive description of atmospheric turbulence.

The need to simulate the atmospheric turbulence as well as the velocity profile over a range of speed has led experimenters to try several novel techniques. In the methods described above, the turbulence is linked to the mean wind speed, but more recent techniques[11] have broken this link. The turbulence here is caused by jets of air blowing into the airstream, as sketched in figs 6.6, 6.7, and 6.8.

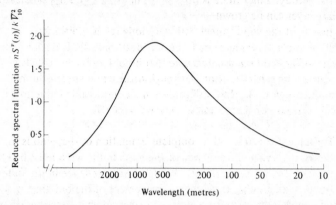

Fig. 6.5 Spectrum of horizontal gustiness in high winds ($nS^v(n)/k\,\bar{V}_{10}^2 = 4\tilde{n}/(1+\tilde{n}^2)^{4/3}$, where $\tilde{n} = nL/\bar{V}_{10}$, L is a scale length, and k is a surface-drag coefficient)

In the first method, jets are blown in from each side of the tunnel, the jet diameters being larger near the floor. In the second technique a vertical jet is used in the entrance to the working section, coupled with fluctuations in fan speed, and in the third method jets are set at an angle facing forward into the flow. Satisfactory simulation of velocity profile and turbulence spectra are claimed for each method.

6.3.6 Wind-tunnel limitations

Constraint. The air flowing around a full-scale building is able to take a path which is determined by the pressure distribution around it. In the wind tunnel, however, the air does not have this freedom. The roof of the tunnel simulates one of the streamlines which is automatically parallel to the floor whatever the size of the model. This constraint modifies all the other streamlines and, in consequence, the velocity and pressure distributions around the model. The modification is not serious provided the model is kept small. It is usual to restrict the model size so that it does not occupy more than 10% of the tunnel cross-section, and to position the model so that its extremities do not come close to the tunnel walls.

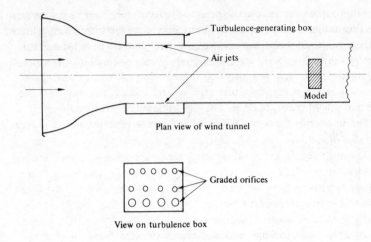

Fig. 6.6

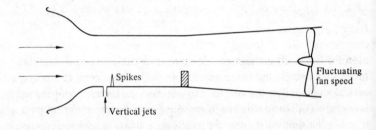

Fig. 6.7

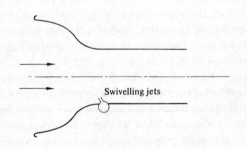

Fig. 6.8

Blockage.   Besides the change in velocity due to the tunnel constraint, the flow is also speeded up by the reduction of area available for the passage of the air past the model. At the low speeds used for industrial testing, the air behaves incompressibly and hence the mean speed around the model is inversely proportional to the cross-sectional area available. Since civil-engineering structures are frequently bluff, the wakes on the leeward side of them are large. This has the result of further speeding up the air outside the wake, which often has a larger cross-sectional area than the model.

The most significant result of this is that the pressures on the leeward surfaces are less than those corresponding to full scale. Unless the appropriate corrections are made, this gives an overestimate of the force in the windward direction. Cowdrey[6] gives a method of correcting force coefficients to allow for blockage and applies the technique to a model giving up to 30% blockage, which is excessively large for normal wind-tunnel work.

6.3.7 Wind-tunnel measurements

Force.   Wind tunnels are usually equipped with either three-component or six-component balances. The three-component balance measures vertical force (lift), normal force (drag), and a (pitching) moment; while the six-component balance measures these together with normal side force, yawing moment, and rolling moment. The measurements needed on building models are usually the forces in the direction of and normal to the main axes of the building, an overturning moment, and a yawing moment. It is not possible to obtain these data from a three-component balance, and it is usually easier to mount the model on a strain-gauged support, or to integrate the pressure distribution around the model to obtain the forces and moments.

The advantage of a strain-gauged support or similar balance is that it can be mounted on the turntable beneath the wind tunnel with the model clamped firmly to it. In this way, the forces can be found directly in directions normal to and tangential to the axes of the model. Although a strain-gauged support is probably the simplest form of balance to construct, three-component balances using strain-gauged transducers have been made.[12] One of the advantages of a strain-gauged balance over the mechanical balance is that it can be used for measuring dynamic loads. The gauges in the balance referred to above were suitable for measuring fluctuations up to 20 Hz frequency. The disadvantage of strain-gauged or transducer-type balances is that they are subject to zero-drift, due to temperature variations.

It should be noted that force and pressure measurements cannot be made at the same time (except by integration), as the pressure tubing invariably interferes with the force measurement.

Pressure. Two types of pressure readings are of interest: time-averaged readings and 'instantaneous' readings. For time-averaged values, pressures can be taken from tubes connected to holes drilled in the surface of the model. The tubes should not interfere with the flow, and the termination of the tube should not significantly modify the model contour. This is sometimes achieved by setting the tubing below the model surface and drilling into it. Cold-setting 'Araldite' is often used *in situ* to position the tubing.

With tubes led away from the model, the pressure can be determined by connecting each tube to, for example, a multi-tube manometer bank if many tubes are involved, or to a single micromanometer if only one pressure tapping is being investigated. Wind-tunnel tests on models of buildings usually involve taking static pressure readings at many points over the model, and hence a multi-tube manometer or similar is frequently used. The pressures which are of interest are seldom greater than 500 mm water, and hence alcohol-filled manometer banks which can be inclined through 60° from the vertical usually accommodate the required range. Two of the tubes on the bank should display the total pressure and the static pressure of the stream, at some reference height. In this way the pressure coefficients for each station displayed can be evaluated. Having obtained the display, the readings can then be recorded manually or photographically. If the tunnel is in demand and expensive to run, photographic recording substantially reduces the time per run. The manometer inclination can cause difficulties, as can staining of the tubes by the manometer fluid. Care must be taken to ensure that the camera is as nearly normal to the plane of the tubes as possible — a feature which is especially important if only one bank is being photographed from a close distance. It should be noted that the photographic records should be read from a projected image of the negative, not a print, as this substantially reduces recording costs and storage problems.

If time-averaged results are required, the effects of tube length and bore do not matter except that with small-bore tubing it takes longer for the pressure readings to reach a steady value. If large-bore tubing is used, some form of damping may be necessary to give a steady reading. The pressure reading may be displayed on an inclined-tube manometer, on a micromanometer, or as the output from a pressure transducer. Because of the expense of transducers, it is usual to connect a number of pressure tubes to a scanner and to survey the pressures one at a time.

Because of the shape of most buildings, the flow around them is usually separated from at least half of the surfaces. In this region the pressure readings fluctuate continuously. If time-averaged values are wanted, the tube bore may have to be restricted, either by adding a length of narrow-bore tubing or by pinching the standard tubing with, say, a burette clip. When time-averaged results are to be taken from a pressure transducer, the signal can be processed electronically to give an r.m.s. value, or a series of readings can be taken and a statistical variation deduced.

Although time-averaged pressures have been used extensively for estimating wind loads on buildings, more interest is now being shown in the way that gusts are distributed over buildings; this is because the worst gust conditions are very unlikely to occur all over a large building at the same time. Further, the data can be used to determine the probability of any given local or overall loading being exceeded 'once in 50 years'.

To establish this it is necessary to know the time history of the pressure coefficients at a series of points distributed over the building. From these time-histories, the variations of instantaneous load and overturning moment (say) can be established. Clearly, for this type of test the atmospheric wind must be accurately modelled. It should be noted that the overall forces predicted by the pressure-integration technique will be the same as those given by a dynamic balance, if the signal is similarly processed.

If the time-history of the pressure is to be accurately established, the simple flush hole and tubing terminating at the manometer have to be replaced by a pressure transducer mounted very close to the model surface. When the tapping is connected to the transducer by a length of tubing, the attenuation and phase shift of the pressure caused by the resonance and other characteristics of the air in the tubing must be established over the appropriate frequency range so that the results can be corrected. The signals may be stored on magnetic tape, say, and then analysed at leisure to produce a plot of amplitude against frequency of occurrence for each point and/or overall force against time for the complete building or a section of it. To find the overall force in this way demands expensive instrumentation, since each pressure tapping needs its own transducer and channel on the tape-recorder. The analysis problem is much more severe if tubing is employed between the tapping and the transducer, the complete tape having to be transcribed before being sampled.

The amplitude–frequency plot can be established for each pressure tapping independently of every other point. This means that only one or two transducers are required, but the time-history of the overall force cannot then be established. One of the significant uses of the amplitude–frequency plot is that it demonstrates the likelihood or otherwise of the assumed local pressure being exceeded during the life of the building.

If the taped signal is analysed to give the variation of power spectral density with gust frequency, then it is possible to see if parts of the structure are likely to have natural frequencies close to those frequencies where the power density is highest. This is particularly important for wall cladding panels and roofing panels.

In the above discussion it has been assumed that the transducer signal can be recorded on magnetic tape and later analysed. Although this is probably the best approach, it does involve considerable instrumentation expense. Two alternative techniques exist. Firstly, the signal can be recorded on light-sensitive paper using a UV recorder. The peaks of the pressure oscillations can then be measured and a plot of 'peak amplitude' against 'frequency of occurrence' may be determined. The reading of peak amplitudes can be done semi-automatically by using commercially available equipment, or a relatively simple rig can be 'home made' for carrying out this task. Alternatively, if only a few traces are to be analysed, the job can be done manually. A third possibility is to leave the tunnel running for a considerable time, say half an hour, and read the peak value attained. This approach, although simple, is expensive in tunnel time and does not give a statistical basis for the design.

The second technique is to sample the signal at a fixed time interval, instead of recording the complete signal. The samples do not, then, represent peaks of oscillations but may be any part of the pressure cycle. Because of this, more points will be needed to establish the plot of amplitude against frequency of occurrence, in order to be confident that a severe peak has not been missed. The advantage of this technique is that the data can be obtained directly as punched-paper tape which is then easily processed. This approach is almost certainly the best if a large investigation is to be undertaken.

Displacement. Measurements of displacement made on models are of significance only if a correctly-scaled dynamic model has been constructed. The parameters for this are set out in section 6.4.

The requirements of any device which measures displacement are that (a) it should not change the inertia of the model building and (b) it should not provide any additional damping. Two basic devices exist which almost satisfy these requirements: these are the inductive-type displacement transducer and the accelerometer.

Various types of displacement transducer exist, but the type sketched in fig. 6.9 is to be preferred as it provides the least damping. The moving core modifies the inductance of the device, and a signal proportional to displacement can be obtained. As with force and pressure measurements, this signal can be recorded continuously or sampled. The advantage of the displacement transducer is that it can easily be calibrated statically and the signal can be displayed on an oscilloscope or recorded on UV paper without expensive intermediate equipment.

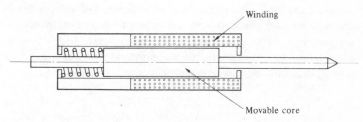

Fig. **6.9** Displacement transducer

The accelerometer has the advantage that it is small and causes very little disturbance to the air flow. The acceleration signal has to be integrated twice to give the displacement before the signal is displayed or recorded. Despite this added complication, the low mass and small size make this a viable alternative to the displacement transducer. The technique chosen will usually depend on the equipment or budget available.

Wind speed and direction. Several techniques have been developed for establishing speed and flow direction in wind tunnels. The principal methods are listed and discussed below. The first four techniques require only a pressure-measuring device to give the velocity, while the last four require more sophisticated equipment.

a) Pitot-static tube
b) Vane anemometer
c) Five-hole probe
d) Claw yawmeter
e) Hot-wire or hot-film anemometer
f) Vortex-shedding counter
g) Laser anemometer
h) Neutrally buoyant bubbles

a) *The Pitot-static tube* (see fig. 4.9) senses the Pitot or total pressure at its open end and the static pressure through holes drilled around the horizontal stem. In an incompressible flow, this pressure difference is proportional to the square of the speed:

$$H - p = \tfrac{1}{2}\rho V^2 \qquad\qquad (4.21) \quad (6.4)$$

where H = total pressure, p = local static pressure, ρ = density of the fluid, and V = speed of fluid.

For this device to be accurate it must be closely aligned to the flow, so that if a Pitot-static tube is to be used for measuring the air velocity close to a model the flow direction must first be established by a flow-visualisation method. Since narrow-bore tubing is used to bring the pressure signal to outside the wind tunnel, this system is not a suitable method of measuring fluctuating pressures, but it is a very useful way of measuring time-averaged values.

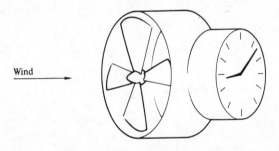

Wind

Fig. 6.10 Vane anemometer

b) *The vane anemometer* is a convenient device for measuring the speed of very light winds. It consists of vanes set on a spindle in a cylindrical tube, fig. 6.10. The action of the wind on the vanes rotates the spindle, and the number of rotations is recorded on a dial on the side of the cylinder. By noting the number of rotations recorded in one minute and referring to the calibration constant, the mean wind speed is obtained.

c) *The five-hole probe* consists of a sphere which has been drilled with one central hole and four equispaced holes around it, fig. 6.11. Fine pressure tubing connects the holes in the sphere to the outside of the tunnel by a hollow rod which also supports the device. When the probe is aligned with the flow, the pressures at the four equispaced tappings will have the same value while the central tapping will record the total pressure. For other wind directions the pressures are all different. The

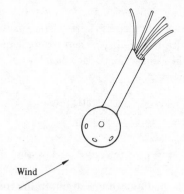

Fig. 6.11 Five-hole probe

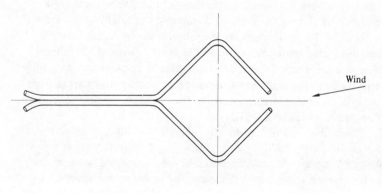

Fig. 6.12 Claw yawmeter

probe can be calibrated so that for any combination of readings the flow direction and speed can be established.

d) *The claw yawmeter* is an easily-constructed instrument for determining the flow direction in any plane (see fig. 6.12). It consists of two open-ended tubes set at right angles to each other. If the yaw-meter is accurately made, the same pressure reading will be given by each arm when the device is aligned with the flow direction. It is usual to calibrate each individual claw yawmeter made, because of the difficulty of ensuring that the open ends of the tubes are identical and that they have been set accurately at right angles.

e) *Hot-wire or hot-film anemometers* rely on the cooling effect of an airstream passing over a heated wire or surface. The hot-wire device (see fig. 6.13) consists of a fine nickel wire, about one micrometre in diameter and about a millimetre in length, attached to two rigid supports through which the heating current is supplied. The two supports are carried in a single stem which enables the wire to be positioned in the flow.

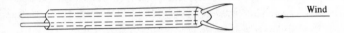

Fig. 6.13 Hot-wire anemometer

There are two basic methods of operation. In the first, the current through the wire is maintained constant and the resistance changes are measured. This is known as a 'constant-current' anemometer. In the second method, the electrical resistance of the wire is maintained constant by varying the current to maintain a constant temperature.

Both of the above methods of operation can be successfully used for measuring fluctuating velocities, but in general the constant-current anemometer is unsuitable where large velocity fluctuations are involved. This is due to the high risk of burning out the wire which arises from the high currents necessary at higher flow rates. A sudden reduction in flow rate then causes wire failure.

The problems which arise in the operation of hot-wire anemometers are due to firstly the difficulty of providing a uniform steady flow of air of known speed for calibration purposes and secondly, when used in the test situation, the likelihood of the probe being damaged by dust particles in the air. Some form of accurate calibration rig, which must be complemented by an adequate repair facility, is essential for successful operation.

Fuller details of hot-wire operation have been published for example by the Institute of Sound and Vibration Research[13,14].

f) One non-pressure device for measuring mean velocities depends on the variation of *vortex-shedding frequency* with wind speed. A counter notes the pressure fluctuations around a cylindrical body and converts these to a velocity. Fortunately the Strouhal number for a circular cylinder is approximately constant for Reynolds number up to 0.8×10^5, and hence a device can be designed which covers the useful speed range of the wind tunnel to be used.

g) *The laser anemometer* offers an opportunity to measure fluid velocities with no interference to the airstream. The device which has been described by P. J. Bourke[15] can be operated in either of two ways (see fig. 6.14).

In arrangement (i), the light from the laser beam is split by a half-silvered mirror and the two beams are then crossed at the point where the velocity is to be determined. The light from the beam is Doppler-frequency shifted in proportion to the velocity component normal to the bisector of the scattering angle. This frequency shift is found by mixing the scattered light with the unscattered light on a photomultiplier which gives an a.c. component at the shift frequency. By moving the detector, the velocity component can be varied.

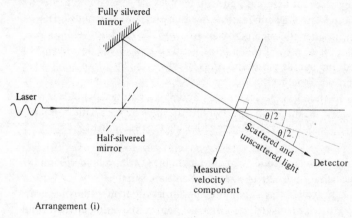

Arrangement (i)

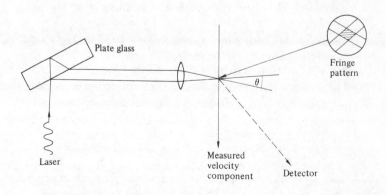

Arrangement (ii)

Fig. 6.14 Laser anemometer

In arrangement (ii), the beam is again split and intersected to give an interference-fringe pattern. Light scattered by particles moving through the fringes is intensity-modulated at a frequency which is in direct proportion to the velocity component normal to the fringes and in inverse proportion to their spacing. The modulation can be detected in light scattered in any direction and gives an a.c. component at the modulation frequency in the output of the detector.

h) Another method of estimating flow speeds with a very small interference to the flow is that of *helium-bubble visualisation*. The small neutrally buoyant helium-filled soap bubbles are generated outside the wind tunnel and are supplied to a head upstream of the model. The bubbles are then illuminated by an arc lamp. To establish velocities, a modulator is employed to chop the lamp current. If the flow is photographed, the bubble paths appear as streaks — the length of each streak being proportional to the local speed.

This method has the advantage of combining flow visualisation with a measuring technique. Areas of interest can be located with normal illumination and then photographed using the pulsed light.

6.3.8 Flow visualisation.   Several techniques have been developed for flow visualisation in the laboratory. Some are suitable only for very-low-speed tests, while others are more appropriate to higher tunnel speeds. These methods are listed and discussed below. The only deliberate full-scale technique is the use of a smoke bomb or canister, but the occasions when such a device may be used are very limited. Full-scale flow patterns may, however, be observed by chance when smoke or mist blows past a building. Effects close to the ground can be noted by observing dust, leaves, and litter as they are blown about. The advantages of the model tests are that preliminary layout schemes can be assessed at low cost, an overall picture of the flow pattern can be gained, and the effect of changing wind direction can be quickly assessed. The full-scale observations are of advantage since they can show the influence of minor architectural features which, due to their small size, may not have been accurately modelled.

The techniques available for flow visualisation during model testing are smoke flows, bubble flows, the use of tufts and wands, and the application of surface flow materials.

Smoke flows are essentially of two types: fine filaments in very-low-speed flows in which very little dispersion of the smoke occurs and coarser plumes of smoke in higher-speed flows which spread out downstream of the smoke nozzle. Although the fine filaments can give a reasonable idea of the flow around the building, the wind speeds necessary to prevent dispersion are so low that it is doubtful if the flow patterns are realistic. Further, the smoke pattern in these conditions can be significantly modified by the exit velocity of the smoke from the nozzle, and extreme care is needed in the operation of the smoke generator.

There are various ways in which 'smoke' can be generated (in reality only the first method below gives smoke; the rest produce vapour). Experimenters have used tobacco smoke, chemical smokes like titanium tetrachloride, the smoke from burning fibreglass material, a mixture of paraffin and oil heated on a plate, and heated cosmetic oil.

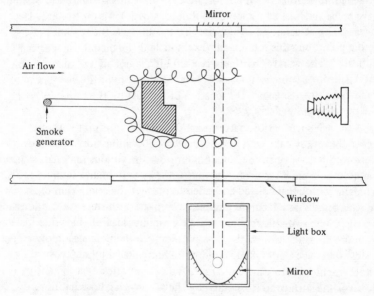

Fig. 6.15 Plan view of illumination arrangement

The latter is the usually preferred method as it is neither corrosive, toxic, nor unpleasant to handle and smell. Another technique is to generate a stream of very fine water droplets, but, although these show up very well when correctly illuminated, their density means that they will not follow the streamlines accurately.

In all 'smoke' flow techniques, the smoke illumination and the viewing background are of vital importance. A matt black background and illumination at right angles to the flow improve the contrast of the photographic record and may well enable finer smoke flows to be used.

Sections through a flow may need to be investigated. These can be recorded by placing the camera downstream of the model and illuminating a section either from above or from the side (see fig. 6.15). The illumination can be greatly improved by placing a mirror opposite the light source, as shown.

The helium-neutrally-buoyant-bubble technique has been described above. Very good flow-visualisation photographs have been obtained with this method, which is particularly suitable for investigating flows around building complexes, the generation of the vortices being particularly clear.

Tufts are short lengths of cotton or nylon-thread about 25 mm long, glued to the surface of the model. Their advantage is that they can be applied quickly with very little expense. Since the tufts are usually attached to buildings or the floor, flow patterns in spaces around buildings have to be established by wands — thin rods with tufts on the end. The tufts can be attached to a fine wire ring to minimise the restraint at the fixing point, but this refinement makes little difference to the pattern indicated. The wand is particularly useful if the line of a vortex is being established. As soon as it has been located, the core of the vortex can be followed along its length, the location of the tuft on the wand indicating the position quite clearly.

Although surface flow patterns are difficult to interpret without experience, they can, with practice, give a good indication of the flow close to the floor or surface of a building. Of the various materials available, the most convenient is probably a suspension of titanium dioxide in paraffin, with a little oleic acid added to prevent the separation of the constituents. The mixture is painted or sprayed onto the model, and the paraffin, being volatile, evaporates fairly rapidly, leaving the white titanium dioxide showing the flow pattern. For the best results the model needs to be black or dark grey and well illuminated so that a clear photographic record can be obtained. The evaporation is sufficiently slow for the surface to be scoured by the air flow, and observation of the process helps in the interpretation of the subsequent record.

6.4 Model design

6.4.1 The scaling parameters. The basis of all model testing is that the ratio of forces, for example the inertia forces and the viscous forces, on the model and on the full-scale structure should be the same. Dimensional analysis is used to establish the non-dimensional groups which represent these ratios. Suppose that the behaviour of a structure under steady uniform conditions depends on the aerodynamic shape and the mass, stiffness, and damping distributions, together with the following eight physical quantities (say), following Whitbread[19]:

E, the modulus of elasticity
ρ, the density of air (or of the fluid in which the structure is immersed)
V, the wind speed
B, a typical external length
μ, dynamic viscosity of the air (or of the fluid etc.)
g, the acceleration due to gravity
σ, the structural density
δ, the logarithmic decrement of the motion

The non-dimensional groups may then be established. These groups and their ratios are tabulated below. It should be noted that the Strouhal number does not appear in this list because the frequency n has been omitted from the eight quantities above. The frequency is fixed by the elasticity E and the mass term σ, and hence n is not an independent variable.

Logarithmic decrement	δ	$= \dfrac{\text{energy dissipated per cycle}}{\text{total energy of oscillation}}$
Elasticity	$E/\rho V^2$	$= \dfrac{\text{elastic forces of the structure}}{\text{inertia forces of the air}}$
Density ratio	σ/ρ	$= \dfrac{\text{inertia forces of the structure}}{\text{inertia forces of the air}}$
Gravitational (Froude) no.	gB/V^2	$= \dfrac{\text{gravitational forces on the structure}}{\text{inertia forces of the air}}$
Reynolds no.	$\rho VB/\mu$	$= \dfrac{\text{inertia forces of the air}}{\text{viscous forces of the air}}$

To include n, we must replace either E or σ, giving nB/V in place of either $E/\rho V^2$ or σ/ρ.

To simulate the wind fully, the wind shear profile, the turbulence intensities $[\sqrt{(\bar{u}^2)}/V,\ \sqrt{(\bar{v}^2)}/V,\ \sqrt{(\bar{w}^2)}/V]$ and the integral scales of turbulence (L_x/B) must all be matched, full scale to model scale. (L_x is a measure of the length of the gusts to which the building is subjected.) In practice it is not possible to satisfy all the non-dimensional parameters simultaneously, and some compromise has to be adopted.

6.4.2 Static models. In the design of static models, the only significant parameter that applies is Reynolds number — except in the case of water flowing round a structure, when the wave-making characteristics at the interface of the two fluids — air and water — would make the Froude number significant. It is usually impossible to obtain the correct Reynolds number in a model test. If it is assumed that the full-scale structure and the model are subjected to wind loads, then ρ, the density, and μ, the viscosity, are approximately the same for each case. The differences in test and full-scale air temperatures may make some small difference, but it will be a minor effect. The implication for similarity is that the product VB must be the same in each case. Suppose the model is of one-hundredth scale (the model size usually being limited by the physical size of the wind tunnel and the blockage problem), then it would be necessary to run the wind tunnel at a speed one-hundred times the full-scale speed for exact (apparent) similarity. Quite apart from the problems of motor size and power consumption, this model flow would be supersonic for any full-scale speed above 3 m/s and hence would be completely unrealistic. A possible alternative is to test in a different fluid, for example water, but test facilities of the size required are not available. Fortunately, it has been shown by tests over a wide range of Reynolds number that the air flow pattern over a sharp-edged body is almost independent of the air speed because the sharp edges, rather than the viscosity, control the flow-separation lines. For bodies with rounded corners, the high-Reynolds-number results can be simulated by roughening the windward faces to ensure that the boundary layer is turbulent. The effectiveness of this technique is open to some doubt, but a more serious reservation with most models is the sharpness of corners on a sharp-edged model. The ratio (r/B) of corner radius r to characteristic length B is likely to be very much greater on the model than on full scale. It is probable that this causes an under estimate of the forces in the windward direction.

In the practice of offering up the model to the wind tunnel, one difficulty that arises with a support-mounted model is that of sealing the gap between the model and the tunnel floor. It is especially difficult to keep this gap small if the model is rotated on a turntable. The usual practice is to seal the gap with nylon fur glued to the base of the model. This will effectively prevent any air flowing under the model edges which might both upset the flow pattern and change the temperature of the strain-gauges. The interference of this material is negligible, and hence the strain-gauge readings will be unaffected by its use.

6.4.3 Dynamic models. There are two types of dynamic model that can be constructed: sectional models and full models. The sectional model is applicable to structures with one long dimension compared to the others, such as suspension bridges, lattice masts, chimney stacks, or grandstands.

The full model is appropriate to structures where the flow is more 'three-dimensional'.

Full models.   The full model has to satisfy all the non-dimensional parameters listed in section 6.4.1. It is found that for a large structure this is extremely difficult to achieve, even if the Reynolds-number parameter is neglected. To fit the complete model of a long bridge into a wind tunnel implies that the model must be to a very small scale, and this in turn demands that the test be conducted at low wind speed if the gravitational parameter gB/V^2 is to be matched, i.e. $V_m/V_f = \sqrt{(B_m/B_f)}$, and for a 1:100 scale model the wind speed in the tunnel is given by $V_m = V_f/10$, so that the tunnel air speed is unlikely to exceed 6 m/s.

Consider now the elasticity parameter, $E/\rho V^2$. It is seen that the modulus of elasticity for the model is given by $E_m/E_f = \rho V_m^2/\rho V_f^2 = B_m/B_f$. For the 1:100 scale model, this means that the modulus of elasticity of the model should be 1/100 of that for the full-scale materials. If these are the usual structural materials of steel or concrete, this is an extremely difficult condition to meet. It can be achieved artificially by reducing the cross-sectional areas of the elastic members and restoring the shape and mass distribution with cladding. Alternatively, the structure can be made up as a series of short rigid segments joined together with springs, to provide the correct overall stiffness. Although full model tests of long suspension bridges have been made, notably that of the Severn Bridge, Frazer and Scruton[16] showed that similar results could be achieved with the simpler sectional models. Full-model tests of radar scanners are essential, however, and in consequence tests are conducted in the largest wind tunnels available, using models of the largest possible scale. Even when the correct elasticity has been achieved, the density ratio σ/ρ (or the Strouhal number nB/V) has still to be matched. With a complex structure the estimation of natural frequency may be difficult, and a range of values will have to be covered.

A more severe problem is that of estimating full-scale structural damping. The usual practice is to make the model damping as low as possible, well below that likely to occur on the full-scale structure, so that the test results are pessimistic.

If dampers have been designed for the full-scale structure then some form of variable damping will be needed on the model. Electromagnetic dampers can be used in this application.

Sectional models.   In tests with sectional models, a typical model cross-section of the structure is built across the wind tunnel or is constructed with large end plates. The part of the structure which is free to move is restrained on the model by springs, the stiffness of which can be changed so that the natural frequency of the model may be modified at will. A sectional model of a grandstand with a flexible roof is sketched in fig. 6.16.

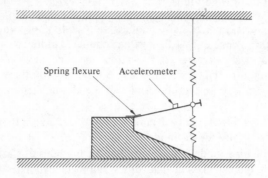

Fig. 6.16 Grandstand sectional model: the wind may blow on either the front or the back of the stand.

In general, if the model is to represent bending and torsion of the full-scale structure, it must be allowed to move up and down and to rotate. With these models the damping, Strouhal number, and density ratios are matched for both the torsional and bending model. These parameters are[19]

Parameter	Torsion	Bending
Damping	δ_{θ_s}	δ_{z_s}
Strouhal number	$n_\theta B/V$	$n_z B/V$
Inertia	$I_\theta/\rho B^4$	$I_z/\rho B^4$

The values of I_θ and I_z are per unit span of the structure. The I_z term means that the mass distribution along the structure must be modelled and is equivalent to $m/\rho B^2$, where m is the mass per unit span. For many structures I_θ will then automatically be close to its correct value if the structure has been accurately modelled, but small corrections can be made by the addition of discrete masses to the model.

6.5 Presentation of data from static and dynamic tests

6.5.1 Data reduction.
Data is collected from model testing in the form of pressures, forces, moments, and displacements. For each test run it is

essential that the velocity profile, and the turbulence spectra if appropriate, should be recorded, together with the tunnel speed and the height at which the speed was recorded. The position of any pressure tappings must be noted and (where the model can be rotated) the wind direction must also be recorded.

The results of wind-tunnel tests should be presented non-dimensionally, so that they are generally applicable. The appropriate non-dimensional groups are obtained as above, by dimensional analysis. The commonly used groups are shown in Table 6.1.

Table 6.1

Item	*Symbol*	*Definition of group*
Direction of wind	ϕ	
Pressure	C_p	$(p - p_0)/\tfrac{1}{2}\rho V^2$
Force	C_F	$F/\tfrac{1}{2}\rho V^2 S$
Moment	C_M	$M/\tfrac{1}{2}\rho V^2 Sh$
Damping	δ	$\ln (y_n/y_{n+1})$
		or $\quad 2M_e\delta a/\rho B^2$
Displacement	ξ	θ or x/B
Frequency	(Str)	nB/V
Viscosity	(Re)	$(\rho VB/\mu)$

B, typical linear dimension
C_M, C_F, C_p, moment, force, and pressure coefficients
F, total wind force
h, linear dimension on which M depends
n, frequency
M, overturning moment due to the wind
M_e, equivalent mass per unit length
p, local surface wind pressure
p_0, free-stream static pressure
(Re), Reynolds number
(Str), Strouhal number
S, characteristic area
V, wind speed
x, linear displacement
y_n, amplitude of nth cycle of an oscillation

δ logarithmic decrement
μ dynamic viscosity of air
ρ density of air
θ angular displacement
ϕ angular rotation

When evaluating the pressure coefficients for a model set in a sheared flow, three possible speeds can be used in evaluating the dynamic pressure $(\rho V^2/2)$. These are (a) the speed in the free stream at the same height as the tapping, (b) the speed at some given reference height, e.g. the top of the structure, and (c) the speed at a point corresponding to a height of 10 metres above the ground away from the structure. The third approach is usually preferred as it enables the structural engineers designing the building to evaluate the loads directly. For the aerodynamicist reducing the results, however, it produces the unconventional condition that pressure coefficients greater than +1 are apparently possible (see section 4.2.3).

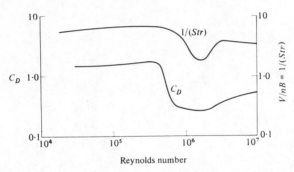

Fig. 6.17 Variation of drag coefficient and Strouhal number with Reynolds number for a circular cylinder

6.5.2 Presentation of results. In most static tests it is usual to present force and moment coefficients graphically, plotting C_F or C_M against wind direction ϕ, and quoting the test Reynolds number if the results are thought to be sensitive to this parameter. The definition of the wind direction should be clarified by a sketch on the graph.

To establish the influence of viscosity, it is usual to plot C_F against Reynolds number over as wide a range of values as possible. It is possible to show the effect of vortex shedding on the same graph by plotting Strouhal number, or its reciprocal, against Reynolds number. A typical plot of C_D and V/nB against (Re) is sketched in fig. 6.17.

Pressure coefficients are usually best tabulated so that graphs around or up and down the structure can be presented as required. There are exceptions to this, as, for instance, when the effect of the proximity of one building to another is being investigated. It would then be reasonable to plot C_p against s/B, where s is the separation distance (see fig. 6.18). In this case the wind direction would have to be quoted, or the results plotted in three dimensions (see fig. 6.19), to show the influence of the three variables. Note that the uncontrolled variable C_p is used for the vertical axis and the spacing of the curves is chosen so that overlapping is avoided. A further advantage is that interpolation is particularly easy with this form of presentation.

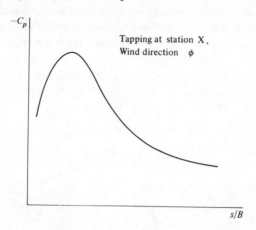

Fig. 6.18 Effect of building proximity on C_p

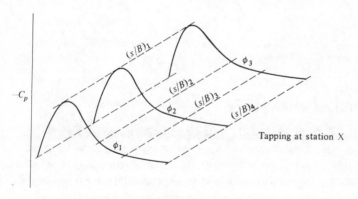

Fig. 6.19

Another interesting way of presenting pressure coefficients is to show C_p contours. A face and a wind direction of particular interest are chosen and the C_p values are marked at the tapping positions. Lines of constant C_p are then constructed which show at a glance the areas of greatest wind loading. Producing such plots manually is usually laborious and inaccurate, but the process may be improved considerably by using an automatic plotter in conjunction with a digital computer.

Although the plot of V/nB against (Re) shows the basic shedding characteristics of a given shape, the designer is interested in the amplitude of the oscillations generated. To demonstrate this, ξ (= deflection ÷ length) is plotted against V/nB for various values of the damping parameter $2M_e\delta/\rho B^2$. An alternative is to construct lines of constant amplitude ξ against V/nB and damping parameter. Such a plot for a circular cylinder is sketched in fig. 6.20. Since the values of M_e, ρ, and B will be fixed for the model, the horizontal scale can also be quoted as values of δ.

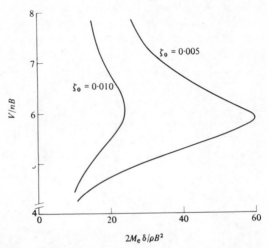

Fig. 6.20 Stability diagram for a circular cylinder

6.6 Further aerodynamic tests

Although most wind-tunnel tests are concerned with loadings on, or vibrations of, structures, an important group of tests is concerned with the environment around buildings. There are three main types of test, concerning (a) winds at ground level, (b) recirculation through heating and ventilating plant, and (c) smoke pollution.

The problem of high winds around buildings has been considered in section 5.4.1. It is usual to establish such wind speeds with a hot-wire anemometer, because in the separated flow regime behind a building the peak velocities will be of as much interest as the time-averaged values. If a single hot wire is being used, the local flow direction is normally established first, usually by a smoke pattern or other similar technique.

The likelihood of recirculation of combustion products with the wind blowing from various directions is important to the siting of chimneys. Of equal importance is the possibility of smoke pollution of the environment before a proper dispersal has occurred. The technique is to photograph smoke plumes emitted from the stack as the model is rotated on a turntable. With these tests, accurate modelling of the surrounding buildings is essential if the results are to be of value, and equally essential is the precise modelling of the characteristics of the plume. Barrett[17] concludes that Reynolds number is not an important parameter, provided it exceeds a value of a few thousand, unless the buildings in the vicinity of the plume are rounded. The model efflux velocity is obtained by reproducing the ratio of momentum flux of the effluent to that of the wind, and model effluent buoyancy is established by using a modified Froude number. For comparison purposes, analytical methods for estimating plume heights and gas concentrations have been quoted by Scruton.[18]

References

Chapter 1

1. Relf, E.F., and Simmons, W. E. G., 'The frequency of the eddies generated by the motion of circular cylinders through a fluid', *Rep. Memo. aeronaut. Res. Coun.* 917, 1924

Chapter 2

1. Houghton, E. L., and Brock, A. E., *Aerodynamics for engineering students,* London, Edward Arnold, 2nd edn 1970
2. Davenport, A. G., 'Rationale for determining design wind velocities', *J. struct. Div. Am. Soc. civ. Engrs*, vol. 86, 1960
3. Ekman, R.V., 'Influence of the earth's rotation on ocean currents', *Arkiv. Mat. Astro. Fysik.,* 1905
4. Panofsky, H. A., 'The structure of atmospheric shear flows', Paper 1, *AGARD Conf. Proc.* CP48, 1969
5. Eaton, K. J., 'Damage due to tornadoes in SE England, 25 January 1971', *Bldng Res. Stn curr. Pap.* CP27/71, 1971

Additional bibliography for chapter 2

Barry, R. G., and Chorley, R. J., *Atmosphere, weather and climate,* London, Methuen, 1971
Day, J. A., *The science of weather*, Reading Mass., Addison–Wesley, 1967
Hare, F. K., *The restless atmosphere*, London, Hutchinson, 1966
Meteorological Office, *Handbook of meteorological instruments. Part 1: Instruments for surface observation*, London, HMSO, 1956
Petterssen, Sverre, *Introduction to meteorology*, New York, McGraw-Hill, 1941
Taylor, J. A., and Yates, R. A., *British weather in maps*, London, Macmillan, 1968
Weaver, J. C., (editor), *An introduction to climate*, New York, McGraw-Hill, 1954

Chapter 3

1. Lumley, J. L., and Panofsky, H. A., *The structure of atmospheric turbulence,* New York, Wiley, 1964

2. Bradshaw, P., *An introduction to turbulence and its measurement*, Oxford, Pergamon, 1971
3. Houghton, E. L., and Boswell, R. P., *Further aerodynamics for engineering students*, London, Edward Arnold, 1969
4. Prandtl, L., 'The mechanics of viscous fluids', *Aerodynamics theory* vol. III (ed. W. F. Durand), Julius Springer, 1935
5. Von Karman, T., *Madw. Ges. Wiss.*, Gottingen, 58–76, 1930
6. Squire, H. B., *Phil. Mag.* 1–20, January 1948
7. Coles, D., 'Law of the wake in a turbulent boundary layer', *J. Fluid Mech.*, July 1956
8. Goldstein, S., (ed.), *Modern developments in fluid dynamics*, New York, Dover Publications, 1965
9. Gibson, C. H., and Williams, R. B., 'Turbulence structure in the atmospheric boundary layer over open ocean', Paper 5, *AGARD Conf. Proc.* CP48, 1969
10. Meteorological Office, *Observer's Handbook* (Met. O. 805), London, HMSO, 3rd edn 1969
11. Davenport, A. G., 'The relationship of wind loading to wind structure', *NPL Symp. 16: wind effects on buildings and structures, 1963*, London, HMSO, 1965
12. Harris, R. I., 'On the spectrum and autocorrelation function of gustiness in high winds', *Elect. Res. Ass.* SP1/T14, 1963

Chapter 4

1. Penwarden, A. D., 'Acceptable wind speeds in towns', *Bldg Res. Establ. curr. Pap.* CP1/74, 1974
2. White, K. C., 'Wind tunnel testing to determine the environmental wind conditions for the proposed centre development at Corby', Paper 34, *Proc. Symp. wind effects on buildings and structures*, Univ. Loughborough, 1968
3. Wilson, P. H., 'Glasgow wind damage', *Bldg Res. Stn curr. Pap.* CP76/68, 1968
4. Carruthers, N. B., Unpublished test results, Hatfield Polytech., 1968
5. Newberry, C. W., Eaton, K. J., and Mayne, J. R., 'Wind loading of a tall building in an urban environment', *Bldg Res. Stn curr. Pap.* CP59/68, 1968 (also *Bldg Res. Establ. curr. Pap.* CP29/73, 1973)
6. Department of the Environment, *Air structures – a survey*, London, HMSO, 1971

Chapter 5

1. Ostrowski, J. S., et al. (Colorado State Univ.), 'Vortex formation and pressure fluctuations on buildings', *Int. Res. Semin. wind effects on buildings and structures*, Ottawa, 1967
2. Maccabee, F. C., (after Drescher, H.), 'The present state of knowledge of flow round buildings', Paper 2, *Proc. Symp. wind effects on buildings and structures*, Univ. Loughborough, 1968

3. Scruton, C., 'The wind-excited oscillations of stacks, towers and masts', *NPL Symp. 16: wind effects on buildings and structures, 1963,* London, HMSO, 1965
4. Johns, D., and Allwood, R., 'Wind induced ovalling oscillations of circular cylindrical shell structures', Paper 28, *Proc. Symp. wind effects on buildings and structures,* Univ. Loughborough, 1968
5. Parkinson, G. V., and Modi, V. J., 'Recent research on wind effects on bluff two-dimensional bodies', Paper 18, *Proc. int. Res. Semin. wind effects on buildings and structures,* Ottawa, 1967
6. Wootton, L. P., 'The oscillations of model circular stacks due to vortex shedding at Reynolds numbers in the range 10^5 to 3×10^6', Paper 18, *Proc. Symp. wind effects on buildings and structures,* Univ. Loughborough, 1968
7. Wootton, L. P., and Scruton, C., 'Aerodynamics stability', Paper 5, *The modern design of wind sensitive structures,* Constr. Ind. Res. Inf. Ass., 1971
8. Richards, D. J., 'Aerodynamic properties of the Severn crossing conductor', *NPL Symp. 16: wind effects on buildings and structures, 1963,* London, HMSO, 1965
9. Scruton, C., Woodgate, L., and Alexander, A. J., 'The aerodynamic investigation for the proposed Runcorn—Widnes suspension bridge', *NPL Aerodyn. Rep.* 29, 1955
10. Scruton, C., 'Aerodynamics of structures', Paper 4, *Proc. int. Res. Semin. wind effects on buildings and structures,* Ottawa, 1967
11. Davenport, A. G., 'Gust loading factors', *J. struct. Div. Am. Soc. civ. Engrs,* June 1967
12. Anthony, K. C., 'The background to the statistical approach', Paper 2, *The modern design of wind sensitive structures,* Constr. Ind. Res. Inf. Ass., 1971
13. Eaton, K. J., 'Damage due to tornadoes in SE England, 25 January 1971', *Bldg Res. Stn curr. Pap.* CP27/71, 1971
14. Hunt, J., 'The effect of wind upon people', *Minutes, 39th int. Fluid Mech. Res. Mtg,* NPL, 1974
15. Davenport, A. G., 'The treatment of wind loading on tall buildings', *Symp. tall buildings,* Univ. Southampton, 1966
16. Vickery, B. J., and Walshe, D. E., 'An aerodynamic investigation for a proposed multi-flue smoke stack at Fawley power station, *NPL Aerodyn. Rep.* 1132, 1965
17. Scruton, C. S., and Flint, A. R., 'Wind excited oscillations of structures', *Proc. Inst. civ. Engrs,* vol. 27, 1964
18. Farquharson, F. B., Vincent, G. S., et al., 'Aerodynamic stability of suspension bridges with special reference to the Tacoma Narrows bridge', *Bull. 16, Univ. Washington Engng Stn,* 1949—54
19. Vincent, G. S., 'Golden Gate bridge vibration studies', *Trans. Am. Soc. civ. Engrs,* vol. 127, part II, 1962
20. Report of the special committee of the board of directors, 'Failure of the Tacoma Narrows bridge', *Proc. Am. Soc. civ. Engrs,* June 1944
21. Frazer, R. A., and Scruton, C., 'A summarized account of the Severn bridge aerodynamic investigation report', *NPL Aerodyn. Rep.* 222, London, HMSO, 1952

22. Richardson, A. S., Martuccelli, J. R., and Price, W. S., 'Research study on galloping electric power transmission lines', Paper 7, *Conf. wind effects on buildings and structures*, NPL, 1963
23. Davis, D. A., Richardson, D. J., and Scriven, R. A., 'Investigation of conductor oscillation on the 275 kV crossing over the Rivers Severn and Wye', Paper 4102P, *Proc. Inst. electl Engrs*, 1962

Chapter 6

1. Morrison, J. G., 'The development of a miniature gust anemometer', Paper 30, *Proc. Symp. wind effects on buildings and structures*, Univ. Loughborough, 1968
2. Newberry, C. W., Eaton, K. J., and Mayne, J. R., 'Wind pressure and strain measurements at the Post Office tower', *Bldg Res. Establ. curr. Pap.* CP30/73, 1973
3. Unpublished papers from *Symp. full scale measurement of wind effects on tall buildings and other structures*, Univ. W. Ontario, 1974 [summarized *J. ind. Aerodyn.*, vol. 1, no. 1, 1975]
4. Mayne, J. R., 'A wind pressure transducer', *Bldg Res. Establ. curr. Pap.* CP17/70, 1970
5. Hunt, J. C., Verbal contribution, *Ind. aerodyn. Res. Mtg*, NPL, October 1974
6. Cowdrey, C. F., 'The application of Maskell's theory of wind tunnel blockage to very large solid models', *NPL Aerodyn. Rep.* 1247, 1967
7. Davenport, A. G., 'Rationale for determining design wind velocities', *J. struct. Div. Am. Soc. civ. Engrs*, 1960
8. Cowdrey, C. F., 'Design of velocity profile grids', *NPL Aerodyn. Rep.* 1268, part II, 1968
9. Davenport, A. G., 'The treatment of wind loading on tall buildings', *Symp. tall buildings*, Univ. Southampton, 1966
10. Counihan, J., 'The structure and the wind tunnel simulation of rural and adiabatic boundary layers', *Symp. external flows*, Univ. Bristol, 1972
11. Euromech 50, *Symp. wind tunnel simulation of the atmospheric boundary layers*, Tech. Univ. W. Berlin, 1974
12. Morgan, D. R., and Chutchlow, M. D., *The design of a three component dynamic wind tunnel balance*, The Marconi Co. Ltd, 1971
13. Davies, P. O. A. L., and Davis, M. R., 'The hot wire anemometer', *Inst. Sound. Vibr. Res. Rep.* 155, Univ. Southampton, 1966
14. Davies, P. O. A. L., Davis, M. R., and Wold, I., 'Operation of the constant resistance hot wire anemometer', *Inst. Sound Vibr. Res. Rep.* 189, Univ. Southampton, 1967
15. Bourke, P. J., 'Laser anemometry for measurement of constant and variable fluid velocities', *Chem. Engng Div. AERE*, Harwell, 1971
16. Frazer, R. A., and Scruton, C., 'A summarized account of the Severn bridge aerodynamic investigation', *NPL Aerodyn Rep.* 222, London, HMSO, 1952
17. Barrett, C. F., 'Dispersion of pollution—experiments on models and at full scale', *Symp. external flows*, Univ. Bristol, 1972

18. Scruton, C., 'A review of the industrial problems related to atmospheric shear flows', Paper 0, *AGARD Conf. Proc.* CP48, 1969
19. Whitbread, R. E., 'Model simulation of wind effects on structures', Paper 21, *Conf. wind effects on buildings and structures*, NPL, 1963

Index